—Multiculturalism—

A Civic Idea
Second Edition

——— Tariq Modood ———

polity

First published in 2007 by Polity Press; second revised edition with new material 2013

Reprinted 2015

Polity Press
65 Bridge Street
Cambridge CB2 1UR, UK

Polity Press
350 Main Street
Malden, MA 02148, USA

ISBN-13: 97807456-6286-2
ISBN-13: 97807456-6287-9 (pb)

A catalogue record for this book is available from the British Library.

Typeset in 11 on 13 pt Sabon
by Toppan Best-set Premedia Limited
Printed and bound by CPI Group (UK) Ltd, Croydon, CR0 4YY

For further information on Polity, visit our website: www.politybooks.com

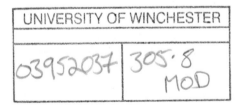

For Glynthea, Ghizala and Yasmin

About the Author

Tariq Modood is Professor of Sociology, Politics and Public Policy, and the founding Director of the Centre for the Study of Ethnicity and Citizenship at the University of Bristol, UK. He is a leading authority on post-immigration ethnicity, racial equality and the theory and politics of multiculturalism. He has written over thirty (co-)authored and (co-)edited books and reports and over 150 articles or chapters in political philosophy, sociology and public policy. He was the principal investigator of the PSI Fourth National Survey of Ethnic Minorities (UK) and has participated in and led numerous research projects, including as co-Director of the Bristol–UCL Leverhulme Programme on Migration and Citizenship. He is a co-founding editor of the international journal *Ethnicities*. His latest books include *Still Not Easy Being British* (2010), and, as co-editor, *Secularism, Religion and Multicultural Citizenship* (2009), *Global Migration, Ethnicity and Britishness* (2011) and *European Multiculturalisms* (2012). He is a regular contributor to the media and to policy discussions in Britain and was a member of the Commission on the Future of Multi-Ethnic Britain (the Parekh Report, 2000) and the National Equalities Panel. He was awarded an MBE for services to social science and ethnic relations in 2001 and elected to the UK Academy of Social Sciences in 2004. His website is <tariqmodood.com>.

Contents

Acknowledgements

This book does not aspire to be a comprehensive theory, detailed comparative study or a policy blueprint. It is written to help us see the wood and not just a bunch of trees; to better identify what multiculturalism might mean as a political project that we might be for or against. The argument is that there is an understanding of civic equality that offers a core vision of multiculturalism that is not only coherent and relevant to the twenty-first century but is also attractive and ought to be a basis for civility, political reform and social research.

The arguments presented in this book have benefited from the opportunities I have had to do a number of presentations and engage with diverse gatherings. The people who have been helpful in these ways are too many to acknowledge individually and I offer them a collective thanks. I would like expressly to thank those who offered comments in writing. Thanks to Yahya Birt, Geoffrey Levey, Nasar Meer, Bhikhu Parekh, Andy Pilkington and Varun Uberoi for reading and commenting on a draft of the book (and also to two anonymous readers). I am also grateful to Veit Bader, Rainer Baubock, Adrian Favell and Jon Fox for the same in relation to Chapter 5. It is a privilege to have so many expert friends and colleagues to be able to call on for constructive feedback; I hope they will forgive me for not always acting on their comments.

I would also like to thank the Leverhulme Trust. Co-directing the Bristol–UCL Leverhulme Programme on Migration and Citizenship perhaps competed for my attention with the writing of this book rather than flowed from it but I am conscious that the Trust's generous funding created a level of activity which provided me with a stimulating context to think about social research in relation to the development of multicultural societies.

As is perhaps true of many university books today, much of the writing was done outside formal work time. Many people could complain that they have a time-IOU from me in their hands but I am most conscious of the diminution of companionship and family life that it has entailed for my wife, Glynthea, and daughters, Ghizala and Yasmin. It is small recompense but I dedicate this book to them, the most important loves of my life.

Second Edition
Acknowledgements

I am pleased that there is a demand for a second edition of this book when its topic is supposed to have intellectually and politically died some years ago. I have made some minor corrections and amendments and added two new chapters, each of which try to take the argument of the book further. Chapter 7 develops the view that integration will remain incomplete without multicultural citizenship. Chapter 8 gives further substance to the view that political secularism is the new, major site for multiculturalism, and while this does not amount to a crisis it means that the current controversies around political secularism are structured by pro- and anti-multiculturalism.

My membership of the two European Union FP7 projects, A European Approach to Multicultural Citizenship: Legal Political and Educational Challenges (EMILIE, 2006–9) and Tolerance, Pluralism and Social Cohesion (ACCEPT PLURALISM, 2010–13), nine and sixteen countries projects respectively, enabled me to continue to explore the nature of diversity and how it was changing across Europe, and I would like to express thanks both for the funding and the stimulating collaboration. The work for chapter 8 was done during an AHRC Fellowship (2010–11) and I am grateful to the AHRC for the award.

I would like to renew the thanks of the original Acknowledgements, in particular to Nasar Meer and Varun Uberoi, who have in this period become co-authors even when not employed to be so, and to Jan Dobbernack for his research assistantship.

I am also pleased to renew the original dedication.

– 1 –

Is Multiculturalism Appropriate for the Twenty-first Century?

The 1960s were a time for asserting the singular character of the human race. Nazism had asserted the irreducible difference between Aryan, Jew, Slav and so on but it had been defeated and anti-racism was on the march. Martin Luther King Jr and his followers proclaimed humanity's essential sameness, that nothing differentiated whites and blacks other than skin colour and few outside the besieged laager of *apartheid* were willing to defend separate development. The imperial idea of 'the White Man's burden' of ruling 'the lesser breeds without the Law' was regarded as an embarrassing anachronism if not a matter of shame amongst white youth. Yet it was also the time for the celebration of difference. A time when people were not only encouraged to 'do their own thing' but when African-Americans started to assert a new black historical pride and the need for a specifically black political mobilization. Some women focused on their sexual differences from men and postulated that women were naturally more caring, consensual and empathetic. For gays the company of co-sexuals became a necessity in order for them to explore the nature of homosexuality and to allow it to be its own thing in its own space without shame or copying heterosexuality.

At the very same moment that the related ideas of humanism, human rights and equal citizenship had reached a new ascendancy, claims of group difference as embodied in the ideas of Afrocentricity, ethnicity, femaleness, gay rights and so on became central to a new progressive politics. It was a politics of identity: being true to one's nature or heritage and seeking with others of the same kind public recognition for one's collectivity. One term which came to describe this politics, especially in the United States, is 'multiculturalism'.

Multiculturalism also has a more restricted meaning, especially in Britain and other parts of Europe. Here we are said to have become a multicultural society not so much by the emergence of a political movement but by a more fundamental movement of peoples. By immigration – specifically, the immigration from outside Europe, of non-white peoples into predominantly white countries. Here, then, the political idea of multiculturalism – the recognition of group difference within the public sphere of laws, policies, democratic discourses and the terms of a shared citizenship and national identity – while sharing something in common with the political movements described above has a much narrower focus. Perhaps the narrower and the broader meanings of multiculturalism – focusing on the consequences of immigration and on the struggles of a range of marginalized groups or on group differences per se – cannot be entirely separated from each other. The narrower meaning might reasonably be construed as a part, a strand, of the larger current. Nevertheless, post-immigration multiculturalism has its own distinctive concerns and sensibilities which can be distorted or obscured if we see it in generic multicultural terms. It may have connections with racism, which may be quite different when the right to settle is not an issue; or, it may have connections with sexism which can only be attended to when there is sensitivity to culturally differentiated sexual norms or gender roles. Moreover, even within the narrower post-immigration phenomenon, the issues can vary between countries. In some countries, racism and the legacy of colonialism may be central; in others, the concern may be how to convert a condition of guest worker into citizen when the former condition offers no opportunity to exercise democratic power. Beginning with a larger idea of multiculturalism tends, as I will illustrate in the next chapter in the case of the philosopher, Will Kymlicka, to distort, even marginalize, some of the specific contemporary issues in relation to the politics of post-immigration, especially in western Europe.

The first countries to speak of themselves as having become multicultural societies were, perhaps not surprisingly, countries which have a long, historical experience of immigration and indeed which have been built up out of immigration, namely, Canada, Australia and the United States. Their previous histories of migration and settlement meant that migrants were more readily seen as prospective co-citizens and the nation was seen as multiethnic in its source, even if till the 1960s and 1970s, assimilation (anglo-conformity) was what was expected from migrants and certainly their children. Most of these historical migrants were of European descent but, as migration policies were loosened to allow non-whites, there was a sense both that the new migrants were more culturally different than many of their predecessors and that assimilation was not acceptable as a policy. As part of, or because of, the wider political acceptance of 'difference' mentioned above, it was felt that the migrants should be able to retain their distinct cultures while they adapted to working and living in their new countries. No doubt some assimilation would take place but it should not be required.[1]

In the decades that followed, some western European societies, especially Britain, the Netherlands and Sweden, began to follow suit. Western Europe had been importing labour, particularly between the late 1940s and the oil crisis of 1973, to rebuild its postwar economies, and the inward flow carried on as dependants and other kin, legally and illegally, joined the migrants, as the economic cycle created new labour demand and refugees sought shelter. Most European countries do not collect data on non-white citizens and residents, only on foreigners, so all figures are guess estimates, but it seems that more than 5 per cent and possibly up to 10 per cent of citizens and residents of EU15 are of non-European descent. Currently most of the largest, especially the capital, cities of northwest Europe are about 15–30 per cent non-white (i.e., people of non-European descent). Even without further large-scale immigration, being a young, fertile population, these proportions will grow for at least one generation more before they stabilize, reaching or exceeding 50 per cent of some cities in the next decade or so. The trend will include some of the larger urban centres of southern Europe. A high degree of racial/ethnic/religious mix in its principal cities will be the norm in twenty-first century Europe, and will characterize its national economic, cultural and political life, as it has done in twentieth (and will do so in the twenty-first) century US. Of course there will be important differences too between western Europe and the US. Amongst these is that the majority of non-whites in the countries of Europe are Muslims; the UK, where Muslims form about a third of non-whites or ethnic minorities, is an exception. With an estimated over 15 million Muslims in western Europe today, about four per cent of the population (Savage 2004), they are larger than the combined populations of Finland, Denmark and Ireland. For this, if for no other reason, Muslims have become central to the merits and demerits of multiculturalism as a public policy in western Europe, though it is to state the obvious that, at least since the attacks of 11 September 2001, Muslim migrants and settlers have come under new political and security scrutiny even in countries in which Muslims form a relatively small proportion of recent settlers, such as the US, Canada and Australia.

The recognition that a society had become multiethnic or multicultural was not simply about demographics or economics. It was an understanding that a new set of challenges were being posed for which a new political agenda was necessary (or alternatively, had to be resisted: the view of certain conservatives, nationalists and French republicans). While this politics was connected with the wider meanings of multiculturalism mentioned above, and was entwined with issues of racial equality, I shall here mean by multiculturalism the political accommodation of minorities formed by immigration to western countries from outside the prosperous West.

A New Idea but not a Comprehensive Political Philosophy

There have been many multicultural societies in the past, especially outside European nation-states, for example, in the Ottoman Empire, where the levels of religious tolerance and accommodation (shown by Muslim rulers towards Jews and Christians) were much greater than those found in western Europe till recent times. Some contemporary societies are much more deeply multicultural than the societies that are the focus of this book. The former include countries like India, which has many millions of followers of most of the major world religions, as well as being the home of many smaller-sized religions, dozens of ethnic groups, over twenty official languages and so on.

The deep communal cultural diversity that characterizes countries like India, no less than the territorial nationalisms of the Quebecois, for instance, or claims of indigenous peoples, is beyond the scope of my theme. The concern here is with the relatively limited diversity caused by large-scale immigration of people perceived to be 'different', who do not simply melt away into the populations they have settled amongst but are ethnically visible and so various multicultural, multiethnic, multifaith urban dynamics come to be and do not seem to be short term only. The 'difference' in question is typically marked by various forms of racism and similar forms of ideologies as the migrants come from societies or groups that have been historically ruled and/or perceived as inferior by the societies into which they have settled. Yet the latter are typically also liberal democracies. That is to say they are places in which – compared to the norm in the world, past and present – an ethical primacy is given to the individual and individual rights are politically fundamental. Relatedly, embedded institutionally are ideas of equality of participation in national self-determination, in democratic processes and public participation, which make up the practice of citizenship and debates – including serious contestations – about how equal citizenship is to be extended.

This is what makes contemporary multiculturalism a new political idea, a new '-ism'. It arises in the context of liberal or social democratic egalitarianism and citizenship whereas earlier manifestations of similar political ideas were in the absence of political citizenship, where the minorities and majorities alike were subjects of the crown/emperor. Hence it is not right to look at the pioneering policy developments in Canada as a 'return to an ancient pattern. . . . Specifically, Canada is finding space for the classical, Islamicate model that existed into the modern era only to be eradicated, not by colonialism, but the triumphalism of the West' (Sardar 2004: 29).[2] This does not mean that multiculturalism is simply a liberal idea, an outgrowth of liberalism. But nor is it a political philosophy in its own right, if by that is meant a comprehensive theory of politics. The closest it has come to that, in my opinion, is in Bhikhu Parekh's *tour de force*, *Rethinking Multiculturalism* (2000). Yet even though Parekh does seem to treat multiculturalism as a philosophy and argues, for example, that all the functions of the state have to be reconceived in the light of it, for they are currently conceived within the ideas that the state represents national and cultural homogeneity, and that citizenship cannot be differentiated other than territorially, he pointedly states that multiculturalism is not a fully fleshed-out political doctrine (Parekh 2000: 336). Moreover, contrary to popular caricature, the multiculturalism I speak of is not necessarily dependent on a general theory about the nature of morality or an epistemology and so is not a form of moral or knowledge relativism. Of course, a political multiculturalism may be part of a larger theory such as moral or truth relativism, liberalism, postcolonialism, (anti-)globalization and so on. My point is that it is possible to construct and defend a more intellectually modest and non-totalistic political perspective, and this is what I endeavour to do here.

While I am not a liberal in the sense of, say, Kymlicka (1995), of wanting to show that multiculturalism can be derived from theories of liberalism,[3] the context of the multiculturalism that I seek to elaborate is, as I have said, democratic; for multiculturalism arises within liberal democracies and its advocacy and critique have to relate to existing, functioning liberal democracies (which of course will not be perfect instantiations of political ideals, let alone of any one '-ism'). This does not mean that an evaluation of multiculturalism is or should be framed by liberalism. My point is that multiculturalism presupposes the matrix of principles, institutions and political norms that are central to contemporary liberal democracies; but multiculturalism is, as we shall see, also a challenge to some of these norms, institutions and principles. In my view, multiculturalism could not get off the ground if one totally repudiated liberalism; but neither could it do so if liberalism marked the limits of one's politics. Multiculturalism is a child of liberal egalitarianism but, like any child, it is not simply a faithful reproduction of its parents. I assume both that liberal democracies are composed of a complex of principles and compromises, open to a number of interpretations and ways forward; and that the right attitude to any of these principles, including liberalism, is not simply take-it-or-leave-it but a respectful and critical engagement. This engagement, however, should be informed by Hegel's insight that tensions or contradictions in our ways of thinking, usually accompanied by or a product of new social relations, can sometimes only be resolved by going beyond our starting '-ism' or '-isms'. This requires creative thinking – not simply the work of theorists – which often takes shape through, indeed is led by, changes taking place in the world, including political struggles, which suggest new ideas and adjustments, or offer what Oakeshott called 'intimations' (Oakeshott 1962), a modest and tentative sense of where we are going and how to get there.

The novelty of contemporary multiculturalism is that first it introduces into western nation-states a kind of ethno-religious mix that is relatively unusual for those states, especially for western European states; though there are some relevant parallels to do with the Jews, blacks, Christian sectarianism and so on. Secondly, it brings to bear notions of democratic citizenship and individual rights on the idea of a co-presence of ethnic and religious communities which goes well beyond the experience of pre-nation-state multiculturalism even if not necessarily approximating to the extent of institutionalized cultural plurality that was achieved by imperial states such as the Ottoman Empire or Muslim Spain or is to be found in contemporary India.

A further specificity of my focus is that my principal reference point will be Britain and then the countries most similar to Britain: those of western Europe on the one hand and north America on the other. This is not because Britain is any more exceptional in regard to multiculturalism than any other country for each has its distinctive history, political culture, divisions and so on. It is important, therefore, not to lose sight of how our analytical and policy frames will have more relevance for some countries rather than others. As it happens, Britain is an interesting example for it combines historical and contemporary features, some of which are most represented in western Europe and others in north America. On the one hand, it has a colour racism and stratification, extreme versions of which are more characteristic of the US; and a nested British identity (hosting national identities of Scottish, Welsh and English and a variable relation to Irish) which allows for a degree of relatively open-textured citizenship and national identities (best exemplified by colonial anglophone settler countries such as the US, Canada and Australia), and which countries like France and Germany, for different reasons, find more difficult. On the other hand, like its western European neighbours, it has a self-image of being an 'old country', a country with a historic character that can, no less than socio-economic and welfare policies, be central to the state; and, also like its neighbours, Britain has to address an anti-Muslim cultural racism as Muslims become a significant feature of its cities, and it seems to be more alive to this than its neighbours.

The starting point of any discussion of multiculturalism today has to be its present crisis, which can be captured well by recording it in Britain.

A Crisis of Multiculturalism?

The New Labour Government, which came into office in 1997, sought in its first term to emphasize the plural and dynamic character of British society by speaking of 'Cool Britannia', of 'rebranding Britain', of Britain being a 'young country' (Tony Blair), a 'mongrel' nation (Gordon Brown) and a chicken tikka masala-eating nation (Robin Cook). The year 2001, however, was a turning point for the idea of multiculturalism in Britain, when in rapid succession over a few months David Blunkett became Home Secretary, there were riots in some northern English cities and the attacks of 9/11 took place in the US. These events, especially the riots and the global 'arrival' of a certain kind of armed, messianic jihadism which some feel that too many Muslims in Britain (secretly) support, led to not just a governmental reversal but to a new wave of criticism against multiculturalism from the centre-left, including from amongst some of its erstwhile supporters. Of course, there have been left-wing critics of multiculturalism from the beginning, from way back in the 1970s, when it was ridiculed as 'saris, somosas and steelbands' by anti-racists (Mullard 1985; Sivanandan 1985; Troyna 1993), let alone those who thought it was a distraction from class struggle or even a scam on the part of global capitalism (Sivanandan 1982; Žižek 1997).[4] The new criticism, however, came from the pluralistic centre-left, people who do not see everything in two-racial or two-class terms, and have been sympathetic to the rainbow coalitional politics of identity and the realignment and redefinition of progressive forces. Examples of attacks on multiculturalism in 2001 from those who have long-standing anti-racist credentials include the Commission for Racial Equality publishing an article by Kenan Malik, arguing that 'multiculturalism has helped to segregate communities far more effectively than racism' (*Connections*, Winter 2001). The late Hugo Young, the leading liberal columnist of the *Guardian* newspaper, went further and wrote that multiculturalism 'can now be seen as a useful bible for any Muslim who insists that his religio-cultural priorities, including the defence of jihad against America, override his civic duties of loyalty, tolerance, justice and respect for democracy' (6 November 2001). More extreme again, Farrukh Dhondy, an Asian one-time Black Panther radical who pioneered multi-cultural broadcasting on British television, wrote of a 'multicultural fifth column' which must be rooted out, and argued that state funding of multiculturalism should be redirected into a defence of the values of freedom and democracy (*City Limits*, 11:4).

By 2004 it was common to read or hear that a challenge to Britishness today is the cultural separatism and self-imposed segregation of Muslim migrants and that a 'politically correct' multiculturalism had fostered fragmentation rather than integration (Meer 2006) – the public view now of no less a figure than the Chairman of the Commission for Racial Equality, Trevor Phillips, who declared that multiculturalism was useful once but is now out of date, for it made a fetish of difference instead of encouraging minorities to be truly British (Baldwin 2004). In 2004 a swathe of civil society fora and institutions of the centre-left or the liberal-left held seminars or produced special publications with titles like 'Is Multiculturalism Dead?', 'Is Multiculturalism Over?', 'Beyond Multiculturalism' etc.[5] This critical, sometimes savage, discourse reached a new peak with the London bombings of 7 July 2005 ('7/7') and the abortive bombings of '21/7'. The fact that most of the individuals involved were born and/or brought up in Britain, a country that had afforded them or their parents refuge from persecution, poverty and freedom of worship, led many to conclude that multiculturalism had failed – or, worse still, was to blame for the bombings. The multinational commentary in the British media included William Pfaff who stated that 'these British bombers are a consequence of a misguided and catastrophic pursuit of multiculturalism' (Pfaff 2005), Gilles Kepel observing that the bombers 'were the children of Britain's own multicultural society' and that the bombings have 'smashed' the implicit social consensus that produced multiculturalism 'to smithereens' (Kepel 2005), and Martin Wolf concluding that multiculturalism's departure from the core political values that must underpin Britain's community 'is dangerous because it destroys political community . . . (and) demeaning because it devalues citizenship. In this sense, at least, multiculturalism must be discarded as nonsense' (Wolf 2005). Francis Fukyama offered a more balanced analysis but concluded that 'countries like Holland and Britain need to reverse the counterproductive multiculturalist policies that sheltered radicalism, and crack down on extremists' (Fukuyama 2005).[6]

As most people will be aware, this disillusionment with and anxiety about multiculturalism amongst the centre-left is neither simply a post-9/11 phenomenon nor confined to any one country. It is however strongly associated with the presence and activities of Muslims. While it is not quite true to say that 'if we put Western democracies on a continuum in terms of the proportion of immigrants who are Muslim, this would provide a good predictor of public opposition to multiculturalism' (Kymlicka 2005: 83; for qualifications see Jedwab 2005), there does seem to be some connection with what has been described as 'a seismic shift' and 'a wholesale *retreat* from multiculturalism in Europe' (Joppke 2004: 249 and 244; emphasis in original). The Netherlands has seen one of the biggest reactions. In many ways it was a pioneer of multiculturalism with its Ethnic Minorities Policy (*Minderhedennota*) of 1983 and generous provisions in relation to state-funded autonomous schools and broadcasting, which it combined not just with its social democratic approach to social housing, unemployment and welfare benefits but also affirmative action in employment. Initially led by the right, anti-multiculturalism spread across the political spectrum as Muslims became associated with sexual repression and political violence. In particular, they were blamed for the murders of the right-wing gay politician, Pim Fortuyn, in 2002 (despite his being killed by an animal rights activist) and the right-wing iconclast, Theo van Gogh, in 2004 (killed by a lone Muslim fanatic for producing a film with verses of the Qur'an superimposed on the exposed flesh of a woman to depict that the Qur'an teaches sexual oppression). An expert came to the conclusion that by 2005 the term 'multiculturalism' had in the Netherlands 'been relegated to the dung-hill of history' (Doomernik 2005: 35). In France, where republican anti-multiculturalism has always been the dominant position across the political spectrum and where Le Pen of the *Front National* got 18 per cent of the vote as a presidential challenger on an explicit anti-Arab platform in 2002, the French parliament banned the wearing of headscarves and other religious dress by pupils in state schools in February 2004 (Kastoryano 2006). Subsequently the Dutch began to explore the banning of the same in universities and the Germans in relation to schoolteachers (Schiffauer 2006). Similar movements of anti-multiculturalist – linked to Muslims – discourses from the right to the centre and left are also noticeable in Australia, the US and Canada (Jakubowicz 2005; for an international review see Bader 2005). In the US, commentators had once speculated that American denominational pluralism, in many ways the civic religion of the country, which from its roots in the plurality of Protestant churches had expanded to embrace Catholics and Jews, creating a self-image of a 'Judeo-Christian civilization', would in the same way come to accommodate Muslims (cf. Casanova 2007). A graphic example of the new, post-9/11 climate in the US and its effect on Muslims can be seen in the case of political participation. According to the American Muslim Alliance, about 700 Muslim Americans ran for public office in 2000; in 2002 it had plummeted to 70 and recovered somewhat in 2004 to 100 candidates (Jones 2006).[7]

Fit for This Century?

Contrary to all those who think that the time to speak of multiculturalism is over, I think it is most timely and necessary, and that we need more not less. Multiculturalism is indeed a prime candidate for 'Themes of the Twenty-First Century', as this book series is entitled. For multiculturalism is a form of integration. It is the form of integration that best meets the normative implications of equal citizenship and under our present post-9/11, post-7/7 circumstances stands the best chance of succeeding. Moreover, contrary to the claims of its critics (and sometimes of its advocates), the key trends and developments are broadly consistent with a moderate, pragmatic yet, inevitably, uneven multiculturalism. I would not go as far as to say that 'multiculturalism is now the ruling idea of Western cities' (Cesari 2004) but I disagree with those who think that multiculturalism in Britain only existed during the years that Ken Livingstone was the Leader of the Greater London Council, 1982 to 1986 (Gilroy 1990, 2005), or that it went awry in the 1990s (Alibhai-Brown 2000). Of the period before the *Satanic Verses* affair of 1989 it just about makes sense to caricature British multiculturalism as 'saris, somosas and steelbands' but the 1990s thinking on multiculturalism not only incorporated aspects of the anti-racist critique of the 1980s but began to take the Muslim challenge with a new and deserved seriousness.

While some readers in a number of countries will (positively) associate the term 'multiculturalism' with an educational reform agenda (e.g., as proposed in Britain by Swann 1985) or (negatively) with the target of anti-racism in the 1980s (Troyna 1993; for Australian parallels see Castles et al. 1992), the meaning that it has come to have is not primarily centred on education, except perhaps in the US. Nathan Glazer, a one-time fierce critic of affirmative action in the US and advocate of liberal 'colour-blindness', had been converted to the merits of the recognition of difference, as captured in the title of his book, *We Are All Multiculturalists Now* (1997). In it he argued that multiculturalism had been or was in the process of becoming a guiding philosophy in the educational systems of the US (in fact he still believes this to be the case but now acknowledges that intellectual opponents of multiculturalism outnumber intellectual supporters (Glazer 2006)). But more generally, multiculturalism came to mean the political accommodation of non-white, mainly post-immigration minorities in ways which went beyond the analyses of colour-racism and socio-economic disadvantage, though it varies between countries (as nicely signalled in the title of the US–Europe comparative article, 'Why Islam is like Spanish', Zolberg and Woon 1999; cf. Modood 2001). Here too multiculturalism seemed not just influential but ascendant by the end of the 1990s, leading Will Kymlicka to claim that 'multiculturalists have won the day' (Kymlicka 1999) and that within that the consensus was towards liberal multiculturalism (Kymlicka 2001a). So, there may be a crisis but it should be clear that the multiculturalism that I speak of is not just a remote or utopian ideal but something that exists as a policy idea qualifying citizenship and informing actual policies as well as relations in civil society.

I am aware that so far I have been quite abstract. While this is necessarily the case when the task is to elaborate and defend a public policy idea, let me at least offer two exemplars of what I mean by multiculturalism and which should be borne in mind as the policy examples of the arguments presented in this book. My first example is a policy dating back to 1971, the Canadian Multi-culturalism Act (1988).[8] This Act declares that the Canadian Government will recognize and promote the understanding that multiculturalism reflects the cultural and racial diversity of Canadian society and acknowledges the freedom of all members of Canadian society to pre-serve, enhance and share their cultural heritage. It asserts that multiculturalism is a fundamental characteristic of the Canadian heritage and identity and promotes the full and equitable participation of individuals and communi-ties of all origins in the continuing evolution and shaping of all aspects of Canadian society and assists them in the elimination of any barrier to that participation. It rec-ognizes the existence of communities whose members share a common origin and their historic contribution to Canadian society, and seeks to enhance their development. It commits Canadian governments to foster the recogni-tion and appreciation of the diverse cultures of Canadian society and promote the reflection and the evolving expres-sions of those cultures. It is important to note that this Act is part of a matrix of legislation which mutually informs and qualifies itself. This includes the Canadian Charter of Rights and Freedom and the Canadian Human Rights Act. The former guarantees fundamental freedoms and demo-cratic rights, including equality rights. The latter extends the laws in Canada to give effect to the principle that all individuals should have an opportunity equal with other individuals to make for themselves the lives that they are able and wish to have and to have their needs accommodated. In each case, discrimination on a number of grounds, including race, national or ethnic origin, colour and religion, are prohibited. Also relevant here is the Employment Equity Act (1995) which asserts that 'employment equity means more than treating persons in the same way but also requires special measures and the accommodation of differences'. Of course these laws and subsequent policies have not necessarily worked to the extent that one might wish but it is notable that the first systematic study of the 'ethnic penalty' in employment found that out of thirteen countries studied, Canada came off best with regard to the situation of second generation of non-European ancestry (Heath and Cheung 2007).

My second example is what I believe to be the best public policy statement on multiculturalism in Britain, the report of the Commission for Multi-Ethnic Britain (CMEB), *The Future of Multi-Ethnic Britain* (also known as The Parekh Report, after its chair, Professor Lord Bhikhu Parekh).[9] Similar to the Canadian case, the CMEB saw the idea of a 'community of communities and individuals' (para 4.19, unfortunately shortened to 'community of communities' in the media and subsequent debates)[10] as undergirded by a human rights framework (CMEB, chapter 7) and by government commitment to substantially decreasing the scale of socio-economic inequalities current in Britain (CMEB, chapter 6). It highlighted the existence of newer and multiple racisms and put a lot of emphasis on identifying and eliminating these. It argued for the need to go beyond the concept of a liberal citizenship, and that a higher goal was the creation in all its citizens of a sense of belonging to the polity. It asserted that this goal could not be realized without a sustained public discussion of what it meant to be British in the twenty-first century. Readers may remember the report primarily for this item for it received massive and hostile press coverage in which it was falsely argued, amongst other things, that the Commission was unpatriotic and was suggesting that most members of ethnic minorities did not feel comfortable being British or that the country should be renamed because the term 'British' meant white (Richardson 2000; McLaughlin and Neal 2004). This was a distortion of the suggestion – which I think is an important aspect of multiculturalism – that the story a country tells about itself to itself, the discourses, symbols and images in which national identity resides and through which people acquire and renew their sense of national belonging, had to be revisited and recast through public debate in order to reflect the current and future, and not just the past, ethnic composition of the country.

Of course I do not endorse these documents in every detail and I go further in one or two important respects (e.g., religion, in particular the focus on the accommodation of Muslims). It will also be seen from the two examples that multiculturalism can have wide policy implications; in particular it connects with other forms of inequality, such as those to do with income, or gender, age and so on. This is worth stressing at the outset because in this book I will only touch on and not pursue these connections. For I am seeking clarity and space for the multiculturalist component of politics, i.e., those elements that arise because of an attempt to address the inequalities of post-immigration socio-cultural formations.

The point of these two illustrations is to show that I am not just discussing a theoretical (misguided or idealistic) abstraction, nor am I working with some idiosyncratic meaning. The multiculturalism I want to elaborate and defend in this book is rooted in recent and ongoing policies, politics and other real-world developments. It consists of ideas that influence policy-makers and public debates and are of great controversy. They have come to have the status that they have because of social and political struggles and negotiations surrounding racial, ethnic and religious differences largely led by immigrants and the second generation. In this book I seek to identify the intellectual core of this political complex. While I believe that these ideas have a certain distinctiveness and coherence to merit the suffix '-ism', they do not, as I have said, represent a comprehensive political philosophy or policy programme.[11] I see multiculturalism, therefore, as constituting an inter-related set of political ideas which are a development out of, and therefore after due modification compatible with, contemporary democratic politics, especially those of the centre-left. Multiculturalism of course challenges certain ways of thinking and certain political positions but the challenge is of inclusion and adjustment, not of giving up one comprehensive politics for another. Interestingly there is a cross-disciplinary irony here (May, Modood and Squires 2004). Social theory and cultural studies were amongst the first disciplines to become interested in 'difference' (e.g., Said 1985, and the collection of essays in Donald and Rattansi 1992) but from about the mid/late 1980s, in an intellectual environment influenced by the French theorists, Derrida and Foucault, criticism of the political discourses and uses of multiculturalism predominated (I discuss some of the key criticisms in chapter 5). Yet this is the period in which political theorists began to discuss and espouse multiculturalism (e.g., Kymlicka 1989; Young 1990; Parekh 1991; Taylor 1992). My own understanding of multiculturalism has been shaped by both these disciplines as well as by empirical socio-cultural and anthropological studies, but above all by the debates around political controversies of the last two decades such as the *Satanic Verses* affair (Modood 2005a). So I shall begin with the most prominent political theorist of multiculturalism, Will Kymlicka. He has perhaps done more than any other author to make the ideas of multiculturalism and multicultural citizenship central to contemporary anglophone political theory; in the next chapter I explain why some of the central aspects of his position are problematic for the project of this book.

In chapter 3 I outline my conception of political multiculturalism based on the ideas of 'difference', 'multi' and a double conception of equality. To further elaborate my concept of multiculturalism I contrast it in chapter 4 with some versions of liberalism and with philosophical multiculturalism. I then go on to argue why the multicultural accommodation of Muslims fits very well with a moderate secularism but not with a radical, ideological secularism. In chapter 5 I consider some social theory critiques which in their different ways argue that the conceptions of group and culture that multiculturalism employs are fundamentally flawed or not pertinent to how ethnic identities are lived today in countries that this book is concerned with. In chapter 6 I bring my argument together in a vision of citizenship that is not confined to the state but dispersed across society; compatible with the multiple forms of contemporary groupness; and sustained through dialogue, plural forms of representation that do not take one group as the model to whom all others have to conform, and through new, reformed national identities. While this multicultural citizenship by itself cannot solve the current crisis, I hope to show that multiculturalism cannot be held responsible for it and we need more not less multiculturalism if the crisis is not to deepen. Having given some substance to what I mean by multicultural citizenship, I return to the concept of integration in chapter 7 and offer a conceptual framework which brings out more fully why integration will remain incomplete without multicultural citizenship. Secularism has become a 'hot' topic in academia, with many speaking in an exaggerated language of 'crisis'. Chapter 8 addresses this specifically by taking further the view of chapter 4 that political secularism is the new, major site for multiculturalism, and while this does not amount to a crisis it means that the current controversies around political secularism are structured by pro- and anti-multiculturalism.

So let us begin by turning to the leading liberal theorist of multiculturalism to gauge his suitability for the post-9/11 crisis in which the integration and loyalty of Muslims are the greatest challenges.

– 2 –

A Liberal's Bias

The single clearest starting point in anglophone political theories of multiculturalism is the work of Will Kymlicka. His book, *Liberalism, Community and Culture* (1989), was one of the very first to raise the issue and his *Multicultural Citizenship* (1995) offered a definitive statement well ahead of most other theorists, and is one of the most cited and discussed texts in relation to political multiculturalism.[1] He works within the framework of John Rawls (1971, 1993) which, while showing some initial concern with the problems of inequality of wealth and distributive justice, had increasingly focused on how persons of diverse beliefs could live together without any imposing their values on the others. Rawls both challenged philosophers to find the moral foundations for liberal democracy and made liberalism dominant in political theory, especially in the US. Kymlicka shared the normative primacy of liberalism but felt there was a gulf between the direction the theory was heading and the route liberal democracies were taking. The theory stressed that the citizens were only free and would rationally only cooperate together if the state – the constitution, laws, government and the services delivered by the state – was neutral between the diverse religious and ethical beliefs of its citizens. No citizen should feel that the state represented a religion or an '-ism' which they did not share and indeed to which they were hostile. It was argued that this could only be achieved if the state remained neutral between all 'conceptions of the good' (Rawls 1971). Kymlicka noted that as a historical interpretation of liberalism, this was a travesty. Liberalism had grown alongside nationalism, combining the view that the state was necessary to and had a duty to promote individual autonomy but also the flourishing of a specific, historical people with their own culture, a nation (Kymlicka 1995: 50–5). Moreover, he noted that in the contemporary world some groups such as conquered nations like the Quebecois, indigenous people like North American 'Indians', ethnic minorities and newly settled migrants were making demands for the state to recognize them as distinct groups with specific historical grievances or cultural needs. They were asking for laws and policies that would enable them to survive as distinct groups. What is more, in practical political terms they were having some effect and their political supporters included people who thought of themselves as liberals and thought that liberals ought to be on the side of the minorities.

Kymlicka argued that academic liberal theory had to be reconceived in the light of this (liberal) politics. His strength lies in attempting to build a theory that was consistent with and attempted to explain the rationale of what liberal democratic states were actually doing. Without offering a sketch of his theory as a whole, let alone evaluate it, I would like to pick out two important features of his theory that I think are valid yet problematic in the way he deals with them, and which mark a point of departure for what I would like to develop myself.

State Neutrality, Ethnicity and Religion

In arguing for his view that a liberal state which is just between adherents of 'different conceptions of the good', between different cultural groups, Rawls explicitly appeals to the founding period of the liberal state, namely sixteenth and seventeenth centuries in western Europe (Rawls 1993: xxvii–xxix). From Luther and the outbreak of Protestant political movements, rebellions and states to the Treaty of Westphalia and beyond, religion was a principal and persistent source of ideology, political identity, oppression, violent conflict and war in western Europe. As an aside we can note that there are interesting parallels between Christianity and Europe then and Islam today. Westerners repeatedly ask if Islam will ever have its Reformation; the fact is that the upheavals and wars that characterize the Reformation are present in the Muslim world today – but with one major difference: non-Muslim powers, especially the US, are major players. (It is an interesting speculation what Muslim Reformation might look like if it took place without imperial intervention or what the European Reformation would have looked like if the Ottoman Empire had been one of the key players.) Returning to the era of religious persecution and destruction in western Europe, on a liberal reading it came to an end as states learnt to tolerate religious dissent within their own jurisdiction and accept the legitimacy of neighbouring states even when based on an opposed version of Christianity.[2] From then on, western European states over the centuries slowly extended this toleration to full religious freedom so that which church one attended, or whether one attended any church (or synagogue or temple), became irrelevant to one's citizenship, legal status, right to property or to hold offices of state and so on. Ultimately, state religion became mainly a matter of edification, pomp and ceremony and for some states became altogether dispensable. Religion gradually but surely became largely a private matter, something the state could not prevent you professing and worshipping in your chosen way. The liberal solution to religio-political conflict was to separate religion from politics; the state would not require any particular form of adherence but would protect the right of all persons to practise their chosen faith as long as they did not seek to use political power to promote their faith or attack another. The practice was never perfectly like this – some states continued to have national or 'established' churches – but by late twentieth century most states that could be categorized as liberal democratic approximated to this (though less than in some of their self-representations, and in quite varied ways, as we shall see in chapter 4).

Religious freedom, toleration and the separation of church and state are then surely amongst the oldest features of liberalism and continue to be at its centre and it is not surprising that in the present crisis they are being reasserted by pundits and politicians. Kymlicka rightly recognizes that the centrality that Rawlsian political theory gives to neutrality, or the non-promotion/imposition of any 'conception of the good', is an extension of the liberal state's strategy for dealing with religious groups to cover ethnocultural groups. He has, however, two objections to this extension. It is unfair to ethnocultural groups; and the strategy is incoherent because neutrality is an impossible goal (Kymlicka 2001a: 50; 1995: 108). Taking the latter first, he argues that any society, including a liberal democracy, will have to make decisions on how many and which languages to recognize as official (cf. the recent making of Welsh as a joint official language in Wales even though more Britons speak Punjabi than Welsh); on the boundaries of its internal units (e.g., treating Scotland as a single devolved polity but England only as an array of regional assemblies); or on official holidays (should only Christian holy days be ones on which employees can expect not to work?). The idea of a completely characterless and value-neutral public space is incoherent. So, the question is does the existing character of a particular polity advantage or disadvantage any group of citizens? Most polities will have a history in which one or more dominant cultural, linguistic or religious groups have fashioned institutions and conventions to suit themselves and then perhaps made adjustments in some specific limited ways to meet the needs of marginalized or newly settled groups. Kymlicka rightly argues that Rawlsian state neutrality, then, is impossible and therefore the injunction to some citizens to simply fit in, to 'when in Rome, do as the Romans do', is to treat them as second-class citizens and to disadvantage them in all sorts of ways. Hence, in any society, it is always pertinent to ask whether the minorities are being justly treated. The strict separation of state and ethnicity is 'incoherent' (Kymlicka 2001a: 50) because the 'state unavoidably promotes certain cultural identities, and thereby disadvantages others' (Kymlicka 1995: 108). He concludes therefore that 'the religion model is altogether misleading as an account of the relationship between the liberal-democratic state and ethnocultural groups' (2001a: 24).

Kymlicka is right on both counts: the model cannot be implemented in relation to ethnocultural minorities and, even if it could be, it would be unfair to them. But what is odd is that he does not think that these two devastating criticisms of 'liberal neutrality' have any interesting implications for the original strategy whose extension is being criticized. For, if neutrality is incoherent, how can we apply it to religious groups? If it is unfair to ethnocultural groups, then is it not unfair to ethno-religious groups?

Kymlicka does not consider these questions. In fact, his silences and manner of talking about religious groups suggest that he thinks that liberal neutrality in relation to religion is correct and unproblematic. For example, regarding religious groups' claims-making in relation to policy, the key term that Kymlicka uses is that such groups seek 'exemptions'.[3] The typical case he has in mind is the granting of an exemption to Sikh men from motorcycle helmet laws and from wearing the uniform helmet in police forces if they feel they have a religious obligation to always wear their uncut hair in a turban (Kymlicka 1995: 31). Of such cases, Kymlicka is usually sympathetic. The point is that for non-religious groups, e.g., linguistic, Kymlicka argues in favour of state support that goes beyond exemptions. For example, he thinks it is reasonable that the Canadian province of Quebec should actively promote the French language and finds himself reluctantly supporting legislation that disbars the use of English in certain contexts (Kymlicka 2001a: 287–8, fn 9). He defends the prohibition that prevents the non-indigenous (non-'Indians') from buying land in certain areas for he recognizes that such purchases would lead to an economic takeover that would mean the end of certain indigenous communities and cultures (Kymlicka 1995). Again, he supports the use of immigrants' 'mother tongues' by the public welfare services and in state schools. In fact most of his theory is directed towards justifying special support or differential rights in relation to language and indigenous people. Yet most matters to do with the needs of religious minorities, with the partial exception of anomalous cases of self-segregated historical groups such as the Amish (Kymlicka 1995: 170), seem for him to fall within the ambit of the traditional freedoms of worship, association and conscience. The only additional questions, for Kymlicka, that political multiculturalism has to consider in relation to religious minorities are exemptions, rather than, as in the case of other cultural groups, demands for democratic participation, for public resources or institutional presence.

It is surely noteworthy that no justification is offered for this stand; it is not even registered that a justification is necessary. We seem therefore to have a certain blindness here; something we might characterize as a secularist bias.[4] A possible argument here is that there is a categorical difference between religion and language. A state must use a language and so a choice must be made, which language? How many languages? Hence state neutrality about language is impossible. Fairness therefore dictates that the state does not pretend to be neutral but pursues an alternative strategy. Religion, on the other hand, is optional. It is not necessary to the functioning of the state and the critique of neutrality does not extend to it.

Moreover, citizens can learn several languages but one cannot be a member of several religions at the same time, so while a multilingual state is an option, a multi-religious state is not, and so that is a further reason why state neutrality in relation to language means addition but in relation to religion it means disestablishment (Baubock 2003: 43–4). These arguments fail to save Kymlicka's theory from the charge of bias and nor do they make practical sense. Firstly, while Kymlicka's theory does centre on language, it extends well beyond language. To repeat the key quote that I cited above, the 'state unavoidably promotes certain cultural identities, and thereby disadvantages others' (Kymlicka 1995: 108). The theory is meant to protect and empower ethnocultural groups (and, as we shall see in a moment, 'societal cultures' and 'nations'), not merely languages; and all cultures contain elements that are no more necessary than religion, and some cultures are centred around religion. Moreover, the idea that a multi-religious state is impossible is a misunderstanding. Countries as diverse as Germany and India could be described as being quasi-multi-establishment states. The German state has various institutional and fiscal ways of supporting and working corporately with the Roman Catholic Church and the Lutheran Churches. The Indian state regulates and incorporates several organized religions and their legal principles. Such recognition of faith communities is a granting of political or legal status and does not mean that state officials or citizens have to believe in any or all the relevant faiths. Indeed, let us take an even more fundamental case of an either/or exclusivity than the case of religion as presented by Baubock above. One cannot be of more than one sex (with extreme exceptions very much proving the point) but it does not follow that a state in all its laws and policies must be gender-blind. Rather, it works to promote the interests of both sexes and needs to ensure that differential treatment, where appropriate, can be justified by reference to differential needs and is consistent with a suitably differentiated concept of equality. So, the argument from the disanalogy between language and religion does not work.

Kymlicka is rightly concerned that toleration and freedom of religion should not simply be seen as an intergroup feature. For example, he is wary, especially in the light of Muslim agitation against Salman Rushdie's novel, *The Satanic Verses*, of proposals for group libel laws or hate speech for religious groups for he believes that some Muslim leaders seek such laws primarily to control apostasy *within* the Muslim community, rather than to control the hostile discourses against non-Muslims (Kymlicka 1995: 43). Reflecting historically, he acknowledges that the toleration and group autonomy that existed for Christians and Jews in Muslim polities, such as the Ottoman Empire, far exceeds how Jews and Muslims have been treated in Christian societies, but argues that Muslim toleration and respect for religions has historically been consistent with intolerance of dissent, of conversion out of Islam (apostasy) and atheism (Kymlicka 1995: 156–8). Ottoman religious multiculturalism, it is alleged, allowed organized religious communities to run their own affairs so that there was no check on what any community did to its own members, such as suppress heterodoxy and apostasy. This, Kymlicka argues, is totally inconsistent with liberal multiculturalism, which is not just about the freedom of religious groups but the freedom of individual conscience. This means that the state must guarantee the rights of not just those who dissent from the dominant religion but also those who dissent from their own religion, or from a particular, institutionalized interpretation of it. Maybe so, and this is an argument in favour of liberal democratic multiculturalism over the *millat* system but it is not an argument for treating groups formed by religion (*millats*) differently from ethno-national groups.

To be clear, Kymlicka generalizes the point about the right to dissent (to being a minority within a minority) into a fundamental principled constraint upon multiculturalism.

He argues that giving the group (or some of its members) the right to restrict the behaviour of its own members can be potentially unjust and so multicultural citizenship should be primarily about giving groups the right to protect themselves from persons or forces external to the group (Kymlicka 1995: 35–8). Leaving aside it might be difficult to separate the two in practice, this distinction does not throw any light on why Kymlicka treats ethnic and religious groups in such a radically different way. For of course he recognizes that denial of individual autonomy is not special to religious groups; indeed, that ethnic internal oppression is just as common; in fact in modern and contemporary times it is perhaps more common. This bias in Kymlicka is not good liberalism, but even if it is not inconsistent with historical liberalism, which we saw has been a movement of escape from religious oppression and conflict in favour of a (unified/hegemonic) national or public culture, it puts religious groups and especially Muslims *outside* multiculturalism as a civic or policy idea. This may possibly work in the US, Canada and Australia but it makes multiculturalism irrelevant in Europe. So, even if we choose to ignore the inconsistency in Kymlicka's multiculturalism, and so do not choose to give up on multiculturalism per se, we still render multiculturalism useless in Europe. This is particularly the case as accommodation of religion is not primarily about conscience, belief and faith. Rather, as vividly illustrated by British government actions in Northern Ireland, it can be about institutionalizing respect for different faith communities, based on the recognition that civil peace and other civic purposes require organized religions to be governmental interlocutors and partners in a routinized, institutionalized way. The state may need to desist from exclusively promoting one religious community but this does not imply the privatization of religion or a separation between religion and the state but may require forging a new, positive relationship with a marginalized religious minority.

National Cultures and Immigrants

So, states are not 'neutral'. What, then, gives them their character? For Kymlicka it is not so much or primarily ethical 'conceptions of the good' as 'cultures' or 'nations' – societal formations as much to do with, say, language as to do with legal norms. I put these terms in quote marks for Kymlicka has his own technical interpretation of what he means by a 'nation'. It certainly does not square with ordinary uses of the term 'nation-state', which generally equates with entities who are members of the United Nations and certainly extends to countries such as the US and Canada. For Kymlicka, the US and Canada are emphatically not nation-states but multinational states. Each of them contains a number of nations such as the Apache, Sioux and Quebecois, though the dominant or conquering nations in these countries have tried to rob these minorities of the status of nations. Yet, by nation, Kymlicka does not simply mean a descent group either, for the nations he wants to highlight are multiethnic, again such as the dominant nations of the US and Canada, which have historically absorbed and grown with migration from all over the world and which he believes should continue to be ethnically open. For Kymlicka, a nation is a 'societal culture': a language, a set of social structures, norms and relationships, institutions, customs and cultural ways (Kymlicka 2001b: 18). While it is linked by a common language, it consists of a whole range of activities housed in a defined territory. They constitute a 'context of choice' in which an individual person develops a sense of social self and group identity and the options for living from which an individual chooses to be their own person (Kymlicka 1995: 82–4).[5] Given this interpretation of nation, it is clear that nations are compatible with liberalism, with a political philosophy that places the freedom of the individual as the highest good. Indeed, for Kymlicka, the political importance of societal cultures or nations is precisely that they are necessary for individual autonomy, for a life based upon one's own meaningful choices. Cultural membership is essential for meaning and choice; and the most politically significant cultures are nations. Hence, a liberal democratic society should be willing to give some degree of self-government and special rights to preserve national minorities.

But where does this leave the claims of post-immigration groups? Kymlicka rightly recognizes that such communities cannot be said to form a societal culture. By definition, migrants have left behind a societal culture and are unable to create a new one as they lack the political, economic and other institutions which form the spine of a societal culture. They are too few and too dispersed in the general population into which they have settled and into which they will gradually integrate. In Kymlicka's view this is not only what is most practical but it is normatively necessary. Those who voluntarily choose to leave their own country in order to make a new and better life in another have a duty to integrate into that country; and that country, having allowed the migration, has a duty to integrate them and their descendants as full and equal co-citizens into the life of the nation. By integration Kymlicka does not mean 'assimilation': migrants or even their children or grandchildren should not be asked to give up their distinct cultures. Indeed, a liberal democratic polity should be willing to provide all necessary support for them to not just maintain their languages and cultures for at least a couple of generations, but should be open to the idea that some of its citizens will have 'hyphenated identities', such as Irish-American or British-Indian, and indeed that the presence of such citizens will to some extent redefine what it means to be American, British and so on (Kymlicka 1995: 96–7, 2001b: 54–9).

Kymlicka is, then, a supporter of post-immigration multiculturalism and argues that 'the institutions of the larger society should be adapted to provide greater recognition and accommodation of these ethnic identities – for example schools and other public institutions should accommodate their religious holidays, dress, dietary restrictions, and so on' (Kymlicka 2001a: 33). In fact, he supports and usually wants to extend what might be called the 'best practice' examples available in countries like Canada and Britain. Yet, the question is, what is the justification for this panoply of policies and for the generous sentiments as regards post-immigration multiculturalism? As I have said, his key argument for the political accommodation of minorities, of what he calls 'multicultural citizenship', is the argument from societal culture. Yet, as he recognizes, the migrants do not have a distinct societal culture and so no argument can appeal to that. But as that is *the* basis for minority rights, one can see why on this theory migrants have a duty to integrate but not why this pill should be sweetened with polyethnic rights. Kymlicka is quite emphatic that one needs to distinguish between conquered or incorporated minorities such as the Navajho or the Maoris or the Welsh, and immigrant minorities, and that the rights of self-government and so on to which the former are entitled cannot be justified for the latter. I do not necessarily dis-agree with this conclusion though I would insist that the dichotomy between voluntary migrants and incorporated peoples is too stark (cf. Carens 1997 and Young 1997). The postwar migrants from the Commonwealth to Britain were clearly a legacy of the British Empire, and as much a migration within an extended polity as between polities, even though some of the imperial territories had recently acquired independence. Hence the view of many migrants of the 1950s was that they were being called to the 'mother country' to assist in its economic reconstruction and in its new health services, just as they or their relatives had recently assisted it in its global war against Germany and Japan.[6] The same is true in different degrees of some of the migration into other former imperial countries such as France, the Netherlands, Spain and Portugal. So, while the national minorities/immigrants distinction is critical to Kymlicka's normative theory, to 'who gets what', he fails to capture the true situation of many immigrants and so the restrictive attitude to the rights of immigrants is based on a false conceptualization. It distorts the circumstances of some kinds of migrants in order to highlight the condition of national minorities and indigenous peoples. However, that is not the main point. The point I want to make is even more fundamental.

As we have seen, Kymlicka is pragmatically generous in addressing the cultural and political needs and insecurities of migrants, even while being theoretically ungenerous. He does not explain why immigrants should get any 'multicultural' rights at all. In his theory, multicultural rights flow out of the fact that individual autonomy depends upon membership of a 'societal culture'. But migrants do not have a distinct societal culture in the relevant sense. For example, newly settled Pakistanis in Britain could be said to have a societal culture in Pakistan but, as that is not within British jurisdiction, it is not the basis of claiming rights from the British state. As these Pakistanis became a settled community in Britain, the only societal culture they could be said to be members of is British society, and so they can hardly claim to be a national minority. In short, Kymlicka's theory – regardless of his own policy preferences – cannot explain why post-immigration communities, let's call them 'ethnic minorities', should have any multicultural rights; it can only explain why they should not have any (Carens 1997: 44). Hence, Kymlicka's theory, besides having a secularist bias, also suffers from what I will call a multinational bias.

These biases may reflect the Canadian or north American provenance of the theory and Kymlicka's own political concerns with the rights of Native North Americans and Quebecois[7] but they do not properly speak to the distinctive, multicultural political challenges in Britain and western Europe more generally. Here, the whole issue of multiculturalism hangs on post-immigration; and within that the political integration of Muslims has emerged as the central challenge. So, a theory whose very understanding of multiculturalism excludes, or at the very least marginalizes, the status and concerns of post-immigration ethnic and religious minorities impedes understanding and dialogue in western Europe. It is undeniably the case that Kymlicka's work has been one of the sources for stimulating, encouraging and framing academic discussion of multiculturalism in western Europe (as elsewhere); we must, therefore, be very careful that in Europe we do not uncritically import a discussion of multiculturalism that is loaded with biases that distort its fit with our circumstances (Favell and Modood 2003).

We need a theory of multiculturalism that does not have an anti-immigrant bias and brings together rather than drives apart ethnicity and religion. The latter needs to be done both at a conceptual level – in our concept of ethnicity – so that we can speak of ethno-religious no less than of ethnocultural and ethno-national groups; and also at a normative level. Rights deemed inadequate for non-religious groups cannot be all right for religious groups. The root of the problem is the idea of the 'context of choice'. It emerges as a central idea, as though it were a question in need of an answer, only because we begin with the liberal assumption that we are searching for individual autonomy. And the 'answer' or endpoint to this search – societal culture – is as we have seen an inadequate basis for founding a theory of post-immigration multiculturalism.

The cultures that multiculturalism should begin with do not need to be 'societal'. They have to be cultures or identities that matter to people who are marked by 'difference' – the latter being a product of exclusionary processes, of impositions from 'outside' one's culture, as well as cultures that are particularly meaningful as 'mine'. Such a concept of difference has to be considered in terms of how the negative element, the stigmatic differentiating from others, can be undone by bringing to bear upon it an extended concept of equality and a sense of belonging with others. I shall elaborate on this in the next chapter.

– 3 –
Difference, Multi and Equality

The Accommodation of 'Difference'

Let us then put to one side Kymlicka's idea of the importance of cultural membership to individual autonomy. A better normative starting point is the politics of recognition of difference or respect for identities that are important to people, as identified in minority assertiveness, and should not be disregarded in the name of integration or citizenship (Young 1990; Parekh 1991; Taylor 1992). Sociologically we have to begin with the fact of negative 'difference': with alienness, inferiorization, stigmatization, stereotyping, exclusion, discrimination, racism, etc.; but also the senses of identity that groups so perceived have of themselves. The two together are the key data for multiculturalism. The differences at issue are those perceived both by outsiders or group members – from the outside in and from the inside out – to constitute not just some form of distinctness but a form of alienness or inferiority that diminishes or makes difficult equal membership in the wider society or polity. There is a sense of groupness in play, a mode of being, but also subordination or marginality, a mode of oppression, and the two interact in creating an unequal 'us–them' relationship. (I hope it will be clear before the end of the book that I do not mean terms such as 'groupness', 'mode of being', 'subordination', 'identity' and so on to denote univocal, internally undifferentiated concepts (see my discussion of Wittgenstein's concept of 'family resemblance' in chapter 5).)

The differences in question are in the fields of race, ethnicity, cultural heritage or religious community; typically, differences that overlap between these categories, not least because these categories do not have singular, fixed meanings. 'Race', for example, can mean different things in different places or different times. For example, in some contexts it is about 'colour' but for many Europeans anti-Semitism has been Europe's primary racism. Again, whilst historically 'race' has been a biological or quasi-biological concept, in the late twentieth century many people, especially social scientists, have come to see it as a social construction, and group behaviour that previously used to be characterized as innate is now seen as socio-cultural. Similarly, 'ethnicity' in the US began life as a description of non-White Anglo-Saxon Protestant settlers from Europe, though it has come to be extended to groups such as east Asians; while in Britain – following a European anthropological tradition in which 'ethnic' meant pre-modern – it primarily denotes varieties of non-whiteness, though in some contexts it can include Jews or the Irish or Italians or others, when they are a minority. So, while in the US, 'ethnic' has typically meant white people and not other 'racial' groups, in western Europe it typically means non-white. In most cases 'difference' does not simply relate to free-floating attitudes and idiosyncratic stereotypes but to ways of thinking, acting and organizing across many if not all social and institutional contexts but not usually to territory (except in the sense of origins). Such a notion of difference fits the situations that are the focus of this book, namely, relatively new urban co-presences in western cities; but co-presences which often have historical roots, usually a relationship of domination–subordination, such as the colonial empires, but while historically the co-presence may have taken place 'over there' in the colonies, it is now within western cities.

These co-presences have a political character and give rise to the processes and outcomes of political struggles and negotiations around the fact of difference. To those struggles and outcomes in which certain kinds of 'differences' are asserted and certain kinds of claims-making takes place, recognition or accommodation is sought and not considered illegitimate. Multiculturalism refers to the struggle, the political mobilization but also the policy and institutional outcomes, to the forms of accommodation in which 'differences' are not eliminated, are not washed away but to some extent recognized. Through both these ways, group assertiveness and mobilization, and through institutional and policy reforms to address the claims of the newly settled, marginalized groups, the character of 'difference' is addressed; ideally, a negative difference is turned into a positive difference, though in most contemporary situations something of each is likely to be simultaneously present.

To speak of 'difference' rather than 'culture' as the sociological starting point is to recognize that the difference in question is not just constituted from the 'inside', from the side of a minority culture, but also from the outside, from the representations and treatment of the minorities in question. Moreover, as I have said, it is also to recognize that the nature of the minorities, and their relationship to the rest of society, is not such that 'culture' is a stand-alone alternative to race, ethnicity, religion and so on. Multiculturalism is not, therefore, about cultural rights instead of political equality or economic opportunities; it is a politics which recognizes post-immigration groups exist in western societies in ways that both they and others, formally and informally, negatively and positively are aware that these group-differentiating dimensions are central to their social constitution.

So, rather than derive a concept of multicultural politics from a concept of culture, it is better to build it up from the specific claims, implicit and explicit, of the postwar extra-European/non-white immigration and settlement and their struggles and the policy responses around them to achieve some form of acceptance and equal membership. Such migrants have not been simply perceived as individuals or new neighbours, fellow-workers or citizens. They have been seen as 'different'; seen in terms of race, ethnicity and so on. So, one of the central features of this politics is the understanding that a collectivity is being targeted and so a collective response is required; that people were being labelled from the outside, for example, as 'immigrants', 'coloureds' or 'foreigners'. These labels had to be contested and rejected through collective protest, the summoning and building up of group pride and the projection of positive labels and images to overcome the stigmatization of involuntary identities. The most famous example of this group pride mobilization has been not by an immigrant group but by African-Americans, who by self-identifying as 'black' turned a derogatory term into a social movement and through slogans such as 'Black and Proud' reclaimed a heritage and history and created a political ethnicity (Omi and Winant 1986). This example was influential in different ways across the world and certainly in Britain where it gave rise to allied black politics and black pride movements and beyond that to other forms of ethnic assertiveness such as that of South Asians in Britain (Modood 2005b), and Latinos and others in the United States (Fox 1996).[1] Indeed, we really only begin to talk about multiculturalism when the groups in question cannot be characterized in 'racial' terms only, when they do not, for example, portray themselves as 'black' or 'brown' but where issues of (perceived) bonds based on community structure, family norms, cultural heritage, religious tradition seem to be equally important as phenotype or descent. In these ways, the assertion, re-imagining and negotiation of difference is central to group formation and evolution and thus to multiculturalism. Nevertheless, anti-colour racism, which in that earlier period was what was meant by anti-racism, has been a key critical element in the evolution of multiculturalism. The fact of racism and of power inequalities tended to be ignored by early conceptions of multiculturalism and came to be rightly rectified in later formulations (May 1999; CMEB 2000).

I have said that the appropriate sociological starting point is that of negative difference and that the politics consists in seeking to turn the negative into a positive, not the erasure of difference but its transformation into something for which civic respect can be won. When we begin to talk of positive difference, it is common to talk of identities. Identities are relational and so, just like difference, are constituted partly from the outside. But the concept of identity (like ethnicity and culture as opposed to race) allows the 'inside' more space, more agency. This is not just in relation to individual self-definition but in relation to the outsider perceptions, treatment and social expectations – indeed the whole social constitution of what is taken to be an Asian, Latino, black, etc., including the inferiorized, imposed status of that group. That is to say, the subordinate group in question does not just begin to take charge of its positive self-definition, of revaluing the group, but also to define the ways it has been inferiorized, its mode of oppression. The group begins to speak for itself, not just in terms of its positivity but also about its pain. Examples of what I have in mind are when British Asians begin to redefine the racism that they experience, from a colour-racism, the experience of not being white in a white society, to a racism which targets Asians in the form of distinctive stereotypes and vilifies aspects of their culture. Or, when black women begin to recharacterize sexism to take account of their distinctive concerns (Carby 1982; Amos and Parmar 1984); or when Muslim women challenge leading forms of feminism which portray the wearing of a headscarf as a form of oppression but regard the sexualization of public space (in terms of dress, visual images, shopping malls) as emancipatory (Bullock 2002). All these are examples of an assertive identity statement because an oppressed group challenges not just its oppression but the prevailing wisdom about its mode of oppression. It claims to know something, to name an experience because the 'difference' is addressed from the 'inside' by the victims. This is a knowledge that can of course be communicated to outsiders, it can be shared with non-victims, including the victimizers, and to allow, enable and welcome such identity communications and learning is to have begun to create a multiculturalist space even before any of the pain itself is treated and further inflictions prohibited. While societal effort, including from dominant groups, will be required to formulate appropriate policies and adjust social relations, this movement from the 'inside', these identity discourses are critical in the formation of a multiculturalist society.

Another advantage of the term 'identity' is that it suggests less assumed behavioural or normative baggage than suggested by 'culture' or even by 'ethnicity'. It means that to speak of the recognition or accommodation of minority identities is not necessarily to advocate the reproduction of the past or customs from far-off places. It is possible for someone to have (and for the public space to recognize) a Pakistani identity without, for example, the Urdu language, observance of the rules of Islam or wanting an arranged marriage. This was a conclusion from a major survey of the 1990s which found that ethnic identification by minority individuals in Britain was almost universal but that adherence to traditional practices was mixed (Modood et al. 1997; discussed further in chapter 5 below). Identities persist even when participation in distinctive cultural practices is in decline or these practices are undergoing considerable adaptation. Not only is there nothing in the idea of multiculturalism that rules out developments of these sorts but they underline a key point. Namely, the primary interest of multiculturalism is not in culture per se but in the political uses of non-European origin ethnic and related identities, especially in turning their negative and stigmatic status into a positive feature of the societies that they are now part of. This means that multicultural-ism is characterized by the challenging, the dismantling and the remaking of public identities.

Multiplicity

If the above is my take on the 'culturalism' of 'multi-culturalism', we now need to spell out what is meant by the 'multi'. It is obviously an appreciation of the fact that the societies in question cannot be conceived in mono-identarian terms (if they ever could have been). More to the point, duality is equally inappropriate as characterization of the societies in question. For countries like most of those of western Europe to continue to think of themselves as 'white' is both inaccurate and a perpetu-ation of an ideology of exclusion. However, for them to think of themselves in dualistic terms, as consisting of two populations, black and white, as became common in Britain in the 1980s, is also to fall short of multi-culturalism (Modood 1988 and 1994). For it overlooks that the people who seek or for whom multicultural inclu-sion is sought are diverse and have different identities, combining elements based on origins, colour, culture, eth-nicity, religion and so on. To group them together as excluded on the basis of 'difference' is to rightly identify that they have something in common, but as a matter of fact such groups can be as different from each other as from white people.

The idea of a 'rainbow coalition' might be a good one politically to harness this diversity but it cannot be reduced to a single identity such as 'black'. The latter will have some positive identity resonance for some – primarily people of sub-Saharan African descent[2] – but not for others, perhaps for whom national origin identities (like Turkish) or a regional heritage (like Berber) or a

religious identity (like Sikh) may be much more meaningful, expressing forms of community and ethnic pride that
are struggling for recognition and inclusion. Moreover, the
'multi' does not just refer to cultural or self-definitional
diversity. The groups in question may have different socio-
economic positions, (dis)advantages, trajectories in, say,
US, Canadian or British society (Loury, Modood and Teles
2005; Heath and Cheung 2007). Nor is it true that they
are all worse off than their white co-citizens. The point is
not that some, say, individual western Indians are better
off than individual whites – that is trivially true. Rather,
that groups such as the Indians, Chinese, Koreans and
some other east Asians, for example, are developing a
more middle-class profile than whites. This complication
of an ethnic stratification model has got to be part of the
parameters of multiculturalism.

The multi has to also apply to our analysis of racism:
there is not a singular racism but multiple racisms. There
are of course colour or phenotype racisms but there are
also cultural racisms which build on 'colour' a set of
antagonistic or demeaning stereotypes based on alleged or
real cultural traits. The ways in which racism works with
Latinos, for example, both in terms of representation but
also in terms of treatment – perhaps they are more likely
to be hired than a black jobseeker but are more vulnerable
in terms of immigration policing and the possibility of
being deported – will be different to how it is for African-
Americans. Similarly, American-Asians may be admired in
distinctive ways (e.g., for their academic and occupational
achievements) but may also be racialized as 'nerds' and
'geeks', not to mention as foreign and un-American (Song
2001). The most important cultural racism today, at least
in western Europe, is anti-Muslim racism, sometimes
called Islamophobia. A multicultural approach, recognizing the plurality of racisms and the distinctive needs and
vulnerabilities of different groups, is therefore what
is needed to tackle racial and religious discrimination
(Modood 2005a).

For all these reasons – differential cultures, identities, economic and skill profiles, racisms, political targeting and so on – we should not expect a single sociological model for a multiethnic or multicultural society. The minority groups that need to be comprehended in such a model are likely to vary not just by dimension such as the above – though of course the nature and degree will vary by society – but also to the extent that they are even groups. It is not just that some groups will see themselves more in terms of regional origins and others in terms of religion; or that some will have the community structures and networks to form economic enclaves and others may not. Rather, some groups will be more mixed in terms of relationships and joint activities with non-group members and may exercise relatively little effort to reproduce the group culturally or politically. For other groups, however, who may not be at all 'separatist' or eschew civic participation, the transmission of a community or a diasporic or faith identity at least into the next generation may be very important. It follows, therefore, that a policy matrix that may suit one type of group may not suit another group. While we can all learn from the experiences and achievements of any one group, and may seek to transfer that for the benefit of other groups, no minority can be a model for all others. We may welcome the interactions that produce cultural hybridity in, for example, the music, dance, videos, TV and entertainment enclaves that characterize certain parts of Los Angeles, New York or London and think they are attractive forms of multiculture, but we have no right to insist that they be *the* form of multiculturalism that other groups should adapt themselves too. Similarly, if other groups are centred more on family, kin, religious education and social welfare, that should be welcomed too, though neither can that be *the* form of multiculturalism. So, the ultimate meaning of 'multi' is that specific policies, complexes of policies and multicultural institutional arrangements have to be customized to meet diverse (as well as common) vulnerabilities, needs and priorities. These points about the 'multi' in multiculturalism are of enormous significance and I shall return to them and their implications in later chapters.

Integration

It is widely said by its critics that 'multiculturalism' is a vague, confused concept whose different meanings to different people render sensible debate and policy orientation difficult. There is some truth in this, but the same is true of its rival ideas or models, 'assimilation' and 'integration'. Thus, a useful debate and reasoned action requires some conceptual ground-clearing in relation to these concepts as well.

The meanings I offer below are not, I believe, arbitrary; rather, they arise out of the public discourses in which the terms assimilation and integration are used, and all these terms are pitted against each other. One way to proceed would be to leave the issues of immigration and ethnic difference aside and begin with a higher level of sociological abstraction – after all, there is a body of sociological theory devoted to the issue of societal integration and the division of labour, most notably in Durkheimian sociology (Durkheim 1964; O'Donnell forthcoming). I believe, however, it is better to stay nearer the phenomenon one is analysing and the issues that need enlightening. The way I define them and establish their interrelationship are however my own, and I am aware that others may prefer to work with other meanings (e.g., Parekh 2005). Examples of alternative use of these words include 'assimilation' in American sociology (as in the 'segmented assimilation' proposed by Portes and Zhou 1993), which is similar to what is meant by integration in Britain. In general, European ethnic groups in the United States are seen as an exemplar for sociological theories and models of assimilation (see Kivisto 2005). Thus, Jews are taken to be a successfully assimilated group but the use of this term includes awareness that they have also changed the American society and culture they have become part of. When politicians in Britain and especially continental Europe speak of integration, the meaning they usually have in mind is what I define below as assimilation.

Assimilation — This is where the processes affecting the relationship between newly settled social groups are seen as one-way, and where the desired outcome for society as a whole is seen as involving least change in the ways of doing things for the majority of the country and its institutional policies. This may not necessarily be a *laissez-faire* approach – for the state can play an active role in bringing about the desired outcome, as in early twentieth-century 'Americanization' policies towards European migrants in the United States – but the preferred result is one where the newcomers do little to disturb the society they are settling in and become as much like their new compatriots as possible.

Integration — This is where processes of social interaction are seen as two-way, and where members of the majority community as well as immigrants and ethnic minorities are required to do something; so the latter cannot alone be blamed for failing (or not trying) to integrate. The established society is the site of institutions – including employers, civil society and the government – in which integration has to take place, and they accordingly must take the lead.

Multiculturalism — This is clearly not opposed to integration. For, as both my exemplars in chapter 1 and my discussion of Kymlicka in chapter 2 clearly show, multiculturalism assumes a two-way process of integration but, additionally, it is taken to work differently for different groups. This is because, as I have argued, each group is distinctive, and thus integration cannot consist of a single template (hence the 'multi'). The 'culturalism' – as we have seen, not an ideal term – refers to the understanding that the groups in question are likely to not just be marked by newness or phenotype or socio-economic location but by certain forms of group identities. Multicultural accommodation of minorities is different from integration because it recognizes the social reality of groups (not just of individuals and organizations). This reality can be of different kinds; for example, a sense of solidarity with people of similar origins or faith or mother tongue, including those in a country of origin or a diaspora. Such feelings might be an act of imagination but may also be rooted in lived experience and embodied in formal organizations dedicated to fostering group identity and keeping it alive. This form of accommodation would also allow group-based cultural and religious practices to be fitted into existing, majoritarian ways of doing things. These identities and practices would not be regarded as immutable, but neither would there be pressure either to change them (unless a major issue of principle, legality or security was at stake) or to confine them to a limited community or private space.

Multicultural accommodation works simultaneously on two levels: creating new forms of belonging to citizenship and country, and helping sustain origins and diaspora. The result – without which multiculturalism would not be a form of integration – is the formation of hyphenated identities such as Jewish-American or British-Muslim (even if the hyphenated nature of the latter is still evolving and contested). These hyphenated identities, on this understanding, are a legitimate basis for political mobilization and lobbying, not attacked as divisive or disloyal. Such minority identities do not necessarily compete with a sense of nationality, e.g., Britishness. Ethnic minority self-concepts can certainly have an oppositional or political character but it is not usually at the price of integration per se, illustrating that integration can take different forms. Indeed, political mobilization and participation, especially protest and contestation, has been one of the principal means of integration in Britain. As activists, spokespersons

and a plethora of community organizations come to interact with and modify existing perceptions, practices and
institutions, there is a two-way process of mutual education and incorporation: public discourse and political
arrangements are challenged but adjust to accommodate
and integrate the challengers. The imperial legacy has,
paradoxically, both been a source of racism and constituted a set of opportunity structures for an easy acquisition
and exercise of citizenship (for ex-imperial subjects), for
political opposition to racism and for an ethnic minority
assertiveness, partly influenced by developments elsewhere,
especially in the US. Ethnic identity, like gender and sexuality, has assumed a new political importance and for some
migrants and their descendants has become a primary
focus of their politics. While 'ethnicity' is disdained on
much of the European mainland and minorities are more
likely to be excluded and cowed, Britain is marked by an
ethnic assertiveness.[3] Arising out of the feelings of not
being respected or of lacking access to public space, it
consists of counterposing 'positive' images against traditional or dominant stereotypes. Indeed, resistance to racism
by each new minority has come to be seen as an almost
necessary path to citizenship and integration with dignity
into British society.

To summarize, multiculturalism or the accommodation
of minorities is different from integration because it
recognizes groups, not just individuals, at the level of:
identities, associations, belonging, including diasporic connections; behaviour, culture, religious practice, etc.; and
political mobilization. It appreciates that groups vary in
all kinds of ways and so will become part of the
social landscape in different ways. This means that they
cannot necessarily be accommodated according to a single
plan and will in different ways change the society into
which they are integrated. I appreciate that there is an
enormous academic and public intellectual critique of
the notion of groups and so I shall have to return to the
topic in chapter 5, but meanwhile we need to ask how can

there be equality across difference. This leads us – theoretically and politically – to an expanded or double concept of equality.

Equality

It should be clear from the above that the concept of equality has to be applied to groups and not just individuals (e.g., Parekh 2000). Different theorists have offered different formulations on this question. Charles Taylor (1992), for example, argues that when we talk about equality in the context of race and ethnicity, we are appealing to two different albeit related concepts – *equal dignity* and *equal respect*. Equal dignity appeals to people's humanity or to some specific membership like citizenship and applies to all members in a relatively uniform way. A good example is Martin Luther King Jr's demand for civil rights. He said black Americans wanted to make a claim upon the American dream; they wanted American citizenship in the way that the constitution theoretically is supposed to give to everybody but in practice fails to do so. We appeal to this universalist idea in relation to anti-discrimination policies where we appeal to the principle that everybody should be treated the same. But Taylor, and other theorists in differing ways, also posit the idea of *equal respect*. If equal dignity focuses on what people have in common and so is gender-blind, colour-blind and so on, equal respect is based on an understanding that difference is also important in conceptualizing and institutionalizing equal relations between individuals.

This is because individuals have group identities and these may be the ground of existing and long-standing inequalities such as racism, for example, and the ways in which some people have conceived and treated others as inferior, less rational and culturally backward. While those conceptions persist they will affect the dignity of non-white people, above all where they share cultural and social life with white people. Such negative conceptions will lead to direct and indirect acts of discrimination – they will eat away at the possibilities of equal dignity. They will affect the self-understanding of those who breathe in and seek to be equal participants in a culture in which ideas of their inferiority, or even simply their absence, their invisibility, is pervasive. They will stand in need of self-respect and the respect of others, of the dominant group; the latter will be crucial for it is the source of their damaged self-respect and it is where the power for change lies (Du Bois 1903).

So, a denigration of a group identity, or its distortion, or its denial, the pretence (often unconscious because it is part of a culture rather than a personal thought) that a group does not exist, the withholding of recognition or misrecognition is a form of oppression (Taylor 1992). It is a form of inequality in its own right but also threatens the other form of equality, equal dignity, the fulfilment of which can be made impossible by stereotyping or a failure to recognize the self-definitional strivings of marginal groups.

The interaction and mutuality between the two kinds of equality runs the other way too. Equal respect pre-supposes the framework of commonality and rights embodied in equal dignity. Hence it is quite wrong to think of the latter in terms of universalism and the former as a denial of universality. For not only does the concept of equal respect grow out of a concern with equal dignity but it only makes sense because it rests on universalist foundations. It is only because there is a fundamental equality between human beings or between citizens that the claim for respect can be formulated. As Taylor says, there is a demand for an acknowledgement of speci-ficity but it is powered by the universal that an advantage that some currently enjoy should not be a privilege but available to all (Taylor 1992: 38–9). Hence we must not lose sight of the fact that *both* equal dignity and equal respect are essential to multiculturalism; while the latter marks out multiculturalism from classical liberalism it does not make multiculturalism normatively particularistic or relativist.

Another way of making the same or similar point, following Iris Young (1990), is to distinguish between:

1 the equality that comes from the impartial and consistent application of a single set of rules or norms or conventions;
2 the equality that comes from a set of rules, norms or conventions that do not (dis)advantage the different parties to whom they are applied for the needs and sensitivities of all the parties have been taken into account and so each of these parties can identify with these rules; that there is a sense that the rules etc. speak to and for all the parties.

The first equality might be realized but egalitarians will still want to ask, 'Whose rules? Who made the rules? Were they jointly made? Do they suit all to whom they apply?' In chapter 2, we discussed Kymlicka's critique of the Rawlsian idea of neutrality. Rawls thought that consideration of (2) above would lead truly rational persons to choose to live in a state that was culturally neutral as that way, while no one was advantaged, no one was disadvantaged (Rawls 1971). Kymlicka rightly pointed out such neutrality is impossible; that any public space, policy or society is structured around certain kinds of understandings and practices which prioritize some cultural values and behaviours over others.[4] They are not fixed but nevertheless always have a specific character. You are inducted into them, though they also change as you participate. It means, for example, that people can argue for extending them. They may appeal for the transferral of one practice, such as elections for political office, to another, in the workplace, say, or in the local community. While some change is always possible and often desirable, no public space is culturally neutral.

If the public space and a particular polity or society that we are members of already has a cultural structure built into it and so is not neutral, where does this come from? Historically, it will have come from a dominant group. Dominant groups can be quite tolerant. They may, for example, allow minorities to live by their own religion, speak their own language, wear distinctive dress and so on but may insist that should be done in 'private' – not in the shared public space of politics, policies, schools and workplaces but only at home or community functions and at weekends. This way of structuring space and of deciding what is public and what is private can be an enormous source of power and inequality. In so far as subordinate, oppressed or marginal groups claim equality, what they are claiming is that they should not be marginal, subordinate or excluded; that they, too, their values, norms, and voice, should be part of the structuring of the public space. Why, they ask, should we have our identities privatized, while the dominant group has its identity universalized in the public space? So the argument is about the public/private distinction and what is 'normal' in that society, and why some groups are thought to be abnormal or different (Young 1990).

For example, many gay people, especially from the 1960s onwards, argue that they do not want to be tolerated by being told homosexuality is no longer illegal and acts between consenting adults done in private are fine. They want people to know that they are gay and to accept them as gay; and for public discussion about gayness to have the same place as discussions about heterosexuality. So when public policy is made, for instance on widows' benefits or pensions, we should not assume an exclusively heterosexual model of society. The same point applies in relation to ethnic and religious minorities. They may have cultural needs and customs which are disregarded by current arrangements and which can be discriminatory; when they try to get that rectified they may be met by racist devaluing of their needs and norms or told that they do not belong in this country – which takes us straight back to respect and recognition. These needs may be to do with bilingual teaching and other aspects of a school curriculum; or, the provision of single-sex schools, which in Britain have been closing across the country in the same period that the South Asian population has been growing and wanting them. They may be to do with dress, whether it is the convention of wearing headdress indoors, as in the case of young African-American men who seem to have created new American norms about the wearing of items such as baseball caps, or the Sikh male turban, the Jewish male yarmulke or the Muslim female headscarf, the hijab. It may be to do with whose holy days are to be recognized as public holidays, when employers cannot demand your presence, when university exams may not be set and which are celebrated in shopping malls, on television and on which public funds are disbursed. As in the gay example above, the area of family structure and size is likely to be central. The construction of new social housing across the western world is based on the premise that households are getting smaller and smaller but where does that leave Bangladeshis in east London, whose need is indisputable but who in many cases are too large as a family to be housed in new stock and so are disproportionately allocated old housing. If a social housing provider in Paris has one definition of family (nuclear and two-generational) and French citizens of Berber origins have another definition (extended and multi-generational), does that mean that they have voluntarily put themselves beyond the obligations of the French state? Who is to decide what is marriage and what is divorce? Most western countries forbid more than one wife at a time but put no limit on the number of girlfriends or live-in partners; some Muslims believe there is a place for up to four simultaneous female partners but not outside marriage. Should only one of these views be recognized by the law courts? In all these cases, whatever specific view we may have on any of them, it is clear that a consistent, impartial application of a single set of rules, norms and conventions by itself is not enough to achieve equality. It can, depending on the content of the laws and of the public generally, create two tiers of citizenship, those who are at home in the rules etc., and those who are all at sea, drowning in a culture of misfit and misrecognition.

This is why the ideas of equal respect and recognition are essential to multicultural equality and multicultural integration. As the variety of the above issues show, some will involve the law and others will not; some will be public policy issues at a national level whilst others will remain local; and sometimes initiatives can be taken by a particular institution – a particular school, hospital, housing association or charity, or by a private sector employer. Yet, while issues of equal respect and recognition do not simply arise at the level of a national state but across society, a legislative framework and governmental leadership may be crucial (CMEB 2000). Nevertheless, it is best to see recognition of positive difference as a civic principle that in general should inform the relations between fellow citizens and ought to be manifest across the varied sites and institutions of civil society (Seglow 2003: 87–8). Hate speech is a good example of where some legislation is necessary but what one needs to achieve goes beyond the practical scope of law, which can be a blunt instrument endangering freedom of speech. Most countries recognize that legal intervention is necessary when there is a serious risk of incitement to hatred; or when the 'fighting talk' is likely to inflame passions and risk public order; or when it is likely to reinforce prejudice and lead to acts of discrimination or victimization. But this falls short of the goal of respect. For that one relies on the sensitivity and responsibility of individuals and institutions to refrain from what is legal but unacceptable. Where these qualities are missing one relies on public debate and censure to provide standards and restraints. Hence where matters are not or cannot easily be regulated by law one relies on protest and empathy, though it will take time for dominant groups to learn what hurts others. This is how most racist speech and images and other free expressions (e.g., the use of golliwogs as commercial brands or *The Black and White Minstrel Show*) have been censured (rather than censored) away and it is how the British media responded to the Danish cartoons affair, recognizing that they had the right to republish the cartoons but that it would be offensive to do so (Modood 2006; for an engaging debate, see Modood et al. 2006a). It is sometimes suggested that a concern with issues of respect is in some sense a diversion from the pursuit of integration or equality, that it is a preoccupation with labels, images and discourse, in short, 'political correctness'. Any serious concern can lead to overzealous, mechanistic application but there is nothing trivial about equal respect. It is certainly not a matter of choosing between difference, integration and equality, for positive difference is necessary to integration that is informed by equal respect as well as equal dignity.

Other Forms of Inequality

The inequalities of 'difference' are of course connected with other forms of inequality, especially those to do with social status and economic opportunities. For example, the groups in question are often disproportionately disadvantaged; the socio-economic disadvantage is one of the sources of, as well as a consequence of, their stereotypical representation as inferior, unintelligent, backward, alien and so forth. Moreover, socio-economic disadvantage can be a basis for an ethnic group solidarity, for enhancing groupness (though it can have the opposite effect too). So neither sociologically nor politically can these groups be seen as classless or as distinct classes in their own right.

Throughout the industrialized world parental class and education are major factors in life-chances, occupational achievements and incomes (Goldthorpe 2000). Their effects today are usually much greater than the effects of race or ethnicity (or for that matter, gender or sexual orientation), and at least some of these effects are independent of race. Yet, that is not the whole story. For class and education have differential effects on different minority groups as these groups have different compositions of pre-migration class origins and educational profiles. For example, the predominantly peasant backgrounds of Bangladeshi migrants to Britain compared to the commercial and professional backgrounds of African-Asian migrants and refugees goes a long way in explaining why today they are differently located by class in Britain, and at the same time have different educational profiles. Their present position can be largely but not wholly understood in terms of class and education; sometimes the unexplained aspects, for example, the higher levels of unemployment, can be partly accounted for by various forms of racial discrimination and disadvantage. At other times, the unexplained aspects are barely explained by reference to race, to a non-white status (Gayle, Berridge and Davies 2002; Platt 2005) though perhaps they do begin to be explained by different attitudes to, for example, self-employment (Modood, Metcalf and Virdee 1998), education and family, including gender roles and the intergenerational nurturing and support of ambition (Modood 2004). So, ethnicity and class interact. Just as attitudes to schooling, higher education and taking out a loan to pay for higher education are influenced by class location so are they also influenced by ethnicity (Connor et al. 2004). This can mean that some minority groups can achieve more social mobility than their class peers and others less; that 'there is evidence of differential processes operating for different ethnic groups that go beyond their class background, but which cannot be attributed to discrimination operating equally against all minority groups' (Platt 2005: 697). So, ethnicity can sometimes be a resource as well as a liability, and while the disadvantages of class and ethnicity can sometimes reinforce each other, ethnicity can sometimes mitigate aspects of class disadvantage (in relation to educational attainment, see Bradley and Taylor 2004).

The sociology of ethnicity or the politics of multiculturalism is, then, only possible because ethnicity and related forms of collectivity are not reducible to or are not just pimples on class (or gender etc.), but they are not meant to analytically or politically displace these other dimensions of social experience as such. Rather, they highlight the social, cultural, economic and political dynamics that are missed when ethnic and related difference is ignored or seen only as a by-product of other sociological determinants.

Multiculturalism, then, is an elaboration of political concerns in relation to certain forms of difference regardless of which other sociological or political analyses it will need to be integrated with.[5] There is no suggestion of monocausal explanations or a one-dimensional politics; on the contrary, an emphasis on ethnicity bespeaks caution about socio-economic generalizations that do not attend to difference and complexity. Sociological multi-dimensionality or intersectionality (Bradley 1996) means taking ethnicity as seriously as class or gender. This requires an elaboration of ethnicity that has some categorical autonomy; that way we can enquire into the varied ways in which it might intersect with class and gender. Otherwise we are likely to see ethnicity subordinated to other social categories, something that I will return to in chapter 5.

Similar points can be made in relation to ethnicity/difference and gender. All groups are gendered; they have distinct as well as related conceptions of gender and gender-roles; indeed, gender is mediated by ethnicity and related cultural norms, no less than by class and generational change. Different ethnic groups are therefore likely to have both similar and distinct forms of gender relations and gender inequalities. For example, Pakistani mothers of young adults may exercise more power over the choice of the marriage partners of their sons and daughters than their white peers but may be more constrained by familial norms about certain types of participation in public activities and paid work outside the home or family business. Even in relation to their treatment by the wider society, it would be too simplistic to assume 'double disadvantage' of non-white women as the universal pattern. It may be a common pattern but one needs to take care to not overgeneralize and homogenize a varied phenomena. For example, if one compares the condition of black women in Britain and the US to that of black men, men (if in work) are likely to be earning higher on average; but relative to whites the position of black women is much better than that of black men (Loury, Modood and Teles 2005). Moreover, there is considerable data showing that it is black men rather than black women that are perceived as threatening – and so likely to suffer unfavourable treatment – by teachers, employers, shop workers, police officers and even by ordinary people in the street fearful of black muggers. Similarly, while hijab-wearing Muslim women are more likely to get hostile stares in the street, it is bearded young Muslim men that are likely to be stopped and searched by the police and experience arbitrary arrest.

This then is my outline of political multiculturalism: it begins with a concept of negative difference and seeks the goal of positive difference and the means to achieve it, which crucially involve the appreciation of the fact of multiplicity and groupness, the building of group pride amongst those marked by negative difference, and political engagement with the sources of negativity and racism. This suggests neither separatism nor assimilation but an accommodative form of integration which would allow group-based racialized, ethnic, cultural and religious identities and practices to be recognized and supported in the public space, rather than require them to be privatized. This is justified by an extended concept of equality, not just equal dignity but also equal respect. While the focus is not on anything so narrow as normally understood by 'culture', and multicultural equality cannot be achieved without other forms of equality, such as those relating to socio-economic opportunities, its distinctive feature is about the inclusion into and the making of a shared public space in terms of equality of respect as well as equal dignity.

– 4 –

Liberal Citizenship
and Secularism

In the previous chapter I outlined the idea of multiculturalism and contrasted it with a simpler form of integration
and a simpler form of equality. I would like to pursue this
further by contrasting the approach being elaborated here
more fully with liberalism and also philosophical multiculturalism. Classical liberalism can take one of two forms.
The older approach is one of toleration, that is to say, one
tolerates difference. Toleration presupposes a number of
preconditions. One is that one disapproves of what one is
being asked to tolerate (Mendus 1989) – if one approves
of, or even if one is simply indifferent to, the attributes,
beliefs or behaviour in question, then there is nothing to
tolerate – the behaviour is simply part of what is normal.
Secondly, one must have the power, or believe one has the
power, to suppress the behaviour in question. That is to
say, there is an alternative to tolerating the disapproved
difference, the deviant behaviour. That is why it makes
more sense to talk of majorities tolerating minorities than
of minorities tolerating majorities (Galeotti 2002). A more
theoretical liberal position but still recognizably classic is
one that we have already touched on in chapters 2 and 3,
namely that developed by Rawls (Rawls 1971). In a just

society, the state expresses no ethical or religious view but is scrupulously neutral between all possible views or, as he later expressed it, between all reasonable views (Rawls 1993). This is clearly an advance on the idea of toleration since the question of moral approval or disapproval is taken out of the frame (even when the frame is limited to reasonable views, these are identified by Rawls as views with which a dialogical consensus can be built rather than because they are worthy). While I think it is impossible for the state to be totally neutral, one can see both toleration and neutrality as classically liberal as liberalism has evolved – in theory and practice – over the centuries, especially in relation to religious dissent.

Multiculturalism is clearly beyond toleration and state neutrality for it involves active support for cultural difference, active discouragement against hostility and disapproval and the remaking of the public sphere in order to fully include marginalized identities. This indeed has become the practice, to some degree or other, of some contemporary liberal democratic countries, and has been theorized by some as the correct liberal response to difference (Kymlicka 1995). Multiculturalism is not only more active in relation to minority identities than sanctioned by classical liberalism but also in relation to majority identities. For it is also concerned to encourage a vision of commonalities, of what is shared across difference, and through remaking citizenship and national identity. This means that far from simply supporting difference, the multicultural state may also need to encourage forms of social mixing and interaction, though this will be a two-way process and not just in relation to simply avoiding minority segregation. Multiculturalism is a form of civic interaction which recognizes the normative and political significance of group identities but is not about merely inward-looking or self-interested communities.

Minorities can also be bearers of distinctive knowledge. They are a primary source about the marginalization and discrimination they experience, and hence of their distinctive location. They have a take on their societies that the majority does not experience and so offers to the majority a very different perspective on their shared society, its institutions, discourses and self-image. They hold a critical mirror up to that society. They are also likely to have sensibilities, ways of thinking and living, heritages they can call upon to widen the pool of available experience and wisdom. In all these ways the presence of diversity is an epistemological condition, a learning experience and the source of the dialogical, two-way character of multiculturalism (Parekh 2000) – except that a multilogue is much more accurate.[1] It underlies that multiculturalism is much more than toleration or the co-presence of mutually indifferent communities. Dialogue necessarily implies openness and the possibility of mutual learning but not uncritical acceptance, and so some kind of mutual evaluation. This is, however, quite a weak sense of 'evaluation'. It can be contrasted with a philosophical multiculturalism which is concerned to develop a frame in which different cultures and religions can come to an understanding of each other and therefore to a richer understanding of humanity. Thus Taylor sees the ultimate frontier of the politics of recognition as being the development – which he sees far off from contemporary capacities – of sensibilities and ways of thinking so that we can understand cultures radically different from our own and thereby evaluate their contribution to human civilization (Taylor 1992). Similarly, Parekh emphasizes that the ultimate value of multiculturalism lies in cross-cultural and cross-civilizational understanding through which we simultaneously appreciate the varied ways to be human whilst more profoundly understanding our own distinctive location (Parekh 2000). While my own formulation of multiculturalism is built on a reading of Taylor and Parekh (amongst others), the philosophical views I have just ascribed to them carry important and controversial philosophical theses which I can leave to one side, for example, Taylor's suggestion that different cultures can be evaluated and ranked by and against each other; or, Parekh's moral inter-subjectivism, the view that values and morality, while grounded in a conception of human nature, ultimately have no foundations independent of reasoning selves (Parekh 2000: 128). These are debates that I do not need to enter. My interest and advocacy is confined to political multiculturalism. While Parekh and Taylor locate their political multiculturalism within a wider, philosophical multiculturalism, I am not locating political multicultural-ism in anything bigger than itself – or more precisely, in nothing bigger than contemporary ideas of democratic citizenship and belonging.

One important implication is that for me the identities and cultures of others are primarily not important for epistemological reasons – except in the sense that all poli-tics involves learning and is epistemological. I can remain agnostic on the ethical and philosophical underpinnings of multiculturalism, or even whether it has any. For me, iden-tities and cultures are important because they are impor-tant to the bearers of those identities, people who are members of our society, fellow citizens, and so have to be included into the polity in ways consistent with respect and equality. As Elisabetta Galeotti puts it: 'Differences should be publicly recognised not because they are important or significant per se, though they may well be, but because they are important for their bearers and because expres-sions of public contempt for them, on the grounds that they depart from the social "norm" are a source of injus-tice' (Galeotti 2002).

There is a distinction between the public recognition and respect for identities and beliefs and the moral evalu-ation of the same; the former is possible without the latter. When we argue for recognition of a difference we are not necessarily morally approving or disapproving of that dif-ference. This does not mean that recognition is beyond the scope of moral principles for moral principles will indeed *limit* what we can recognize: child sacrifice, cannibalism and sati (widows' self-immolation) would be unacceptable for just about everybody and cliterodectomy would also be unacceptable for many. Recognition should not infringe the fundamental rights of individuals or cause harm to others. What this means in practice will sometimes be unclear and contested. The important point is that the instancing of unacceptable cases does not damage or undermine the argument for recognition. All laws and public policies have these kinds of limits but nevertheless most laws and policies are accepted as legitimate without a moral evaluation of their content – a law requires compliance from all, regardless of how different individuals may evaluate it. Another way of putting this is that laws and the policies of legitimate governments have a moral standing or at least a public legitimacy without each law or policy being subject to a moral evaluation – though the legitimacy can be undermined if they are shown in any specific case to be immoral by reference to a higher morality. Similarly, the legitimacy of recognition does not depend upon a moral evaluation of the difference in question; but recognition works within moral limits. This distinction between the legitimacy of recognition *as such* and of any specific claim is then on the same footing as law or taxation or war. The claim I am defending is that there is nothing illiberal or inegalitarian or anti-citizenship about recognition.

We are not being asked to approve or disapprove in an ultimate way but allow co-presence, public support, interaction and societal redefinition. Of course the giving of a new public status to an identity group is not just to legitimize their presence and to include them in the self-definition of one's society or country; it is also to allow them to influence the attitudes, mores and practice of the rest of society. For example, encouraging greater public participation by women, gays or Muslims may come to mean that their critical perspectives upon existing practices and values are openly discussed, that marginalized sensibilities become de-stigmatized and come to be more influential and that certain concerns, styles, aesthetics, discourses and literatures come to be produced and shape the mainstream. In these various ways, the broader culture and specific minority perspectives will interact and mutually influence each other. The mainstream will not simply be dominated by one or a few groups, or by people who think alike, a kind of mutual admiration society, but will have a more plural and composite character in which learning is a two-way, or better, a multilogical process.

3+1 Implications for Liberal Citizenship

In the previous chapters I have argued that multiculturalism arises within contemporary liberal and social democratic egalitarianism but it is at the same time in tension with and a critique of some classical liberal ideas. I would now like to elaborate this critique further.

The multiculturalism or politics of difference that I have been advocating has four major implications for liberal citizenship. Firstly, it is clearly a collective project and concerns collectivities and not just individuals. Secondly, it is not colour-, gender-, or sexual orientation-'blind' and so breaches the liberal public–private identity distinction which prohibits the recognition of particular group identities so that no citizens are treated in a more or less privileged way or divided from each other. These two implications are obvious from the discussion so far but the next two implications are less obvious and more controversial. The first of these is that multiculturalism takes race, sex and sexuality beyond being merely ascriptive sources of identity, beyond mere categories. Liberal citizenship is not interested in group identities and shuns identitarian politics; its interest in 'race' is confined to anti-discrimination and simply as an aspect of the legal equality of citizens (Barry 2001). Strictly speaking, race is of interest to liberal citizenship only because no one can choose their race; it is either a biological fact about

them or, more accurately, is a way of being categorized by
the society around them by reference to some real or perceived biological features, and so one should not be dis-
criminated against on something over which one has no
control. But if, as I have argued, equality is also about
celebrating previously demeaned identities (e.g., taking
pride in one's blackness rather than accepting it as a merely
'private' matter), then what is being addressed in anti-
discrimination, or promoted as a public identity, is a
chosen response to one's ascription, namely pride, identity
renewal, the challenging of hegemonic norms and asserting
of marginalized identities and so on. Of course this is not
peculiar to race/ethnicity. Exactly the same applies to sex
and sexuality. We may not choose our sex or sexual orientation but we choose how to live with it politically. Do
we keep it private or do we make it the basis of a social
movement and seek public resources and representation
for it? In many countries the initial liberal – and social
democratic and socialist – response that the assertions of
race, political femininity, gay pride politics and so on were
divisive and deviations from the only political identity that
mattered (citizenship; and/or class, in the case of socialists)
soon gave way to an understanding that these positions
were a genuine and significant part of a plural, centre-left
egalitarian movement.

Marginalized and other religious groups, most notably
Muslims, are now utilizing the same kind of argument and
making a claim that religious identity, just like gay identity,
and just like certain forms of racial identity, should not
just be privatized or tolerated, but should be part of the
public space. In their case, however, they come into conflict
with an additional fourth dimension of liberal citizenship.
This additional conflict with liberal citizenship is best
understood as a '3+1' rather than merely a fourth difficulty
because while it is not clear that it actually raises a new
difficulty, for many on the centre-left this one, unlike the
previous three, is seen as a demand that should not be
conceded.[2] One would think that if a new group was
pressing a claim which had already been granted to others

then what would be at issue would be a practical adjustment not fundamental principle. But as a matter of fact,
the demand by Muslims not just for toleration and religious freedom but for public recognition is indeed taken
to be philosophically very different to the same demand
made by black people, women and gays. It is seen as an
attack on the principle of secularism, the view that religion
is a feature, perhaps uniquely, of private and not public
identity.

Before we discuss the issue of secularism, however, it is
best to get an argument out of the way which, if valid,
would prevent the issue arising at all. This is, and it is
commonly found in the op-ed pages of the broadsheets,
that Muslims (and other religious groups) are simply not
on a par with the groups with which I have aligned them.
It is argued that woman, black and gay are as a matter of
fact ascribed, involuntary identities while being a Muslim
is about chosen beliefs, and that Muslims therefore need
or ought to have less legal protection than the other kinds
of identities. I think this is sociologically naive (and a
political con). The position of Muslims today in countries
like Britain is similar to the other identities of 'difference'
as Muslims catch up with and engage with the contemporary concept of equality. No one chooses to be or not to
be born into a Muslim family. Similarly, no one chooses
to be born into a society where to look like a Muslim or
to be a Muslim creates suspicion, hostility, or failure to get
the job you applied for. Of course how Muslims respond
to these circumstances will vary. Some will organize resistance, while others will try to stop looking like Muslims
(the equivalent of 'passing' for white); some will build an
ideology out of their subordination, others will not, just
as a woman can choose to be a feminist or not. Again,
some Muslims may define their Islam in terms of piety
rather than politics; just as some women may see no politics in their gender, while for others their gender will be at
the centre of their politics.

I put to one side, therefore, the contention that equality
as recognition (uniquely) does not apply to oppressed

religious communities. Of course many people's objections may be based on what they (sometimes correctly) understand as conservative, even intolerant and inegalitarian, views held by some Muslims and others in relation to issues of personal sexual freedom. My concern is with the argument that a commitment to a reasonable secularism rules out extending multicultural equality to Muslims and other religious groups.

I proceed on the basis of two assumptions, firstly that a religious group's view on matters of gender and sexuality, which of course will not be uniform, is open to debate and change; and secondly, that conservative views which do not lead to harmful or unlawful actions cannot be a bar to multicultural recognition.[3] Those who see the current Muslim assertiveness as an unwanted and illegitimate child of multiculturalism have only two choices if they wish to be consistent. They can repudiate the idea of equality as identity recognition and return to the 1950s' liberal idea of equality for instance as colour-, sex-, religion-blindness (Barry 2001). Or they must appreciate that a programme of racial and multicultural equality is not possible today without a discussion of the merits and limits of secularism.

Secularism can no longer be treated as 'off-limits' or, as President Jacques Chirac said in a major speech in 2004, 'non-negotiable' (Cesari 2004: 166). Not that I believe, as I shall now go on to argue, that it is really a matter of being for or against secularism; but rather of a careful, institution by institution analysis of how to draw the public–private boundary and further the cause of multicultural equality and inclusivity.

Secularism: Different Public–Private Boundaries in Different Countries

At the heart of secularism is a distinction between the public realm of citizens and policies, and the private realm of belief and worship.[4] Secularism as an ideology might consist of an uncompromising separation between religion and state, perhaps even of an atheistic, materialist analysis of religion as the opium of the unenlightened masses, which reason and material progress will consign to the dustbin of human history. Yet that is not what we mean when we talk about secular institutions in western democracies. Ideological secularism may have motivated some of the participants of the French, Soviet and Maoist revolutions and been responsible for some of the brutality and totalitarian excesses that they gave rise to. Its twin, ideological anti-secularism, is an uncritical and unwarranted extension of an opposition to ideological secularism into an opposition to all forms of secularism. Both perspectives have little empirical or normative purchase on the secularism as it has actually come to develop in most democracies, what we might call moderate secularism, by which I mean the relative autonomy of politics so that political authority, public reasoning and citizenship does not depend upon shared religious conviction and motivation. Such a moderate secularism can be institutionalized in many different ways but is not hostile to nor characterized by an absolute determination to expel religion from the political, let alone expunge it from the world. While all western countries are clearly secular in many ways, interpretations and institutional arrangements diverge according to the dominant national religious culture and the differing projects of nation-state building. The result is that what is taken to be the practice of secularism in one country is thought to be overly permissive or overly restrictive in another.

For example, the United States has as its First Amendment to the Constitution that there shall be no established church and there is wide support for this and in the last few decades there has been a tendency amongst academics and jurists to interpret the church–state separation in continually more radical ways (Sandel 1994; Hamburger 2002). Yet, as is well known, not only is the US a deeply

religious society, with much higher levels of church attendance than in western Europe (Greely 1995), but there is
a strong Protestant, evangelical fundamentalism that is
rare in Europe. This fundamentalism disputes some of the
new radical interpretations of the 'no establishment clause',
though not necessarily the clause itself, and is one of the
primary mobilizing forces in contemporary American politics; it is widely claimed that it decided the presidential
election of 2004. The churches in question – mainly white,
mainly in the South and mid-West – campaign openly for
candidates and parties, indeed raise large sums of money
for politicians and introduce religion-based issues into
politics, such as positions on abortion, HIV/Aids, homosexuality, stem-cell research, prayer at school, the teaching
of creationism at school and so on. It has been said that
no openly avowed atheist has ever been a candidate for
the White House and that it would be impossible for such
a candidate to be elected. It is not at all unusual for politicians – in fact for President George W. Bush, it was most
usual – to publicly talk about their faith, to appeal to
religion and to hold prayer meetings in government build-
ings and as a prelude or epilogue to government business.
On the other hand, in 'establishment' Britain, bishops sit
in the upper chamber of the legislature by right and only
the senior Archbishop can crown a new head of state, the
monarch, but politicians rarely talk about their religion. It
was noticeable, for example, that when Prime Minister
Blair went to a summit meeting with President Bush to
discuss aspects of the Iraq War in 2003, the US media
widely reported that the two leaders had prayed together.
Yet, Prime Minister Blair, one of the most openly professed
and active Christians ever to hold that office, refused on
his return to answer questions on this issue from the
British media, saying it was a private matter. The British
state may have an established church in England and a
national church in Scotland and in Wales but the beliefs
of the Queen's first minister are his own concern. In

disestablished America when President Bush says God told him to invade Iraq, a sizeable popular reaction might be 'Jesus be praised!' but in the British state it is the Archbishop of Canterbury that publicly interprets God's will – and on matters of war, as on other political matters, God is not always supportive of government policies, and when this is the case it is the duty of the bishops to let the public know, not just in the churches but on national media. In both countries, churches and priests can be not just major providers of (sometimes state-funded) social welfare and pastoral care but also leaders of political movements on issues such as anti-racism, international social justice, third-world debt relief, nuclear weapons, world peace and so on.

France draws the distinction between state and religion differently again. Like the US, there is no state church but, unlike the US, the state actively promotes the privatization of religion. While in the US, organized religion in civil society is powerful and seeks to exert influence on the political process, French civil society does not carry signs or expressions of religion. This is particularly the case in state schools where the radical secularist idea of *laïcité* is interpreted as the production of future citizens in a religion-free zone, hence the popular banning of the *foulard*, the headscarves worn by some Muslim girls. Yet, the French state, contrary to the US, confers institutional legal status on the Catholic and Protestant Churches and on the Jewish Consistory, albeit carefully designating organized religions as *cultes* and not communities. Through state-sponsored institutions such as the Jewish Consistory and the recently formed French Council of the Muslim Faith (*Conseil Français du Culte Musulman*), the state gives some recognition to organized religions but largely on its own terms: selected religious leaders have regular liaisons with the state but on a narrowly religious and non-political set of issues. Indeed, such an institutional framework is as much a form of state control as it is of recognition and

Table 4.1 Religion vis-à-vis state and civil society in three countries

	State	Religion in civil society
England/Britain	Weak establishment but churches have a political voice	Weak but churches can be a source of political criticism and action
United States	No establishment	Strong and politically mobilized
France	Actively secular but offers top-down recognition/control	Weak; rare for churches to be political

Adapted from Modood and Kastoryano 2006.

falls far short of any kind of social partnership. We might want to express these three different national manifestations of secularism as in table 4.1.

So, what are the appropriate limits of the state in a liberal democracy? Everyone will agree that there should be religious freedom and that this should include freedom of belief and worship in private associations. Family too falls on the private side of the line but the state regulates the limits of what is a lawful family – for example, polygamy is not permitted in many countries – not to mention the deployment of official definitions of family in the distribution of welfare entitlements. Religions typically put a premium on mutuality and on care of the sick, the homeless, the elderly and so on. They set up organizations to pursue these aims, but so do states. Should there be a competitive or a cooperative relationship between these religious and state organizations, or do they have to ignore each other? Can public money – raised out of taxes on religious as well as non-religious citizens – not be used to support the organizations favoured by some religious taxpayers? What of schools? Do parents not have the right to expect that schools will make an effort – while pursuing

broader educational and civic aims – not to create a conflict between the work of the school and the upbringing of
the children at home but, rather, show respect for their
religious background? Can parents, as associations of religious citizens, not set up their own schools and should
those schools not be supported out of the taxes of the same
parents? Is the school where the private (the family) meets
the public (the state); or is it, in some Platonic manner,
where the state takes over the children from the family and
pursues its own purposes? Even if there is to be no established church, the state may still wish to work with organized religion as a social partner, as is the case in Germany,
or to have some forum in which it consults with organized
religion, some kind of national council of religions, as in
Belgium. Or, even if it does not do that because it is
regarded as compromising the principle of secularism,
political parties, being agents in civil society rather than
organs of the state, may wish to do this and institute
special representation for religious groups as many do for
groups defined by age, gender, region, language, ethnicity
and so on. It is clear then that the 'public' is a multi-faceted
concept and in relation to secularism may be defined differently in relation to different dimensions of religion and
in different countries.

We can all be secularists then, all approve of secularism
in some respect, and yet have quite different ideas, influenced by historical legacies and varied pragmatic compromises, of where to draw the line between public and
private.[5] It would be quite mistaken to suppose that all
religious spokespersons, or at least all political Muslims,
are on one side of the line, and all others are on the other
side. There are many different ways of drawing the various
lines at issue (Parekh 2000: 321–35). In the past, the
drawing of them has reflected particular contexts shaped
by differential customs, urgency of need and sensitivity to
the sensibilities of the relevant religious groups (Modood
1994, 1997). Exactly the same considerations are relevant
in relation to the accommodation of Muslims in Europe

today – not a battle of slogans and ideological over-simplifications.

Moderate Secularism As an Implication of Multicultural Equality

Multicultural equality, then, when applied to religious groups means that secularism *simpliciter* appears to be an obstacle to integration and equality. But as we have just seen secularism pure and simple is not what exists in the world. The country by country situation is more complex, and indeed, far less inhospitable to the accommodation of Muslims than the ideology of secularism – or, for that matter, the ideology of anti-secularism – might suggest (Modood, Triandafyllidou and Zapata-Barrero 2006b). All actual practices of secularism consist of institutional compromises and these can, should be and are being extended today to accommodate Muslims and others, just as in the past they have been extended to accommodate rival churches and the Jews. The institutional reconfiguration varies according to the historic place of religion in each country. Today the appropriate response to the new Muslim challenges is pluralistic institutional integration, rather than an appeal to a radical public–private separation in the name of secularism. The approach that is being argued for here, then, consists of:

1 The extension of a politics of difference to include appropriate religious identities and organizations.
2 A reconceptualization of secularism from the concepts of neutrality and the strict public/private divide to a moderate and evolutionary secularism based on institutional adjustments.
3 A pragmatic, case by case, negotiated approach to dealing with controversy and conflict, not an ideological, drawing a 'line-in-the-sand' mentality,

with a view to pluralizing the contemporary
institutional arrangements in relation to church–
state linkages.

Certainly this involves recognizing the normative significance of religion, namely, it offers identities that matter to
people. But this is an idea at the heart of political multiculturalism and involves no theological or ethical evaluation of any particular faith or even religion as such. This
institutional integration approach can then be used as a
basis for including Islam into the institutional framework
of the state, using the historical accommodation between
state and church as a basis for negotiations in order to
achieve consensual resolutions consistent with equality
and justice. As these accommodations have varied from
country to country, it means there is no exemplary solution, for contemporary solutions too will depend on the
national context and will not have a once-and-for-all-time
basis. It is clearly a dialogical perspective and assumes the
possibility of mutual education and learning. Like all negotiation and reform, there are normative as well as practical
limits. Aspects of the former have been usefully characterized by Parekh as 'society's operative public values' (Parekh
2000: 267). These values, such as equality between the
sexes, are embedded in the political constitution, in specific
laws and in the norms governing the civic relations in a
society. Norms, laws and constitutional principles concerning the appropriate place of religion in public life
generally and in specific policy areas (such as schools or
rehabilitation of criminals) consist of such public values
and are reasoned about, justified or criticized by reference
to specific values about religion or politics as well as
more general norms and values in a society, such as fairness, or balance or consensus and so on. I, therefore,
recognize that the approach recommended here involves
solutions that are highly contextual and practical but they
are far from arbitrary or without reference to values. While
the latter are not static because they are constantly being

reinterpreted, realigned, extended and reformed, neverthe-less they provide a basis for dialogue and agreement.

An example is the development of a religious equality agenda in Britain, including the incorporation of some Muslim schools on the same basis as schools of religions with a much longer presence. It also includes the recom-mendations of the Royal Commission on the Reform of the House of Lords (2000) that in addition to the Anglican bishops who sit in that House by right as part of the Anglican 'establishment', this right should be extended to cover those of other Christian and non-Christian faiths. The same point can be made in relation to the fact that as early as 1974 the Belgian state decided to include Islam within its Council of Religions as a full member, or to the way that Muslims in the Netherlands have long had state-funded religious schools and television channels as a progressive step in that country's traditional way of institutionally dealing with organized religion, namely, 'pillarization'.[6] Similarly, a 'Muslim community' is becom-ing recognized by public authorities in Germany by appeal-ing to the historic German idea of a 'religious society' (*Religionsgesellschaft*). Again, a series of French Interior Ministers have taken a number of steps to 'normalize' Islam in France by creating an official French Islam under the authority of the state in ways that make it identical to other faiths (for more on these cases see Modood and Kastoryano 2006; Cesari 2004).

The recognition of Islam in Europe can, as some of these examples suggest, take a corporatist form, can be led or even imposed by the state in a 'top-down' way and can take a church or ecclesiastical model as its form. This may be appropriate for certain countries or at certain moments and could be – usually is – consistent to some degree or other with the conception of multiculturalism I have out-lined. However, it would not necessarily represent the multicultural experience and its potentialities at its best. A corporatist inclusion might require, for example, Muslims and their representatives to speak in one voice and to create a unified, hierarchical structure when this is out of character in Sunni Islam, especially the South Asian Sunni Islam espoused by the majority of Muslims in Britain, and of the contemporary British Muslim scene. Corporatism would very likely consist of state control of the French kind, with the state imposing upon Muslims its own template, plans, modes of partnership and chosen imams and leaders. My own preference, then, would be for an approach that would be less corporatist, less statist and less churchy – in brief, less French. An approach in which civil society played a greater role would be more comfortable with there being a variety of Muslim voices, groups and representatives. Different institutions, organizations and associations would seek to accommodate Muslims in ways that worked for them best at a particular time, knowing that these ways may or ought to be modified over time and Muslim and other pressure groups and civic actors may be continually evolving their claims and agendas. Within a general understanding that there has to be an explicit effort to include Muslims (and other marginal and underrepresented groups), different organizations may not just seek this inclusion in different ways but may seek as representatives Muslims that seem to them most appropriate associates and partners, persons who would add something to the organization and are not merely delegated from a central, hierarchical Muslim body. The idea of numerical or 'mirror' representation of the population might be a guideline but it would not necessarily follow that some kind of quota allocation (a milder version of the corporatist tendency) would have to operate. Improvisation, flexibility, consultation, learning by 'suck it and see' and by the example of others; incrementalism and all the other virtues of a pragmatic politics in close touch with a dynamic civil society can as much, and perhaps better, bring about multicultural equality than a top-down corporatist inclusion. 'Representation' here would mean the inclusion of a diversity of backgrounds and sensibilities, not delegates or corporate structures.

Recognition, then, must be pragmatically and experimentally handled, and civil society must share the burden of representation.

While the state may rightly seek to ensure that spiritual leaders are not absent from public fora and consultative processes in relation to policies affecting their flocks, it may well be that a Board of Jewish Deputies model of community representation offers a better illustration of a community–state relationship. The Board of Deputies, a body independent of, but a communal partner to, the British state is a federation of Jewish organizations which includes synagogues but also other Jewish community organizations and its leadership typically consists of lay persons whose standing and skill in representing their community is not diminished by any absence of spiritual authority. It is most interesting that while at some local levels Muslim organizations have chosen to create political bodies primarily around mosques (e.g., the Bradford Council of Mosques), at a national level, it is the Board of Deputies model that seems more apparent. This is certainly the case with the single most representative and successful national Muslim organization, the Muslim Council of Britain (MCB), whose office-holders and spokespersons are more likely to be chartered accountants and solicitors than imams. Most mosques in Britain are run by local lay committees and the mullah or imam is sometimes, perhaps usually, a minor functionary. Very few of those who aspire to be Muslim spokespersons and representatives have religious authority and are not expected to have it by fellow Muslims. This is as it should be because the accommodation of religious groups is as much if not more about the recognition and support of communities rather than necessarily about ecclesiastical or spiritual representation in political institutions. The state has a role here which includes ensuring that Muslim civil society is drawn into the mainstream as much as it is to seek forms of representation within state structures.

In my preferred approach it would be quite likely that different kinds of groups – Muslims, Hindus and Catholics for instance, let alone women, gays and different ethnic minority groups – might choose to organize in different ways and to relate differently to key civic and political institutions. While each might look over its shoulders at what other groups are doing or getting and use any such precedents to formulate its own claims, we should on this approach not require symmetry but be able to live with some degree of 'variable geometry'. I am unable to specify what this degree of flexibility might be but it should be clear that sensitivity to the specific religious, cultural and socio-economic needs in a specific time and place and political context is critical to multiculturalism. This indeterminacy leaves something to be desired but I hope it is evident that it can be a strength too. It also underlines that multiculturalism is not a comprehensive political theory but can and must sit alongside other political values and be made to work with varied institutional, national and historical contexts.

The critical issue of principle, however, is not how but *whether* religious groups, especially those that are marginal and underrepresented in public life, ought to be represented. I have explained why I think a 'neutralist', difference-blind approach is inadequate if equality is our goal. The real problem today, however, is with an approach that eschews difference-blindness in general but would not dream of being anything other than religion-blind. Take the BBC – an organization with a deserved reputation for public service and high standards, an aspect of which is manifested in the remark by a serving Director-General, Greg Dykes, that the organization was 'hideously white'. Relatedly, for some years now it has given political importance to reviewing and improving its personnel practices and its output of programmes, including its on-screen 'representation' of the British population, by making provision for and winning the confidence of women, ethnic groups and young people. Why should it not also use religious groups as a criterion of inclusivity and have to demonstrate that it is doing the same for viewers and staff defined by religious community membership? Muslims, Hindus and Sikhs should be treated as legitimate groups in their own right (not because they are, say, Asians), whose presence in British society has to be explicitly reflected in all walks of life and in all institutions; and whether they are so included should become one of the criteria for judging Britain as an egalitarian, inclusive, multicultural society. That there is no prospect at present of religious equality catching up with the importance that employers and other organizations give to sex or race in Europe (outside Northern Ireland) and north America is a measure of the distance we have to travel.

Conclusion

The emergence of Muslim political agency has thrown multiculturalism into theoretical and practical disarray. The fear of it has led to policy reversals in the Netherlands and elsewhere, and has strengthened intolerant, exclusive nationalism across Europe. We should in fact be moving the other way and enacting the kinds of legal and policy measures that are necessary to accommodate Muslims as equal citizens in European and other polities. These would include anti-discrimination measures in areas such as employment, positive action to achieve a full and just political representation of Muslims in various areas of public life, the inclusion of Muslim history as European history and so on. Critically, I have been arguing that the inclusion of Islam as an organized religion and of Muslim identity as a public identity are necessary to integrate Muslims and to pursue religious equality (and the same would apply to other religious minorities). The civic and institutional expression of this multicultural inclusion will be manifested in the formation and activities of pressure groups, consultations at various governmental levels and across civil society, in political party outreach, autonomous representation in trade unions and so on but it can and sometimes should take on a more corporate form too. While this inclusion runs against certain interpretations of secularism, it is not inconsistent with what secularism means in practice in Europe. We should let this evolving, moderate secularism and the spirit of compromise it represents be our guide. Unfortunately, an ideological secularism is currently being reasserted and generating European domestic versions of 'the clash of civilizations' thesis and the conflicts that entails for European societies. That some people are today developing secularism as an ideology to oppose Islam and its public recognition is a challenge both to pluralism and equality, and thus to some of the bases of contemporary democracy. It has to be resisted no less than the radical anti-secularism of some Islamists. While the Christian right is emerging as a potential domestic obstacle to the civic integration of Muslims and Islam in the US, we must prevent radical secularism playing the same role in Europe.[7]

− 5 −
Multiculturalism and Essentialism

The difference-blind approach to equality (perhaps never absolutist in relation to women's representation) has steadily given ground in recent decades – at least in practice – as certain aspects of differential or multicultural representation have made gradual inroads in, for example, mainstream politics and workplaces. Often led by socialist organizations such as the British Labour Party and some of the larger trade unions, each of the British main political parties has women's 'sections' and ethnic minority 'sections' with budgets, separate meetings and national conferences and sometimes reserved places on regional and national executive committees. Amongst some employers, including my own, Women's, Ethnic Minorities, Gay, Lesbian, Bisexual and Transexual (GLBT) and Disability networks have been set up and there are special consultative and training opportunities for people eligible for group membership. Collecting data on such groups (except those defined by sexual orientation), for example, ethnic monitoring based on form-filling by individuals, and using it in public debates and in relation to equality policies is common in many countries.[1] While in the US the most prominent form of political difference-sightedness has been in relation to 'race', in the European Union it has been in relation to gender, such that for many years the brief of the Equal Opportunity division of the European Commission was confined to gender equality. Some western European political parties have introduced affirmative action policies to increase office-holding amongst women members and to increase the number of women representing them in the national legislatures, initiatives that in Europe have been particularly developed in the Nordic countries. Quotas were initially introduced at a party level in western Europe in the 1970s (Krook, Lovenduski and Squires 2006), but increasingly also take the form of legislative quotas and are now present throughout the rest of the world, particularly in Latin America (Araujo and Garcia 2006) and Africa (Tripp, Konate and Lowe-Morna 2006).

These developments are uneven in relation to the dimensions of difference, across countries and in time – sometimes they are very recent – but they constitute a definite and conspicuous political trend. Nor have they been without opponents – and sometimes the argument has been fierce. Moreover, the measures are sometimes opposed because they are seen as divisive. For example, socialist organizations have often initially argued that such forms of recognition and remedial measures are divisive of working-class solidarity.[2] When there has been a campaign, however, the argument for recognition and differential representation has been won and a suitable institutional compromise achieved – till the next time the argument flares up. Since these matters are dynamic and the gains are incremental, we should expect the issues to remain alive throughout the next decades.

These difference-recognizing measures do not necessarily constitute a great deal of power and some people think we still need to go further while others think the opposite but the principle has broad support: the egalitarian acknowledgement of difference has been incorporated into mainstream political and managerial consciousness in most countries that I am concerned with and has made steady progress through the 1990s and into the twenty-first century (though sometimes it is still confined to gender). It is a trend that begins on the left and advances to include the centre and even the centre-right such as the British Conservative Party. Yet in the same period of time institutional multiculturalism has been under sustained social science criticism. Attending to such criticism is both necessary to justify the conception of multiculturalism that I have been elaborating and helps me to elaborate more the notions of group and identity that I am using.

The central theoretical criticism is that 'cultures' or 'groups' do not exist in the ways presupposed by multiculturalism. It is said that the positing of minority or immigrant cultures, which need to be respected, defended, publicly supported and so on, appeals to the view that cultures are discrete, frozen in time, impervious to external influences, homogeneous and without internal dissent. Cultures are seen as a fact of nature, perhaps like a 'race', so that people of certain family, ethnic or geographical origins are always to be defined by their origins and indeed are supposed to be behaviourally determined by them (Feuchtwang 1990; Gilroy 1990; Schierup and Alund 1991; Yuval-Davis 1992; Al-Azmeh 1993; Dirlik 1990; Baumann 1996). In this critique it is said that group membership falsely implies the existence of some shared essential characteristics, an essence, and multiculturalism is portrayed as 'a picture of society as a "mosaic" of several bounded, nameable, individually homogeneous and unmeltable minority uni-cultures which are pinned onto the backdrop of a similarly characterised majority uni-culture' (Vertovec 1996: 5; recently characterized as 'plural monoculturalism', Sen 2006). So, the most fundamental problem with multiculturalism is that the cultures or groups it speaks of do not exist.

Are Groups Less Real than Individuals?

This critique sometimes assumes a philosophical or onto-logical character. It seems to deny the existence of some-thing that we might otherwise think exists. Thus Gerd Baumann states that 'culture is not a real thing, but an abstract and purely analytical notion' (Baumann 1996: 11). Similarly, Rogers Brubaker argues that 'ethnicity, race and nation are not things in the world but perspectives on the world; ways of seeing, interpreting and representing the social world' (Brubaker 2005: 17, 79 and 219 and cover flap; cf. 11, 65). One way to interpret this claim might be to conclude that there is something false, ficti-tious and illegitimate about appeals to culture, ethnicity and so on in understanding oneself, let alone others or society. Stuart Hall's words sometimes lend themselves to this sceptical conclusion: 'If we feel we have a unified identity . . . it is only because we construct a comforting story or "narrative of the self" about ourselves . . . The fully unified, completed, secure and coherent identity is a fantasy' (Hall 1992a: 277).

However, these authors and other anti-essentialists do not necessarily mean their words to bear such a radical interpretation. For example, in the above quote from Hall, the term 'we' presupposes an underlying self behind all the stories. Brubaker explicitly states that to deny that ethnic-ity, race and nation as things in the world is 'in no way to dispute their reality' but to argue that their reality 'does not depend on the existence of ethnic groups or nations as substantial groups or entities' (Brubaker 2005: 12).[3] Baumann quotes in aid the sociological classic, Berger and Luckmann 1967, to the effect that: reification is 'apprehen-sion of human phenomena as if they were things . . . as if they were something other than human products – such as facts of nature . . .' (Berger and Luckmann 1967: 106; quoted in Baumann 1996: 12; cf. Brubaker 2005: 206, endnote 6). Of course Berger and Luckmann were offering a constructionist view of social reality; they were contrasting the social and the natural; they were not contrasting social reality with social fantasy. So, their argument that the social world is a human product applies no less to the concepts of individuals, citizens and workers than it does to race, ethnicity and so on. But then that's not an argument against political multiculturalism. I have not claimed any naturalistic status for any aspects of culture, ethnicity or identity that I argue require a multiculturalist political response; and nor do I know of any multiculturalists that have.[4] When Margaret Thatcher said 'there is no such thing as society' some political implications were meant to follow. Anti-reification, however, is no more anti-multiculturalism than it is anti-society. It places phenomena like ethnicity no higher than – but no lower than – other social phenomena like class or gender, over which it has no privileges but which in turn have no higher ontological or sociological status. Ethnicity may only be a 'human product' but that does not mean that it is less sociologically real or less normatively important than other 'human products'.

Who Essentializes?

Brubaker and Baumann do have a more specific claim about reification, namely that it is 'central to the *practice* [as opposed to the analysis] of politicised ethnicity', (Brubaker 2005: 10; italics in original) to the creation of the political fiction that constitutes the sense of belonging to an ethnic group. Baumann has a more qualified thesis: people in multiethnic locations sometimes speak as if everybody belonged to one or another ethnic group, constituted by their participation in uniform customs and practices with co-ethnics, but at other times they are more savvy and appreciate that there is considerable internal diversity, overlap between members of so-called different groups and that not only do individuals belong to more than one group but different groups will be salient in different contexts (sometimes it might be ethnicity, or colour or youth or neighbourhood, etc.) (Baumann 1996). Nevertheless, Baumann too holds that reification, homogenization and essentialism are a characteristic of British official and political discourses of multiculturalism (Baumann 1996). Indeed, some claim that this characteristic has grown and is central to the CMEB Report, which I offered in chapter 1 as a model of multiculturalism (Alexander 2004: 533–4). Others assert that the same is true of some forms of black politics (Gilroy 1990, 2000), of Muslim political 'fundamentalism' (Yuval-Davis 1992 and Al-Azmeh 1993), of official discourses in European countries (Schierrup and Alund 1991, Vertovec 1996 and Baumann 1999) and of US racial discourses (Hollinger 1995). Sometimes it is also contended that this reification, homogenization and essentialism is part of a manipulative strategy on the part of some political agents. An extreme version of this view is found in a book by the Nobel Prize winning economist, Amartya Sen: 'The imposition of an allegedly unique identity is often a crucial component of the martial art of fomenting sectarian confrontation' (Sen 2006: xiii).

The wariness about some discourses of culture, ethnicity and so on is right but it does not follow that the ordinary, non-theoretical discourses are vitiated by philosophical errors. In talking about other people's cultures it is not uncommon to assume that a culture has just the kind of features that anti-essentialists identify. When non-Chinese people, for example, talk of 'Chinese civilization', their starting point often is that it has coherence, sameness over centuries and a reified quality. Sometimes, as Ayse Caglar notes of minority intellectuals, one slips into such a mentality when talking of one's own cultural traditions (Caglar 1997). Hence, rich, complex histories become simplified and collapsed into a teleological progress or a unified ideological construct called French culture or

European civilization or the Muslim way of life. But the political uses of ethnicity or culture do not depend upon erasing this sense of change and internal complexity – upon believing that a culture has a primordial existence or a singular, deterministic, essential quality. In the case of a living culture that we are part of, that we have been inducted into, have extended through use and seen change in our own lifetimes, it is easier to better appreciate the processes of change and adaptation, of borrowings from other cultures and new influences, and yet at the same time appreciate what is the subject of change. There cannot merely be flux and fluidity, for change implies the continuation of something which has undergone change.[5] It is the same in the case of a person: at the end of one's life one might reflect on how one's personality changed over time and through experience, and see how all the changes constitute a single person without believing that there was an original, already formed, essential 'I' prior to the life experiences. As with a person, so with a culture. A culture is made *through* change; it is not defined by an essence which exists apart from change, a *noumenon* hidden behind the altering configurations of phenomena. In individuating cultures and peoples, we neither need nor for the most part resort to the idea of an essence. Yet we must, however, insist on the possibility of making historical connections, of being able to see change *and* resemblance. If we can trace a historical connection between the language of Shakespeare, Charles Dickens and Winston Churchill, we call that language by a single name. We say that it is the same language, though we may be aware of the differences between the three languages and of how the changes are due to various influences, including contact with and borrowing from other languages, and without having to make any claim about an 'essence' or a language being a natural rather than a human product. The same applies across geography: not all primary users of a language, even in the same time, use it in a uniform way, as would be true of New York and York.

Again, Urdu is as hybridized a language as one could find, derived as it is from Arabic, Farsi, some central Asian Turkish languages and north Indian languages, especially Hindi and its predecessors. Yet it would be hard to deny that Urdu is a distinct language. This is the case even though orally it overlaps with a number of contemporary South Asian languages – a plural overlap that used to be called 'Hindustani' but might best now be called 'Bolly-woodese', given that Bollywood film-makers think they are making films in Hindi but many who will say they are not Hindi speakers, which includes most Urdu speakers, under-stand the films as native speakers. So, Urdu is a human product, is hybridic and fluid (as the growing entry of English words and phrases testifies) but no one would deny it has an identity as a distinct language.

So, what kind of cultures does multiculturalism speak of? Well, one illustration is cultures like Urdu. This is particularly apposite because languages can be transported and can, including under conditions of conquest, become the secondary (or tertiary, etc.), or even the primary lan-guage of others; the latter case is exemplified by English, for not only is it a language that has borrowed from so many others (including Urdu-Hindi), but its development, whether at the level of slang or literature, has been and continues to be profoundly influenced by those whose ancestors were not English speakers (recent examples include South Asians but historical examples include the Scots, the Irish and African-Americans). So, there can be identifiable, distinct cultures even under conditions of domination, interaction and hybridity, and multicultural-ism can be a political response to such a legacy.

In the points that I have been making I have been influ-enced by Wittgenstein's anti-essentialism. In the 1930s and 1940s Wittgenstein thoroughly revised the philosophy of his earlier work, the *Tractatus* (Wittgenstein 1922). In the *Tractatus* Wittgenstein had assumed that all languages aspired to a single ideal structure. In his later work he assumed that languages were of many different kinds, reflecting different histories, purposes and forms of life and could not be judged against an ideal standard. But he did not think it followed that *anything* could be a language; he thought that specific languages could have a unity in the way that different elements of a game hang together and makes sense to the players. The point applies to the relations between the elements that give to a particular game its distinct identity and it equally applies to what different games have in common in order for each to be a game (i.e., members of the same group). Wittgenstein went through a list of possible essential characteristics that a game must have (Wittgenstein 1967: paras 65–7). For example, must it be competitive? (no, some games are played for fun); involve teams? (no); players? (no, games can be played by just one person – patience) and so on. He concluded that there was no single essential characteristic that all games shared. Rather, there were a number of important characteristics and most games had some or other combination of these characteristics. The result was that different games resembled each other in the way that different members of the family do: 'I can think of no better expression to characterize these similarities than "family resemblances"; for the various resemblances between members of a family; build, features, colour of eyes, gait, temperament, etc. etc. overlap and criss-cross in the same way. – And I shall say: "games" form a family' (para 67). Moreover, while there is always change over time, there are different levels of changeability; some things are structurally deeper to a language or way of thinking, 'deep grammar', and under normal conditions would change much more slowly and perhaps imperceptibly so.

The first key point, then, is that one does not need an idea of essence in order to believe that some ways of thinking and acting have coherence; and so the undermining of the ideas of essence does not necessarily damage the assumption of coherence or the actual use of a language (Wittgenstein 1967: para. 108). The coherence of small-scale activities (for example, games) is of course easier to see and describe than those of histories and ways of life, but as long as we do not impose an inappropriately high standard of coherence (for example, the coherence of a mathematical system, as assumed to be the ideal of language in the *Tractatus*), there is no reason to be defeatist from the start. If we do not expect actually existing ethnic groups to measure up to some idealized notion of being 'things in the world', or judge ethnic identities in terms of falling short of a 'fully unified, completed, secure and coherent identity', then we will not be tempted into asserting absences in ways which confuse rather than illuminate. Family resemblance may be enough to characterize group membership.

The second key point I draw from Wittgenstein is that theorists should be wary of reading philosophical errors into non-theoretical activities. If we, as non-philosophers, can understand what languages or games are (or, to cite some other of Wittgenstein's examples: knowledge, mind, memory, time), we can successfully operate in the world – play the appropriate 'language-game' – without positing essences or indeed philosophical theories. Philosophical ideas about, for example, what is knowledge or consciousness, can be drawn out of our ordinary activities and uses of language, but the activities in question operate without needing those ideas. Most of us – perhaps all of us – are unable to answer the question, 'what is knowledge?', and yet are successfully able to make, check and revise a multitude of knowledge claims daily (e.g., I know that Christmas Day fell on Tuesday in 2007). Similarly, we can talk of there being ethnic groups or a cultural plurality without having clear-cut ideas of what is an ethnic group or a culture. Confused or false theories or absence of theories about culture are compatible with the ordinary language games in which someone being culturally different has a meaning. Quite simply, we do not have to essentialize or reify cultures to be multiculturalists; successful politics of difference-recognition may (or may not) be accompanied by crude, confused, unreflective notions of culture.

Not only is there no inherent reification in politicized ethnicity but for theorists to latch on to the reification in the confused or crude accounts that agents give of their activities and beliefs is actually to over-homogenize and essentialize the beliefs that people have. Taking the two key points together, the coherence of a group – its group-ness – is neither a fiction nor an essence but more akin to family resemblance.

The charge of essentialism then is itself essentialist. It rightly identifies some elements of essentialism in the political discourses of identity and culture but attributes a false importance to them. It gives them the status of being *the* beliefs that constitute the understanding of culture, identity and so on in multiculturalism, when in fact multicultural discourses may be, indeed invariably are, based on a variety of beliefs and assertions about culture. While some of these are essentialist, others are not – as critical anti-essentialists themselves record. For example, as already noted, Baumann (1996) records just such a discursive mix. But he dichotomizes – in an essentialist way – multicultural discourse so that the bad essentialist kind is the public, official one, while the more mixed one, capable of subtlety, is called demotic (Baumann 1996). Rather than seeing that our discourses at both (overlapping) levels are mixed and pull us in different directions, this essentializing by some theorists of anti-essentialism is made worse by their failure to see that multicultural politics, official or otherwise, is not dependent on theoretical clarity; it can proceed, be reformed, qualified, extended and so on without the deconstructivist strictures of the theorists (cf. Fuss 1989). In many ways, it is the misguided search for a discursive coherence which – like the search for an ideal language in the *Tractatus* – constitutes the essentialist move; sometimes more than the social and political phenomena which is charged with essentialism. Essentialist ideas are present in ordinary social discourses but it is the theoretical critique of ethnicity, race and multiculturalism that affixes these ideas to multiculturalism.

This inevitably leads to the conclusion that political multiculturalism is inherently essentialist, reificatory, etc. and so we need to go 'beyond multiculturalism', 'beyond race' and so on. If, however, we continue to be interested in a refined, sophisticated, self-critical and moderate multiculturalism, then multiculturalism is strengthened, not destroyed by anti-essentialism.[6]

Multi-dimensionality

Having considered a philosophical objection to ethnicity/cultures – namely, that they only exist as reified, essentialized constructs, especially in politics – let us now consider two related sociological objections. The first is general, and the second is much more specific and contemporary. The first objection is that social factors external to a group are much more likely to influence its behaviour, indeed its existence as a group, than features which are distinctive or internal to it. It is not language, religion and customs which explain cultural difference and give rise to multiculturalist politics but economic structures, power relations or the results of self-interested calculations and decisions which more or less affect all agents in the same way and so are external to or independent of ethnicity or culture. At one level the distinctions necessary to sustain this argument cannot be made. For example, markets or at the least the scope of markets are cultural products; they require the presence of certain attitudes such as the willingness to calculate social goods and services in terms of money. The same is true of how relations of power are perceived and institutionalized, the extent of resistance, the capacity for them to change and so on. Again, identification of certain interests as 'self-interest', their prioritization in relation to other interests, the capacity to act on them, especially given the unsaid, unwritten constraints and inhibitions on behaviour, these too will all vary in a way which will limit the power of accultural sociological generalizations. As these remarks are all at a very abstract level and suggest degrees of cultural constitution which go well beyond what applies at the level of multiculturalism, let us consider something more specific and small-scale.

Between the mid-1970s and early 1980s self-employment amongst South Asian men in Britain more than doubled, whilst nationally there was just a small increase, and since then it has become a marked feature of South Asians, visible in the 'corner shops', restaurants and taxi ranks, as well as amongst the self-made rich (Metcalf, Modood and Virdee 1996: 1). One cannot explain this fact in terms of a primordial ethnicity, for while there is some evidence of family businesses, most of those who took to self-employment did not have a direct background in self-employment, let alone the specific business sectors just mentioned, and certainly did not come to Britain with plans to do so (Metcalf, Modood and Virdee 1996: 33–4). A stimulus to this self-employment was the economic recession at the time which, combined with racial discrimination in the labour market, meant that the Asians had to create their economic opportunities. Moreover, the fact that there were opportunities for self-employment is also relevant. But these socio-economic facts about Britain are by themselves not enough to explain the unusual scale of the self-employment. To do that one would need to take account of intra-ethnic relations, including the pooling of savings, information, support of co-ethnics through lines of credit, familial organization of labour and a higher level of motivation amongst individuals who sought to better themselves and their families and were willing to work exceptionally hard and forgo or defer consumption to do so. Also relevant is an imported cultural norm in relation to opening in the evenings and on Sundays when native-owned shops closed. So, while clearly there is economic rationality, migration-based motivations, avoidance of racial discrimination and other factors at work here, one could not conclude that any group 'in these circumstances' (which themselves are difficult to fully specify without mentioning ethnic group characteristics) would do the same, e.g., the African-Caribbeans did not. Yet, this is not 'ethnic determinism', which is supposed to be a denial of agency (Baumann 1996: 1) for I am actually highlighting agency. Rather, the argument is that this agency cannot be understood purely in external or 'objective' terms, without reference to cultural norms and ethnic identities. Moreover, it suggests that not only can ethnic resources be a source of opportunities, but analytical attention to ethnicity can help free analysts from economic or other determinism.

Or, consider a more political example. At about the same time as the above, an anti-racist political movement asserting a 'black' identity developed in Britain amongst African-Caribbeans and South Asians. It spread from African-Caribbean intellectuals and activists to other African-Caribbeans; yet Asian intellectuals and activists were not able to achieve the same in their own communities (Modood 1994b), presumably because in the one case it resonated with a group's sense of itself and in the other case it did not; to explain which one would have to know a lot more about these groups than just what was happening in Britain at that time, i.e., what could be characterized as the 'circumstances'. Indeed, I would say that the reason South Asians gave as much interest to colour identities ('brown' as well as 'black') as they did was because of the prior presence and anti-colour racist activism of the Caribbeans and the support it got from sections of British society. If supposing that the group that had preceded the South Asians had not been the African-Caribbeans, but had been the Chinese, the South Asians would probably have given even less weight to colour identities. Instead, they might have emphasized a common Asian identity or alternatively might have sought to distinguish themselves from a Chinese Asianness and highlighted a non-Chinese Asianness. The point is that a sense of identity and the assertion of identities depend upon circumstances, including the presence of other group-ings, but cannot be reduced to such. So, we can, indeed must, acknowledge contingency while acknowledging that for different groups some responses are more likely than others. Playing the 'what if . . .' game is consistent with the recognition that there is a limit to the variations; we can imagine that the African-Caribbeans might have grouped around an identity other than black or their African descent.[7] Or even that their sense of groupness might have been fragmentary and eclipsed by other identities, includ-ing religious, e.g., Christian; they would not have thought of themselves, for example, as Hindus. The total possibili-ties for one group are different than for another; and the same is true of the probabilities.

So there is contingency and considerable openness as to which of a possible set of developments materialize. Moreover, the two examples above give some idea of how any social phenomenon is shaped by a multiplicity of factors. These factors – ethnicity, racial discrimination, economic opportunities, religious norms, political opposi-tion and so on – cannot be reduced to each other or pre-dicted in advance. The relevance of factors, possible combinations of them and prioritization amongst them is not to be derived from an ethnic essentialism nor from any other postulated uniformity about behaviour or a general theory of society. For all such generalities will at best approximate and typically crudify real situations. For what is wrong with essentialism is wrong with all theoreti-cal homogenization, abstraction and reductionism. They miss out the diversity, complexity and open-endedness of social phenomena.

As my two examples above show, features 'internal to a group', features 'internal to other groups' and 'external circumstances' are not readily distinguishable and exclu-sive; and even where some distinctions can be made, there is no single direction of causality (from 'external' to 'inter-nal' or vice versa). Nor is there a uniform, a priori, hierarchy of causality that allows us to conclude that external circumstances are more important than groupness. Sometimes it may be one set of causes that are most relevant, sometimes another set; none of the social dimensions are more real than the others. One of the implications of calling them 'dimensions' is to underline that they do not exist apart from each other except for analytical or other specific purposes. Moreover, social phenomena are intrinsically dynamic and interactive and so we must allow for and seek inter-dimensionality (cf. Bradley 1996 on 'intersectionality'). It is one thing to connect aspects of a phenomenon, for example, religion and politics in the Rushdie affair, but quite another to reduce one to another. Reduction and complexity begin in the same place: they connect two different kinds of phenomena between which a relationship is postulated, arguing that one kind of phenomenon cannot be understood without an understanding of the other kind. In reductionism one kind of phenomenon is always privileged, whereas for complexity what is sought is not reduction to one kind (e.g., competition between community leaders or over economic resources) but the broadening out of a phenomenon into its multi-dimensionality. Reduction is not an over-enthusiastic friend of 'always connect', but its enemy. Of course it does not follow that all factors are always equally important: that would be a denial of explanation. Rather, the determining of the relative importance of factors is contingent, specific and sociologically variable.

Goodbye to Old Ethnicities?

I turn now to the second sociological objection. This does not necessarily take issue with the idea of ethnic groups but argues that such an idea no longer fits contemporary reality in at least certain parts of the world. Stuart Hall's essay (1992b), originally given as a public lecture in 1988, is a seminal text in this regard. Aptly entitled 'New

Ethnicities', it identified a shift in black cultural politics such that, while it might have made sense to talk about black people as a singular group in Britain in the 1960s and 1970s, in recent decades they have to be understood in a much more plural and nuanced way, as bearers and creators of multiple cross-cutting identities. This is an analysis that has been extremely influential not just in sociology but also in cultural studies and geography; for example, in the latter it is argued, without denying that groups of a more traditional kind may exist elsewhere, that in 'global cities' like New York and London 'urban melange' and 'multiculture' are the new reality (e.g., Amin 2002; Keith 2005). An allied reading of the same spaces is the idea that at intellectual-imaginative levels non-white, usually postcolonial, settlers in the former imperial nations of the West are neither of one culture nor another but are hybrids occupying a 'third space' (Bhabba 1994; Gilroy 1987, 1993). Beyond the anglophone world, it has long been argued that those born in France of Maghrebian descent cannot be understood in terms of Arab culture and ethnicity but as a French phenomenon (self-designated as *beur*, that is to say, as turning the French pronunciation of 'Arabes' back to front); and that Islam in France owes as much to processes of globalization, such as individualization and secularization, as to any internal factors (Roy 2004, 2005).

Leaving aside the virtues of the differing theoretical ways of capturing the fact, there is considerable qualitative research evidence for the view that many ethnic minority people today do not understand themselves as having singular group identities or merely in terms of 'difference' and 'otherness' (e.g., Back 1996; Cohen 1999; Mac an Ghaill 1999). Systematic, quantitative support for this can be found in the PSI Fourth Survey (Modood et al. 1997; for France see Tribalat 1995 and Tribalat 1996). It found very high levels of ethnic self-identification, with nearly 90 percent assenting to 'In many ways, I think of myself as being as . . . [respondent's ethnic group]'. Yet this identity was not seen as in competition with being British; nearly two-thirds assented to 'In many ways, I think of myself as being British' (Modood et al. 1997: 328–9). Moreover, identities are more fluid than they used to be. Some of those who said they were black at the start of the 1980s might be Bangladeshis at the end of that decade and might today be British Muslims. A recent major study of self-identities amongst teenage children of immigrants to the US (the second generation) found not just a variety of forms of self-identification amongst people of similar origin (e.g., Mexican, Hispanic, Latino, Mexican-American, American and so on) but, when the same young people were interviewed a few years later, reflecting both the persistence of minority identities and their malleability, more than half chose a different label or combination (Rumbaut 2005).

Perhaps even more significantly than the finding of non-oppositional, hyphenated identities like British-Indian or Cuban-American, or even of identity shifts, is that the continuation of a group, the identification with a group, does not depend on the participation of activities and behaviour associated with the group in question. For example, some Indians, especially second-generation, did not wear Indian dress, regularly attend a temple or gurd-wara or mosque, or regularly use an Indian language but that did not stop them continuing to think of themselves as Indian in many ways. Behaviour of course often did correlate with self-identity descriptions but in many cases it did not. If the traditional conception of ethnicity is about behavioural conformity, the Fourth Survey found that this is present in contemporary Britain, but it also found what might be regarded as evidence of new forms of ethnicity. Namely, strong forms of group identification with moder-ate or even weak behavioural conformity to traditional group norms and practices; associational group identities that do not see group belonging as implying stasis, cul-tural purity or internal uniformity (Modood et al. 1997: 334–8).

It may be thought that in some ways the latter pattern is reminiscent of the ways that earlier migrants to the US from various parts of Europe culturally blended in over three or four generations into a white mainstream American identity and their identity became largely 'symbolic' or an 'ethnicity of the last resort' (Gans 1979) or simply an option that they might care to exercise, mainly in nostalgic and personal ways (Waters 1990). This may turn out to be true for some non-white groups at some point in the future, but it is not the case today and not likely in the near to mid-term. The non-white groups that are the focus of multiculturalism have a visibility and are subject to forms of exclusion that continue to sustain group identity; above all, there can be passionate commitments to those identities in personal, institutional and political ways that belie that these identities are symbolic or cultural heirlooms.

What the 'new ethnicities' or hyphenation argument or the distinction between behavioural and associational identities underlies is that when we speak of an ethnic group or an ethno-religious identity, we can be talking about quite different kinds of groupings or identities. It is not just – as was emphasized in chapter 3 – that for example Sikhs and African-Caribbeans are different kinds of groups, but also that there are different ways of being Sikh and being African-Caribbean. 'Group' and 'identity' are not univocal concepts; no less than 'game', what unites a diverse set of instances is not an essential (set of) characteristic(s) but what Wittgenstein called family resemblance. Indeed, 'identity' has come to be a useful concept because it seems more suited than the idea of a group (given some of the resonances of discreteness, boundedness, fixity and homogeneity that it has for some people) to stretching widely enough to encompass both behaviour-based and associational conceptions of group membership. In order to capture the sense of group membership that cannot just be read off from behaviour but involves a sense of membership amongst otherwise diverse individuals, useful concepts such as 'imagined community' (used by Anderson 1983 to analyse national belonging) and 'political subject' (Laclau 1994) can be employed to analyse the uses of identity in relation to group formation and mobilization.

There is then considerable contemporary purchase in the 'new ethnicities' approach and one can also see why it should lend itself to political critiques that multiculturalism is out of date, having been overtaken by hybridic, fluid and more individualistic identities (e.g., Alibhai-Brown 2000). The problem with the 'new ethnicities' approach, however, is the tendency to overgeneralize, to suppose that the new comprehensively replaces the old. After all, what the Fourth Survey showed was the emergence of associational identities alongside more traditional ethnic community behaviour and that, though there was a temporal trend, it varied amongst groups. For example, even after controlling for age, birth/time in Britain, educational qualifications and social class, Pakistanis and Bangladeshis were more culturally conservative than Indians and African-Asians (Modood et al. 1997: 332–6; cf. Modood, Beishon and Virdee 1994).

Moreover, 'new ethnicities' sometimes seems to be about the embrace of a particular kind of ethos, perhaps someone who enjoys the challenge of confronting 'a bewildering, fleeting multiplicity of possible identities, any one of which we could identify with – at least temporarily' (Hall 1992a: 277). It also fits with aspects of contemporary globalization with its emphasis on consumerism, recreational culture, flexible employment and personal 'make-overs'. This is attractive to some but not to others. Some groups stress one aspect of their self and others see that as unrealistically narrow but then go on not to stress radical multiplicity and flux but to shift primacy from one aspect to a few. For example, in June 2002, a *Guardian/ICM* opinion survey asked 500 Muslims in Britain whether they would describe themselves as Muslim or British or British-Muslim (Travis 2002). The answers were:

Muslim	37%
British	3%
British-Muslim	54%
Other	6%

What is interesting is not just that the majority of Muslims selected a hyphenated identity but that the overwhelming number of respondents were able to answer a question that gave them such a limited choice and so few – indeed only two – identity elements.[8] It may be thought that this was entirely to do with the context of being asked an opinion poll question, i.e., they understood the 'game' they were being asked to play and cooperated, and so the answers are nothing more than an opinion poll contrivance in the background context of suspicions about the loyalty of Muslims in Britain eight months after the 9/11 attacks in the US. This would however be to overlook the qualitative research in which Muslims are frequently quoted as making – in sincere, thoughtful and passionate ways – statements such as 'I am first and foremost a Muslim' or 'I am a Muslim first and British second' (Modood, Beishon and Virdee 1994; Jacobson 1997; and Saeed, Blain and Forbes 1999). Now of course each and every one of these respondents has numerous identities based on sex, age, place of birth, neighbourhood, employment, recreational activities, membership of various kinds of organizations and so on and so on – indeed, one could not possibly enumerate all such past, present and future identities. Yet, no one would suppose – for themselves or as a theoretical proposition – that all these identities are of equal value. Some are of much more significance than others; in which case we must recognize the possibility that those which are valued, how many and in what combination will vary between people. This will be the case in general but even amongst those identities that fundamentally shape people's lives and which people usually give primacy to. This prioritizing of identities is particularly likely to occur amongst the minorities we are concerned with.

Some people so comfortably meld into their society that they are not marked – by others or by themselves – by 'difference' (or even by conviction such as socialism or atheism) and so often the question of identities, let alone prioritization, does not even arise. Our specific concern with 'difference' is typically with that based on or linked to racial and ethnic descent in a context where it shapes life-chances and how people relate to each other, is connected to a heritage or important belief system that governs one's personal life and/or is the basis of political debates, alliances, enmities and projects. Typically the physical basis and the ideational orientation are linked in the way that the social image of a Middle Easterner is linked with Islam or, to use examples from other contexts, women can be linked with feminism, or even working-class people with socialism. These linkages are of course shaped by contemporary contexts and social movements and are not just 'given'. Nor are these identities discrete and many different kinds of syntheses occur (e.g., a woman for whom being a black feminist is central to her self-definition). Moreover, we can allow that some people who in the eyes of others have a visible primary identity may not wish to embrace it but look for ways and means to deprioritize it in their lives; in particular, given that the identities under discussion typically straddle politics and non-politics, some people may seek to depoliticize their identity or at least to remove themselves from the political allegiances others, including co-members, foist upon that identity. All of these are matters of contingency and empirical inquiry; none of them are critiques of groupness, old ethnicities or 'identity politics'. So while there is evidence of strong identity prioritization, whether consciously, at an associational level or implicit at a behavioural level, it means the presence of groups that cannot be framed in terms of 'new ethnicities' and 'beyond multiculturalism'.[9]

The Politics of (Anti-)Essentialism

It is generally part of the theoretical critiques of group identities that the role of politics in their constitution, promotion and recognition is viewed with suspicion and even regarded as illegitimate. The consideration of these critiques began by seeing how essentialism is seen to be intrinsic to official multiculturalism or certain kinds of politics. We noted Brubaker's view that 'reifying groups is precisely what ethnopolitical entrepreneurs are in the business of doing. When they are successful, the political fiction of the unified group can be momentarily yet powerfully realized in practice' (Brubaker 2005: 10). I doubt actually that reifying (defined by Berger and Luckmann as 'apprehension of human phenomena as if they were things . . . as if they were something other than human products – such as facts of nature . . .' (Berger and Luckmann 1967: 106) is necessarily what group mobilizers of, say, British Pakistani Muslims or Bosnian Muslims are trying to do. In any case, as we have seen, ethnopolitical entrepreneurs can employ a concept of groupness without it being reificatory. The point I now want to make is they may or may not achieve a necessary degree of unity for their political purposes, but if they do then there is nothing fictive about the unity (unless *pace* family resemblance one imposes an essentialist-perfectionist Platonic meaning on 'unity').

One of Brubaker's concerns is to distinguish between a social group and a social category.[10] Just because we have a category that covers a selected population, e.g., the category 'black', it does not follow that black people form a single group. They may be divided into more than one group (e.g., Africans and Caribbeans, or young and old, or men and women) or they may consist of some group fragments and others who are very loosely, perhaps not at all, connected to one or more of these fragments. Brubaker takes this point to its logical conclusion: if categorizing does not create a group then self-categorization does not create a group (Brubaker 2005: 206, note 10). I think this is too narrow an interpretation of category, group and self-categorization. We have seen how prevalent ethnic self-identification is in countries such as Britain and the US. Sometimes these self-identifications are based on new labels, including pan-ethnic groups such as 'Asians' in Britain or 'Hispanics' or 'Latinos' in the US (Rumbaut 2005) which often have their origins in majority, administrative or colloquial categorization, but come to be embraced by the relevant minorities. Indeed, self-identification can be a political act and can be the basis of the (re)creation of a political subject. Such transformations of categories cannot be achieved *ex nihilo* but they suggest that Brubaker does not appreciate how contemporary ethnicities and minority political identities are related to categories. The most dramatic example is how black people transformed the category 'black' through a politics which invested it with new meaning (Omi and Winant 1986). In this respect minority categories are like Marx's distinction between a 'class-in-itself' (an observer's or an analyst's positing of a class) and a 'class-for-itself', a class that thinks and acts, especially politically, with self-consciousness (Marx 1955). As with class, so with other forms of groupness; politics can play a large role in creating a certain kind of collective identity and action but would be unlikely to succeed if some element of shared circumstances and/or ways of living were not already present and could be drawn upon to weave a political project. When political activists and identity entrepreneurs rouse a targeted population, there must be a 'target' and individuals who constitute the target must be able to understand that they are being addressed and have to 'respond' (even if it is by rejecting the call). The use of categories, symbols, the group-making discourses and so on all suggests that some kind of, some elements of, groupness already exists, albeit latent. One can see how such active identification and self-consciousness is creative – a group takes shape and new

imagined relationships materialize as new collective claims-
making and representation is articulated. In a democratic
context this activity will, as suggested in earlier chapters,
take the form of debate, pressure group organization,
agitation and protest, seeking the right to be included in
consultations and decision-making and so on, in short a
politics of recognition. It is difficult to see how such group
identities are more or less 'fictive' than non-ethnic
collectivities.

Of course, as has already been said, this does not mean
that every person is a member of a group, let alone that
people are members of only one group (for the same individual can be black, working-class, Christian, a Manchester United supporter and so on). Nor am I claiming that
the relevant groupings or forms of groupness are in any
sense complete (as, for example, in Kymlicka's (1995:
76–9) idea of a minority nation as a 'societal culture').
Certainly the post-immigration cultures that are of interest
to my argument are almost by definition partial and fragmentary – albeit to different degrees – and capable of
growth or decline in the significance they have amongst a
base-line membership. Moreover, while some identities
operate on different planes, for example, working class
and Muslim, and so in one sense do not compete with each
other, in the sense that Muslim and Hindu do in India,
nevertheless one has to note the competition between the
claims that different groups, identities and belongings
make upon the same individual or same population. The
same set of individuals can be asked, if not directly then
certainly in effect, to prioritize working-class or Muslim
membership, especially in relation to support for political
causes. Often the outcome of such competition is a non-
uniform distribution of prioritization across contexts.
Nevertheless, some groupness succeeds in certain times
and places, if not absolutely then disproportionately. There
is a temptation to say that the variation in political consciousness and organization will depend upon 'external
social circumstances' rather than on internal social and

cultural features (Ngata 1981: 96). It is better, however, not to be wedded to a single-factor explanation or to generalize from one case to a general truth, and above all to avoid an analysis in terms of either/or.

Brubaker and Sen are of course right to point to the political motives of identity entrepreneurs. But critical, anti-essentialist social theory is not without political motives either. A political orientation manifest for instance when either anti-essentialism is selectively applied to 'debunk' certain but not other group claims. For example, the initial targets of anti-essentialism were what may be called the first wave of identity politics, namely, feminism, blackness and gayness (e.g., Gates 1986; Butler 1990; and Gilroy 1993). Some of these critiques were theoretically contested and certainly caused some political dismay amongst advocates of some of the above causes but the interesting point is that the critiques were delivered as appropriately tempering the demands of representation. They were not intended to say (and certainly did not have the effect of saying) 'no right of way' to the idea of special measures to increase black representation or institutional innovation in relation to giving voice and power to, say, women. Yet this is often what the entailments of these critiques is taken to be in relation to Muslims, latecomers to identity politics in western polities. When Al-Azmeh argues that 'Muslim' and 'Islam' are falsely constructed monoliths that impede social inquiry for there are too many different kinds of Muslims and Islams for the singular versions of these terms to be at all helpful (Al-Azmeh 1993); or it is argued that 'categorisation of minority communities in primarily religious terms assumes them to be internally unified, homogenous entities with no class or gender differences of conflicts' (Yuval-Davies 1992: 284), and therefore creates the false impression that there is a 'seemingly seamless (and supra-racial) Muslim consensus in Britain' (Connolly 1990: 6), it is no longer about tempering but about rejecting the demands of representation, voice and power (Sen 2006).

Conclusion

I have argued that ethnic groups are not natural but simply a feature of society and so have no higher – but no lower – ontological status than, say, class or gender. Wittgenstein's concept of family resemblance enables us to identify distinct groups and appreciate membership over time and space and in the absence of internal homogeneity. The distinctness of a group is neither a fiction nor an essence. It is true that we cannot understand group membership, group goals and group behaviour as if they were something discrete and independent of wider socio-economic structures and processes, but again, such multi-dimensionality is characteristic of social phenomena as such and not distinctive of ethnicity. Moreover, multi-dimensionality emphatically does not warrant any form of sociological reductionism. For what is wrong with essentialism is wrong with all theoretical homogenization, abstraction and reductionism. It misses out the diversity, complexity and open-endedness of social phenomena. The important thing in relation to the argument of this book is that multiculturalism is not damaged by a rejection of essentialism and the conceptualization of ethnic and cultural groups without essences. Those who insist that ethnicity, groups and multiculturalism cannot be saved without essentialism, and so must be left behind, are themselves essentialists.

While there is much about contemporary post-immigration ethnicity and religious formations in western societies that is better understood in terms of hybridity, associational and multiple identities, some ethnic and religious identities are being manifested as having a primacy rather than sitting alongside an individual's other identities. Even such identities, however, usually are being asserted in ways that connect with a national citizenship as expressed in self-designated hyphenations such as Cuban-American, black-British and French-Muslim. Such identities are of course thoroughly political – as are critiques of them – but no less real for that. These divergent trends in post-immigration identities underlie, however, the importance of not conceiving culture, group, identity and so on in a uniform, fixed way – not just as if groups had an essence but as if the concept of a group did too. As if African-Caribbeans, Hindus and Chinese in Britain were all groups in the same way. It follows that a difference-based policy response, a multiculturalism, must be sensitive to the forms that groupness is taking in the relevant society and no one preferred form – for example, youth culture based hybridity or Muslim communalism – should be used as a straitjacket for all groups. This indeed has been one of the themes of this book and shall now be developed further in the next chapter.

– 6 –

Multicultural Citizenship

One of the underlying sociological arguments for multiculturalism, for establishing the fact of 'multi' that requires a political response, is that there are groups in our society marked by 'difference' but another is that not all groups are constituted in the same way. The latter covers not just the fact that the marked groups' 'difference' from the dominant society can vary (e.g., it could be 'race', religion or a combination of the two) but also that not all groups are groups in the same way. Some might have a much more organized community structure than others; one might have strong economic networks based on religious affiliation, another on endogamy, and yet another may be much more economically dependent upon the possession of educational qualifications or on shaping popular culture. Taking these forms of difference into account can illuminate not just how members in different groups can relate differently to their group(s) and have different attitudes to group identity; but also how they can exhibit different priorities and responses (as in my example of different reactions to self-employment in chapter 5) and so different trajectories and modes of integration. One implication is that social mobility is a heterogeneous process (Loury, Modood and Teles 2005). For example, in Britain African-Caribbeans may be culturally valued in some contexts but not able to convert this into economic advantage, while South Asians may build up economic advantage without being culturally valued. Nor should we overlook that a comparable kind of divergence and diversity may already be present in the dominant society with some, for example, valuing the hedonism of a youth culture over middle-class concerns with social mobility and vice versa. In which case, it is very likely that different minorities may seek to reach out to and connect with different aspects or parts of mainstream society; if they are successful there will be a form of integration but the overall result will be plural, overlapping forms of integration; not the disappearance of 'difference' but multiple forms of integration.

To these layers and forms of multiplicity could be added a number of others, not least some degree of individual variability. Groups might be observed to have differential reactions and trajectories, but these will also vary between individuals within and across groups. This does not just mean that any generalizations about groups can – like the rest of social science – only achieve probabilities at the level of individuals, but more importantly that not all group members, even in the case of any one group, are all members in the same way. We have already noted this in relation to behavioural-based group identities and associational identities in chapter 5 and we can allow that variety in forms of membership or group identification can go beyond just that distinction. The individual variability, however, is not usually random but shaped by demographic, social and economic dimensions that were mentioned in chapters 3 and 5 such as age, education, class, gender and so on. As I pointed out in chapter 5 in relation to ethnicity in general, so now also in relation to the fact of individuality, the recognition of complexity qualifies rather than damages multiculturalism. For it applies to all collectivities, not just those associated with multiculturalism. It is only in abstract schemas and typologies that all members relate in a uniform way to a category or class that they are members of. This is really an extension of the point made about 'family resemblance' in the last chapter. Just as not all members of a family give equal priority (amongst their various relations and activities) to being members of that family (as opposed to being young or living in a certain part of the country) or have the same experience of and status within the family, or have the same normative conception of 'family' and of what is due to family members, so in each of these cases the same point can be made about membership of a group.

So, the Multi family resemblance has five levels:

1   There are differences/groups.
2   These are based on different social attributes (e.g., race, religion, etc.).
3   Not all groups are groups in the same way.
4   They have different 'priorities' (e.g., different reactions to unemployment, different trajectories).
5   The above will vary between individuals within groups and so not all group members are members in the same way.

The acknowledgement of this latter, additional form of multiplicity does not cancel out giving sociological and political importance to the ideas of group and identity. For example, it does not mean that it is necessarily woolly to talk of a British-Indian identity. For the singularity of that label does not denote a monism or homogeneity but marks a generic term, leaving open what variety it does or does not contain, a contingent matter to be determined by empirical inquiry.[1] It is just like talking of, for example, 'French society' without implying any monism or homogeneity. Or talking about 'scientific method' without implying that there is only one thing worthy of the name. Of course, some things will be more central to science (does merely using the singular term 'science' imply homogeneity?) than others, e.g., empirical testing of hypotheses; and so the statement that a generic term can cover a variety of non-uniform cases does not imply that 'anything goes' or even that all cases are equally significant.

A more substantial objection might be that in arguing for group representation I have implied that, while minority groups differ from each other, each minority should be offered its own appropriate mode of representation and this sounds like a singular mode. Actually I have not suggested that each minority should be offered one mode of representation, let alone one voice. What I do think we have to appreciate is that this argument for internal differentiation and heterogeneity can have the character of an infinite regress. Of any group, e.g., Indians, it may be important to recognize differences between middle and working classes; within each class there will be important sub-class differences; within these there will be differences between men and women, who will also be differentiated by age, by geography, by religious affiliation, by cultural heritage . . . at each step the referent population would get smaller and smaller. Indeed, we could go on and on till all we have are individual biographies. Perhaps we could not even rest there as we have also encountered the suggestion that the unity of a self is a fiction (Hall 1992a: 277). Yet most people would acknowledge that this or a Thatcherite-'there is no such thing as society'-individualism is a very poor understanding of the social world. So, at any level of conceptualization and generalization there may be some sociologically and politically valid generalizations even though there will always be scope for internal differentiation, complexity and qualification. The point is that while sometimes the movement towards analytical complexity and differentiation will suggest the relative vacuity of a particular category, this cannot always or even usually be the case for we would indeed then be caught in a destructive infinite regress in which the social world 'disappears'.

So, the important fact of intra-group difference, even to the level of individual variability, is not a reason to disregard the various levels of the 'multi' that I have sketched above. It does not dissolve the political argument for contemporary democratic societies to recognize and accommodate some of the new forms of groupness that have now become part of these societies. It does mean that we have to be flexible to the form that this takes. Hence, multiculturalism can take a hybridic, multiculture, urban melange form; but it does not have to and indeed should not exclusively do so if one or some groups are not comfortable with that (for the time being). The latter should not, however, be able to impose their groupness-based multiculturalism on other minority groups – or on their own co-ethnics or co-religionists – who relate or want to relate to each other and the mainstream in a different way; but similarly, the latter version of multiculturalism must not be normative for the former type of group. Hence the importance of the 'multi'; and the eschewing of a single theoretical paradigm or policy template as 'multiculturalism'. So, the justification – both normative and pragmatic – for multiculturalism is the need to give respect to stigmatized or marginalized identities that are important to people and cannot be disregarded in the name of the individual, or for that matter, social cohesion, integration or citizenship. I have already argued this does not require any monistic notion of group or culture, as for example in Kymlicka's idea of a 'societal culture'.

Citizenship

It is particularly important to distinguish between the varied kinds of difference, for multiculturalism, like all policy ideas, ought to be not just about genuine issues but to be grounded ideas. They must fit not just the facts but have to work with the grain of the institutional and normative contexts that they seek to inform, utilize and reform. It is common to distinguish between the mere fact of the presence of a multiethnic population – something that can be captured in statistics or in the look of a city – and multiculturalism as a set of policies or a way of politically ordering the population in question. But the data that policy ideas must address are not merely demographic or sociological descriptions, though they can be approached descriptively. What one is describing is a public order, a normative set of relations, which one may approve of or not; or, more realistically, approve of in some respects and disapprove of in others; find something which should be developed and other things which should be reformed or eliminated. For example, in the contemporary western context the sociological description will already have implicit in it certain normative ideas such as various interpretations of fairness, equality, market and so on. The ideas of equality that are implicit in the practice of citizenship can be used to highlight how certain challenges to those ideas of equality are not being met, or need to be rethought, of how the facts and mechanisms of negative difference have to be more seriously explored and highlighted and overcome by allowing the flourishing of positive difference. Such critique can be and is largely likely to be internal, namely, we will point to problems within existing practice (e.g., racisms) by utilizing and developing other aspects of contemporary practice (e.g., anti-racisms).

The point is that multiculturalism is not an abstract ideology but is grounded in a specific set of socio-political realities and is developed out of a broadly accepted framework of norms, policies and politics, especially amongst the centre-left and especially in anglophone and some western European countries. It works to reform the status quo by selecting, developing and organizing ideas, tendencies and 'intimations' (Oakeshott 1962) that are already present in the world that is being reformed. This 'world' of course includes the presence of ethnic minorities and their grievances against that world and their distinctive discourses, modes of protest and mobilizations, which too modify and expand the field of analysis and policy. The object of our concern is a very specific set of realities, namely, the dynamic outcome of social and political struggles and negotiations surrounding racial, ethnic and religious differences in relation to non-white migration into white countries. The terms of engagement are the ideas of equality, respect, integration, accommodation and so on. These are about the relations between citizens, about the proper attitudes to fellow citizens, about identifying and overcoming the obstacles to the extension of citizenship across difference. The multiculturalism in this book has this focus on citizenship and so, amongst the normative projects on offer in the field of multiculturalism or 'post-multiculturalism', the definition and project I am defending, whilst not necessarily inconsistent with some of the others, is relatively modest; but I believe able to stand on its own two feet without the larger conceptual frames offered by some of the others, and so without having to take on unnecessary and complicating commitments.

It is not part of a grander theory or political project. It, therefore, has the merit of being more compatible, with suitable modifications where necessary, with a wider variety of intellectual and political viewpoints. It is drawn out of contemporary political struggles within western democratic societies. This does not necessarily mean uncritically accepting contemporary democratic societies with their normative and institutional limitations – let alone their racisms and other inequalities – but is a more restricted formulation of multiculturalism than most others in the literature. I have distinguished it from Kymlicka's societal-culture-based notion of multiculturalism which embraces multinationalism and rights of indigenous peoples besides the post-migration polyethnicity that I am concerned with.

My position is also more modest than other well-known accounts of multiculturalism. I mentioned in chapter 4 that some notions of multiculturalism imply ideas about cross-civilizational understanding and aspire to evaluate cultures and civilizations as contributions to humanistic knowledge, and so for them political multiculturalism is derived from, or at least is part of, a philosophical humanism (Taylor 1992; Parekh 2000). Another example would be Paul Gilroy's planetary humanism which he glimpes in the convivialities of hip-hop, bands like The Streets and comedians like Ali G (Gilroy 2004). Or, the view that the kind of multicultural policies that are being developed in countries like Britain are excessively narrow and Eurocentric (Sardar 2004: 29), or need a global postcolonial formation which does not yet exist and which will need to take into account the existence of diasporas and global solidarities like those of the Muslim ummah but also reverse the western domination of the globe (Sayyid 2000, 2007). The latter view can also be found without any special foregrounding of Muslims but a return to a Marxist political economy in the form of a 'revolutionary multiculturalism' (McLaren 2001), or in the claim that the rise of 'religious ethnicities' has to be seen in the context of a Christian right attack on 'secular humanism' which is symptomatic of the fact that the modern world-system is in a crisis of transition (Wallerstein 2005). I am sympathetic to some of the views just listed but none of them are presupposed by or follow from my conception of civic multiculturalism which therefore does not depend on the validity of any of them. Yet it is perhaps compatible with most of them and many other positions too.

Having asserted the relative modesty of my project and that it lies in its focus on citizenship, I need to say something about citizenship in addition to what was said in chapters 3 and 4, in the process showing that my understanding is different from some other conceptions of citizenship. Citizenship is not just a legal status and set of rights but is amplified by a certain kind of politics. I have nothing specific to say about the former, the basic, foundational levels of citizenship, except that they are necessary – in the way of a skeleton to a living body – to all wider meanings of citizenship. T. H. Marshall (1973) famously conceptualized a wider citizenship as a series of historical-logical developments, each necessary to later stages, by which legal rights such as habeas corpus were gradually extended to include rights of political participation and then later social rights such as the right of citizens to receive health care funded by the citizens as a whole. These developments were a long process of centuries, involved a history of political struggles, not least in extending the body of citizenry, the rights-holders, from an aristocratic male elite to all adults. With some plausibility it has been argued that through egalitarian movements such as the politics of difference the second half of the twentieth century has seen the emergence of a fourth stage in the form of a demand for cultural rights (Roche 1992; Turner 1993), while also seeing an erosion of some social rights. Social citizenship has certainly not been accultural; rather it has been informed by an assumption of cultural homogeneity, such as its support of a male breadwinner model of the nuclear family (Lister 2003). The homogeneity has been particularly exposed by social change and change in attitudes and critiqued by feminists whose work – as with the public–private distinction discussed in chapter 3 – others have built upon. I would, however, here like to outline an understanding of this historically developing citizenship – which has not been a simple linear process – in terms of certain overarching characteristics rather than by types of rights. Like Marshall I believe the citizenship I speak of is particularly informed by British history, though it can be seen at work in many other places too.

1   Non-transcendent or pluralist

Citizens are individuals and have individual rights but they are not uniform and their citizenship contours itself around them. Citizenship is not a monistic identity that is

completely apart from or transcends other identities important to citizens, in the way that the theory – though not
always the practice – of French republicanism demands.
The creation of the UK created new political subjects (for
my purpose citizens, though, strictly speaking, for most of
the history of the UK subjects of the Crown) but did not
eliminate the constituent nations of the UK. So a common
British citizenship did not mean that one could not be
Scottish, English, Irish or Welsh, and so allowed for the
idea that there were different ways of being British – an
idea that is not confined to constituent nations but also
included other group identities. The plurality, then, is ever
present and each part of the plurality has a right to be a
part of the whole and to speak up for itself and for its
vision of the whole.

2   Multilogical

The plurality speaks to itself and it does not necessarily
agree about what it means to be a citizen; there can be a
series of agreements and disagreements, with some who
agree on X while disagreeing on Y, while some who disagree on X may agree and others disagree on Y and so on.
But there is enough agreement and above all enough interest in the discussion for dialogues to be sustained. As the
parties to these dialogues are many, not just two, the
process is more aptly described as multilogical. The multi-
logues allow for views to qualify each other, overlap, synthesize, modify one's own view in the light of having to
co-exist with that of others', hybridize, allow new adjustments to be made, new conversations to take place. Such
modulations and contestations are part of the internal,
evolutionary, work-in-progress dynamic of citizenship.

3   Dispersed

Related to citizenship not being monolithic is that action
and power are not monopolistically concentrated and

so the state is not the exclusive site for citizenship. We perform our citizenship and relate to each other as fellow citizens, and so get to know what our citizenship is, what it is composed of, not just in relation to law and politics but also civic debate and action initiated through our voluntary associations, community organizations, trades unions, newspapers and media, churches, temples, mosques, etc. Change and reform do not all have to be brought about by state action, laws, regulation, prohibitions, etc., but also through public debate, discursive contestations, pressure group mobilizations and the varied and (semi-)autonomous institutions of civil society.

Citizenship, then, consists of a framework of rights and practices of participation but also discourses and symbols of belonging, ways of imagining and remaking ourselves as a country and expressing our sense of commonalities and differences, and ways in which these identities qualify each other and create – should create – inclusive public spaces. It is this understanding of citizenship that is at the basis of my use of the term, 'moderate', e.g., as in moderate secularism, moderate multiculturalism, moderate Muslims: namely, positions advanced which embrace or at least are compatible with this conception of citizenship. By multicultural citizenship I mean my characterization of multiculturalism or the politics of difference, as in chapters 3 and 4, emerging and taking shape through the form of citizenship just outlined.

The Danger of Ideology

This does not mean that all is rosy harmony and there is conflict. Nor is it the case that conflict is temporary; conflict and its management, recurring conflict and recurring reconciliation are built into these societies and so into the citizenship possible in these societies. In fact citizenship is not so much a way of overcoming conflict in some ultimate transcendent way but a way of moderating and handling it with some openness and in a relatively peaceful way.

Ideology, however, is a tendency also implicit in these struggles and if not checked threatens multicultural citizenship. It is a recurring danger because it is not an uncommon tendency, though it takes a different form in different times and places, and is a cause of concern in the case of the politics of difference as in most politics.[2] I will exaggerate it a little in order to identify it better.

By ideology I understand a perspective upon the social world that does not sufficiently attend to the concrete context(s) to which it is directed; rather it operates as a set of ideas that are only tangentially or only partially connected to the set of social and political arrangements that it is concerned to critique or defend (Oakeshott 1962). These ideas and the mode of reasoning which holds the ideas together and produces specific critiques and justifications are to a large degree derived either from the workings of another society (e.g., some ideal construction of a past society) or an imagined and wished-for society. In each case an ideology sees its object of critique or defence, usually a contemporary society or movement, in very crude terms which distort the object. Its diagnoses and prescriptions can often be exciting and appealing to a certain population but are not a good basis for diagnosis of problems and strategies for reform because they are too abstract and disconnected from a specific society, its institutions, norms and ways of working. This is often hidden from those who subscribe to a particular ideology, especially if it is a well-developed ideology, for it works as a total, self-referring, closed or semi-closed system. An ideology can achieve quite sophisticated levels of internal coherence, as in certain forms of Marxism, but still have a poor sense of connection with any existing society.

It would be too crude to divide all available social and political perspectives into the ideological and non-ideological. It is better to see ideology as a tendency in our politics which may become too great in any one of those perspectives – perhaps afflicting different perspectives at different times or all of them at any one time depending upon the wider intellectual and political climate. It is easy to see how certain ideologies, above all racism and nationalism, can be a danger to multicultural politics but my point is that ideology itself is such a danger. It may produce debates and proposals which are not only impractical or not likely to achieve their stated goals but, even in achieving them, do not address key issues or create problematic side-effects and so lose the political support necessary for reform. Additionally, ideologies can be a danger to the pluralist and multilogical nature of citizenship. This is particularly the case because typically ideologies dichotomize the social world into key actors or groups. These may be workers and capitalists, nation and aliens, male and female, black and white, and so on. Each of these dichotomies has a certain validity but an ideological working of them totalizes them so that each member of the pair is totally different – and usually opposed – to the other and all possibilities of overlap, hybridity and plurality is deemed secondary and minor; and the paired identities are said to have a sociological primacy which lends support to claims that for members of these groups the relevant identity should always trump all others. It should be easy to see that such totalized dualistic perspectives, even where they exist only as a significant tendency and not as a pure form, are not conducive to fostering dialogue, respect for difference, to seeking common ground and negotiated accommodation, in short to citizenship in general and above all to multicultural citizenship. Our attitudes to such ideologies is well put by Hall when he say that in the contemporary context when we are faced with discourses of equality, on the one hand, and of difference, on the other, we must reject the ideological liberalism that presses an 'either/or' upon us and demand a 'both/and' (Hall 2000; cf. Laclau 1996).

As should be apparent from the characterization of the current crisis of multiculturalism in chapter 1, the current

ideologies which are the greatest danger to multiculturalism are those formed around a totalistic dichotomization
of West-Islam/Muslims. On one side is Islamophobia or
anti-Islamism as a set of attitudes, prejudices and stereotypes which are being developed into an ideology in the
context of a neo-conservative geopolitical strategy to dom-
inate Muslims. Talk of a clash of civilizations; of Islam
being deeply opposed to the ethos of democracy and
gender equality; of the presence of too many Muslims
amongst migrants and new citizens as a problem for
democracy and so on are some examples of these discourses. Obverse discourses to these which assert the civilizational superiority of the West are those which simply
see the West as decadent compared to the civilizational
superiority of Islam and its products, or characterizes the
West as a colonial overlord. The two sets of discourses are
asymmetrical in being sustained by quite unequal intellectual, political, economic and military forces but each
has a similar dichotomizing, distorting logic. The dichotomizing obscures, for example, that there are a variety of
views in the West, including those which are hostile to the
western geopolitical domination of the Muslim world; just
as there are a variety of views amongst Muslims. With
each ideological tendency, the totalizing of West and
Muslim into radical opposites undercuts the efforts to
build cross-cutting connections, syntheses, alliances and so
on which multicultural citizenship facilitates and needs.
Just as earlier exclusivist dichotomies of British/alien, or
even the political blackness that divides the British people
into black or white, had to be challenged, so similarly
some versions of Islamism are not sufficiently respectful of
fellow British citizens and the aspiration of a plural Britain
and have to be challenged even while the legitimate grievances of Muslims are being expressed and addressed.
Indeed, attending to the latter is necessary to any effective
challenge.

In identifying Islamist ideologies as one of a set of ideologies (another being Islamophobia) that multicultural

citizenship must challenge, I must (re)emphasize there is no special problem with Islam, let alone with religion as such; it is religious ideologies, not religion, that can threaten the free, healthy working through of multicultural citizenship. Secular ideologies are no less – in the twentieth century, were much more – dangerous than religious ideologies. Indeed it is central to the contention of this book that one of the current dangers to multicultural citizenship is a radical secularism that seeks to destroy the historic compromises with organized religion which is a characteristic of twentieth-century citizenship, especially in western Europe, and a promising basis for the accommodation of Muslims in those countries.

Muslims and Identity

I have argued that groups marked by difference may need modes of political and civil society representation and that this may have to take varied forms in order to accommodate some of the difference between members of a group. I have also warned of the need to be alert against the ideological tendency that creates monoliths out of groups (and usually places them in confrontation with another totalized group). It may be, however, that there is a further problem left unaddressed. We can get to this problem by the Nobel laureate prizewinner Amartya Sen's question, 'why should a British citizen who happens to be Muslim have to rely on clerics and other leaders of the religious community to communicate with the Prime Minister?' (Sen 2006: 78). Nothing in what I have said implies that Muslim citizens should not be part of mainstream democratic processes – to the contrary. My argument is about what additional forms of recognition and representation may be necessary to empower excluded groups and to meet their distinctive needs. Nor am I arguing in the case of Muslims that they should be represented by clerics and religious personages – though I want to allow for that as one possibility amongst others against those who want to rule it out. Nevertheless, I appreciate that talk of Muslims needing representation can easily have an exclusively religious inflection. So, the problem left unaddressed is that when one identifies some people as a group one inevitably pulls out one feature of a complex set of features and gives it a primacy. In arguing that Muslims deserve some recognition and representation one is almost inevitably prioritizing religious over other features (such as occupation or locality, for example) and promoting religious Muslims as the representatives of Muslims as a whole.

In dealing with this as an objection to forms of representation demanded by some Muslims I follow a strategy that should by now be quite plain: seek consistency and do not demand that Muslims (or other minorities, as the case may be) have to satisfy a higher standard than those in current use. Accordingly, we must first recognize that the point made about Muslims applies to any social description, e.g., if we substitute 'black' for 'Muslim' then those who identify most with that description will step forward and say they represent the group designated 'black' and their claim may indeed seem greater than those of black individuals who do not foreground their blackness. And we are not talking about something that is just a flaw in recent 'identity politics'. The same problem arises when we use allegedly non-identity categorizations like class.[3] As in one case, spokespersons can play a more-black-than-thou game, so in the other putative leaders will put down their rivals using a more-working-class-than-you rhetoric. 'Muslim', like the identity categories that set the scene for identity politics – woman, black, Asian etc. – emerged politically because existing forms of recognition and representation were inadequate and marginalized some people who were poorly or not at all represented by the left vs. right discourses of the third quarter of the twentieth century. No doubt the emphasis on any particular identity can be overdone in some contexts and can overly circumscribe agendas, choice of spokespeople and so on. But this can only be dealt with in the context of specific political debates; there is no general remedy. In any case, as a danger it is true of any identity formation, there is no specific problem with religion or Muslims. We should not apply double standards to Muslims, i.e., think of class politics or feminist projects as universalist and Muslim politics as particularistic, reductive and one-dimensional.

With any identity, for some it will be a background, while others will often foreground it, although much will depend on context. So it is with Muslims. Even with those for whom a Muslim identity is in many contexts not just a background, it does not follow that it is the religious dimension that is most salient:[4] it can be a sense of family and community; or for collective political advancement, or righting the wrongs done to Muslims. Indeed, we cannot assume that being 'Muslim' means the same thing to them. For some Muslims – like many Jews in Britain today – being Muslim is a matter of community membership and heritage; for others it is a few simple precepts about self, compassion, justice and the afterlife; for some others it is a worldwide movement armed with a counter-ideology of modernity; and so on. Some Muslims are devout but apolitical; some are political but do not see their politics as being 'Islamic' (indeed, may even be anti-'Islamic'). Some identify more with a nationality of origin, such as Turkish; others with the nationality of settlement and perhaps citizenship, such as French.[5] Some prioritize fund-raising for mosques, others campaigns against discrimination, unemployment or Zionism. For some, the Ayatollah Khomeini is a hero and Osama bin Laden an inspiration; for others, the same may be said of Kemal Ataturk or Margaret Thatcher, whose policies created a swathe of Asian millionaires in Britain, brought in Arab capital and Islamist exiles and who was one of the first to call for NATO action to protect Muslims in Kosovo. So it is no more plausible to ascribe a particular politics (religious or otherwise) to all Muslims as it is to all women or members of the working class.

So when we speak of allowing Muslims to politically organize as Muslims without any sense of illegitimacy and for them to raise distinctive concerns, to have group representation in political parties, trades unions, various public bodies and so on, this means allowing Muslims to organize in ways they think appropriate at different times, in different contexts and for different ends. The result will be a spectrum of activity, a democratic constellation reflective of the 'family resemblance' of a group discussed in chapter 5. The idea that such a constellation of participation can be summed up as 'fundamentalism' (as in the view of Women Against Fundamentalism 1990) simply because it represents some of the public/political aspirations of religions is scaremongering; or, relatedly, is to tar moderates and ideologists with the same brush. Religious fundamentalism, like all fundamentalisms and ideology, is a potential threat to democratic civic life but it cannot be equated with the participation of religious groups in multicultural citizenship (Casanova 1994).

I do not accept, therefore, that the recognition of religious groups like Muslims will necessarily mean the promotion of religious leaders. I do not rule out that in some contexts it could have that effect but ultimately the issue is not whether we should have more or fewer religious leaders in our civic life. Muslims – or any other group – should be free to appeal (or not) to religious discourses but it should be as participants in multicultural citizenship, a citizenship in which other kinds of discourse will also be present and will engage, qualify and synthesize with each other. Religious discourses are legitimate civic discourses; religious leaders are legitimate civic leaders if their presence is a result of the civic participation of fellow citizens who must be included and respected as fellow citizens. As Peter Jones says, 'the recognition that is demanded is recognition directed at a group of people rather than at a system of belief . . . [e.g.,] . . . what the majority is called

upon to recognise is not Islam but Muslims – not a religious faith but those who subscribe to it' (Jones 2006: 29).
Even 'subscribe' is probably too strong; or at least it does
not mark where recognition begins, for that is (in the
present case) not those who subscribe to a faith but those
who identify with the Muslim family of communities.

Those who think we are beyond such identity politics
may see a confirmation of this in Sir Iqbal Sacranie's
valedictory speech as Secretary-General of the Muslim
Council of Britain (MCB) in 2006. Describing Muslim
community development over a quarter of a century in
terms of three stages, he labels the period since 1997 – the
period of New Labour and of the MCB itself – as 'identity
politics' and suggests the way forward lies in thinking
of the good of society as a whole, of Britain, which, in
his view, means the end of identity politics (MCB website;
see also Masood 2006a). I do not, however, see identity
politics as being antithetical to political perspectives
focused on the good of society as a whole. British Muslim
identity politics had been stimulated by the *Satanic Verses*
affair. It was a crisis that led many to think of themselves
for the first time as Muslims in a public way, to think
that it was important in their relation to other Muslims
and to the rest of British and related societies. This is
for example movingly described by the author, Rana
Kabbani, whose *Letter to Christendom* begins with a
description of herself as 'a woman who had been a sort
of underground Muslim before she was forced into the
open by the Salman Rushdie affair' (Kabbani 1989: ix).
Yet such shocks to Muslim identity are hardly a thing of
the past. The present situation of some Muslims in Britain
is nicely captured by Farmida Bi, a New Labour parlia-
mentary candidate in Mole Valley in 2005, who had not
particularly made anything of her Muslim background
before 7/7 but was moved by the London bombings to
claim a Muslim identity and found the organization, Progressive British Muslims. Speaking of herself and others as
'integrated, liberal British Muslims' who were forced to

ask 'am I a Muslim at all?', she writes: '7/7 made most of us embrace our Muslim identity and become determined to prove that it's possible to live happily as a Muslim in the west' (Bi 2006).

This sense of feeling that one must speak up as a Muslim is of course nothing necessarily to do with religiosity. Like all forms of difference it comes into being as a result of pressures from the 'outside' as well as the 'inside'. In this particular case, both the 'inside' and the 'outside' have a powerful geopolitical dimension. The emergence of British Muslim identity and activism has been propelled by a strong concern for the plight of Muslims elsewhere in the world, especially (but not only) where this plight is seen in terms of anti-imperialist emancipation and where the UK government is perceived to be part of the problem – tolerant of if not complicit or actively engaged in the destruction of Muslim hopes and lives, usually civilian. Political activity, charitable fund-raising, the delivering of humanitarian relief and sometimes the taking up of arms has taken place in connection with Palestine, Kashmir, Bosnia, Chechnya, Kosovo, Afghanistan and Iraq, just to mention the most prominent cases. As a consequence, Muslims have been perceived by some other Britons as disloyal and have experienced recurring and deepening tensions connected with dual loyalties and alienation from New Labour, initially seen as a champion of British Muslims (Werbner 2004). It is not that unusual, even for successful, integrated and respected minorities, to be strongly identified with an international or a 'homeland' cause; British and American Jews in relation to Israel and Cuban-Americans in relation to Cuba are notable exam-ples. Yet, as these latter cases demonstrate, these causes are usually where one's government is either neutral or on your side. The western Muslim identification with the international ummah has a clear parallel with how postwar Jewish identification has come to be more centred on heri-tage and Israel than Judaism. Nevertheless, the fact that British, American and Australian (perhaps to some extent most western) Muslims are having to develop a sense of national citizenship, to integrate into a polity which has a confrontational posture against many Muslim countries and is at war with or occupying some of them in what is perceived by all sides to be a long-term project, is an extremely daunting task and I suppose one has to say that success cannot be taken for granted. Moreover, domestic terrorism, as well as political opposition, has become part of the context. The danger of 'blowback' from overseas military activity is, as 7/7 has already shown, considerable and capable of destroying the movement towards multicultural citizenship.

This is of course where the book started; the crisis of multiculturalism, that I have been arguing must not be responded to in panic but with a cool reappraisal of what multiculturalism is and what is needed for it to succeed. One of the reasons why I do not think we should simply give up and pursue a less attractive political goal is that I am impressed by how most British Muslims have responded to and are responding to the crisis. Despite this dependency on overseas circumstances outside their control and so where one might anticipate passivity and a self-pitying introspection, what is clear from many Muslims is their dynamism, energy and confidence that they must rise to the challenge of dual loyalties and not give up on either set of commitments. Ideological and violent extremism is indeed undermining the conditions and hopes for multiculturalism but, contrary to the multiculturalism blamers cited in chapter 1, this extremism has nothing to do with the promotion of multiculturalism but is coming into the domestic arena from the international. The government, having created the political extremism through its foreign policies, by blaming multiculturalism and the Muslim communities for the crisis, is losing the one sure resource that is necessary for a long-term victory over domestic terrorism: namely, the full and active 'on-side' cooperation of the Muslim communities. (That at least would be the lesson from Northern Ireland.)

Debating Muslims

It is ironic that Muslims are experiencing the pressures to step up and be British Muslims in the same context in which members of other minorities might be coming to feel an easing of identity pressures and feel free to mix and match identities on an individual basis (as partly captured in the theorizing of 'new ethnicities' discussed in chapter 5). Perhaps as a result of a combination of these two factors – the public avowal of a socio-political Muslim identity and the general loosening of unitary definitions of identity – 7/7, and before it 9/11, accelerated and heightened a trend that was already visible, namely the proliferation of Muslim organizations, each seeking to create a public platform for a distinctive point of view and to display – to other Muslims, to co-citizens, to the government – and promote a particular Muslim identity. Sometimes the distinction is based on doctrine and tradition (e.g., Sufi vs. Wahabbi), sometimes on politics (e.g., the degree of critical distance from New Labour, MCB or international Islamism), sometimes on a combination, but in each case what is being sought is not some private belief but a working out of what it is to be a Muslim in a public space called Britain. Some of the most interesting developments are the emergence of organizations – the scale of which is currently still relatively small – which want to belong to the family of public Muslims but are thoroughly critical of a religious politics. I have already mentioned Progressive British Muslims; another is Muslims for a Secular Democracy. Such groups have to be distinguished from those who see themselves as anti-Islamic or as ex-Muslims (like Salman Rushdie or Aayn Hirsi Ali), and while the former may be part of the broad swathe of contemporary Islamic modernism,[6] what is particularly distinctive about them is the relative thinness of their appeal to Islam to justify their social democratic politics. They could just as easily seek to privatize their Muslimness but feel a socio-political obligation to do the opposite. They manifest the general truth that identity politics is not necessarily undermining citizenship and can be propelled by a sense of civic as well as communal duty. In addition, there is the more specific truth that in many western countries today even those Muslims distant from Islamic discourse, let alone Islamism, feel they must stake a claim in the growing Muslim identity. There is a felt need to join the public constellation of Muslim identities rather than walk away from them. Some contemporary Muslim identity politics, then, takes the form of what might be called 'existential Muslims', where Muslims argue about what it is to be a Muslim in an existential and pragmatic way, e.g., by bridging the communities and institutions that one belongs to, say, Muslims and the Labour Party, or Muslims and racial equality institutions (Modood and Ahmad 2007). It is to treat being 'British-Muslim' as a hyphenated identity in which both parts are to be valued as important to oneself and one's principles and belief commitments. Of course to bring together two or several identity-shaping, even identity-defining, commitments will have an effect on each of the commitments. They will interact with each other, leading to some reinterpretation on both (or all) sides, for example, on what is highlighted in each identity. This has certainly been happening with Muslims in Britain, and the West generally, especially in the United States (Leonard 2003). Often this has been happening in a practice-led way as indicated in those cases that Fauzia Ahmad and I have called 'existential Muslims' (Modood and Ahmad 2007). Sometimes it can go well beyond this and involves scholarly engagement with the Islamic intellectual heritage.

One of the key areas of renewal and reinterpretation has been equality and related concepts. This can be seen in debates about gender equality in which Muslim cultural practices and taken-for-granted assumptions have been subjected to severe critique through fresh readings of the Qur'an, the sayings and practice of the Prophet

Muhammad and Muslim history, tracing the emergence of conservative and restricted interpretations at moments when other interpretations could and should have been favoured (Mernissi 1991; Ahmed 1992; Wadud 1999). In relation to issues to do with minorities, namely groups such as themselves, Muslim impulses and sensibilities, including the experience of negative difference, of Islamophobia, are clearly entering our citizenship but they are adjusting to and being translated into contemporary, western civic discourses and practices (Modood 2005a). A very good concrete example of this translation is how protestors against the *Satanic Verses* initially spoke of apostasy, then blasphemy and in due course most settled on the policy goal of creating a legal offence of incitement to religious hatred. The notions of minorities and groups that Muslims are deploying are generally on a par with those employed by other equality-seeking groups such as women and ethnic minorities and are reflective of the national political culture. Thus the normative conception of 'minority' and 'minority rights' used by most Muslims in Britain is grounded in British political discourses and notions of equality and not the classical Muslim idea of 'dhimmi' (non-Muslims in Muslim-ruled states who enjoy legal protection but not equality with Muslims). On the other hand, plurality is emerging as an important Muslim idea. Despite certain ideas that one might associate with Saudi Arabia or the Taliban, most Muslims have no theological or conscientious problems with multifaith citizenship – after all the Prophet Muhammad founded just such a polity. The first organized, settled Muslim community was in the city of Madina which was shared with Jews and others and was based on an inter-communally agreed constitution. The late Sheikh Dr Zaki Badawi, widely regarded as the most learned Muslim theologian in modern Britain, has described it as the first example in history of a multicultural constitution in that it guaranteed autonomy to the various communities of the city (Badawi 2003; see also Wyn Davies 1988; Khan 2002; and Asani 2003 for 'ideas that form the seeds for a theology of pluralism within Islam').[7]

There is a general understanding amongst the authors mentioned and their readers that these projects of recovering and reinterpreting Muslim precedents and texts has to be done within a framework of democratic citizenship. Citizenship and politics narrowly interpreted have not had the importance in the Muslim world that they have come to have in the West for, while participation in communal governance is a feature of Muslim thinking and practice, participation in state governance is much less so. Using 'citizenship' in the wide sense outlined earlier in this chapter, Muslim notions of citizenship are more communitarian than state-centred, but this is generally true of traditions outside the West (cf. Parekh's discussion of human rights and Asian values, 2000: 136–41). Islam has a highly developed sense of social or ethical citizenship in which, in line with contemporary western communitarian thinking, duties as well as rights are emphasized. This is illustrated in one of the 'five pillars of Islam', namely, zakat, the obligation to give a proportion of one's income or wealth to the poor and needy. This is not an act of charity, that is to say something left to the discretion and goodwill of the individual, for the amount is specified, but nor is it a legal compulsion like a Christian tithe or a state tax; it has a civic character for it is not simply a responsibility to one's kith and kin or to those known in face-to-face relationships such as those in one's neighbourhood or at one's workplace. It extends to strangers, to an 'imagined community'. The idea that it needs a state to enforce social citizenship or religious law more generally is very much twentieth-century theology – one of the innovative ways in which thinkers such as the radical Sunni, Mawdudi, and the radical Shi'a, Khomeini have sought to modernize the Islamic heritage. What is interesting in this move is that it seeks to place the political over the legal (the shariah); another strand of Islamic modernity has countered this authoritarian tendency by seeing the shariah not as a body

of unchanging law, but as a set of ethical principles with
legal conclusions that apply to specific places and times
only and so have to be continually reinterpreted, and so
placing the ethical over the legal and the political (Sardar
1987; Ramadan 2004).

Variable Group Representation

Such ethical perspectives on shariah and citizenship are
examples of how western Muslim sensibilities are mani-
festing themselves and drawing on extra-European heritages, while at the same time reinterpreting them in a
context of a democratic citizenship and thereby pluralizing
it and making it one's own.[8] The process, both in method
and goal, is illustrative of what Parekh has theorized as
the multiculturalizing of liberalism and of western societies
in general (Parekh 2000). As Muslims discuss these matters
and as Muslim discourses become part of British debates,
these things will become more openly considered and
political maturity could mean that when we seek Muslim
voices or civic participants we will not seek exclusively one
or even a few kinds of Muslims. This is easier to achieve
at the level of discourses, more difficult in terms of institutional accommodation, but not impossible. After all, it
seems to work to some degree in relation to other groups,
e.g., the Jews. A variety of Jewish people can be taken to
represent one or another strand of Jewish opinion and may
be consulted as such, whether as organizations like a federation of synagogues or the Board of Deputies or as
individuals. So we must not set the bar too high for new
groups of ethnic and religious minorities. To take the
severe view that for a group to enjoy public representation
they must all agree, otherwise no representation is possible, is either to use double standards or to succumb to an
essentialism about that group. Moreover, it is a positive
virtue that there is internal variety within any group and
that (organized) members of any one group will want to

locate themselves in different parts of the representational landscape – secular, religious, close to government, distant from mainstream political parties – for that is true integration; new groups should have similar opportunities to old groups and will not need to conform to a singular minority perspective. They will spread themselves across society in ways that suit them and also create or give rise to new discourses, new patternings in political activity and in social organization. This is not going back on the idea of group representation but making it consistent with the understanding of groupness, its variability and transmutations, that has been present in this book. The result will be a democratic constellation of organizations, networks, alliances and discourses in which there will be agreement and disagreement, in which group identity will be manifested by way of family resemblances rather than by the idea that one group means one voice.

We must, however, also avoid simplistic and reductive models of democratic citizenship. Overcoming the marginality of a minority and integrating it into the political structure might indeed require some degree of corporatism in the way that the Anglican Church as an organization is guaranteed representation in the House of Lords; or the Catholic Church is a partner in the state educational system; or the trades unions have substantial representation in the Labour Party and formal and semi-formal representation on a panoply of public bodies and advisory government committees. I argued for such possibilities – and why they will take different forms in different countries – in chapter 4, and how we may reasonably be guided by some existing ways in which churches and Jews are represented, though avoiding top-down state control of religious organizations and facilitating lay community, not just 'clerical', representation. Such corporate representation is not necessarily undemocratic but can be pillars in the extensive architecture of participation in the multilevel decision-making processes of a democratic society in which power is shared and not overly concentrated in the hands of career politicians and state bureaucracies. There are two points here to underline. First, that the 'recognition' of difference can be institutionalized in varied ways which can include (but does not have to include) some degree of corporate representation depending on the circumstances, especially whether the minority in question is capable of and willing to institutionalize itself in that way. Secondly, the formalized partnership with government that I am speaking of here is, no less than the election of legislatures or governments, part of the participative structure of self-governing societies, and as such something in which identity groups should be accommodated.

National Identity

Multiculturalism has been broadly right and does not deserve the desertion of support from the centre-left, let alone the blame for the present crisis. Some advocacy of multiculturalism has, however, perhaps overlooked or at least underemphasized the other side of the coin, which is not just equally necessary but is integral to multiculturalism. For one can't just talk about difference. Difference has to be related to things we have in common. The commonality that I have been emphasizing, in common with most multiculturalists and others, is citizenship. I have emphasized that this citizenship has to be seen in a plural, dispersed and dialogical way and not reduced to legal rights, passports and the franchise (important though these are). I would now like to go further in suggesting that a good basis for or accompaniment to a multicultural citizenship is a national identity.[9]

Many multiculturalists and others for whom equality and difference are politically important do not agree with me but national identity seems to be relevant here. This is partly because conceiving of citizenship in the very broad way that I have outlined already begins to overlap with much of what we mean when we speak of the 'national', as in, for example, the national news, national history, national dynamism, national malaise, national agenda and so on. Indeed, modern democratic citizenship has nearly always – if not in theory, then in fact – been accompanied by a national identity. Of course, these national identities have not usually been welcoming of difference and sometimes have actively suppressed it, so I am not simply recommending unreformed historical models of nationhood. Many people today think that the dynamics of globalization are fatally undermining national identities for, in a context of global economic organizations and instant international communications, migrations as part of globalization are giving rise to diasporas, transnational and cosmopolitan identities which are dissolving nations in terms of both objective structures and personal sentiment. There is some truth in this, though it is easily exaggerated. In any case, the developments just referred to do not so damage national citizenship that it cannot be a container for multicultural currents.

We in Europe have overlooked that where multiculturalism has been accepted and worked as a state project or as a national project – Canada, Australia and Malaysia for example – it has not just been coincidental with but integral to a nation-building project, to creating Canadians, Aussies and Malaysians, etc. Even in the US, where the federal state has had a much lesser role in the multicultural project, the incorporation of ethno-religious diversity and hyphenated Americans has been about country-making, civic inclusion and making a claim upon the national identity. This is important because some multiculturalists, or at least advocates of pluralism and multiculture (the vocabulary of multiculturalism is not always used) – even where they have other fundamental disagreements with each other – argue as if the logic of the national and the multicultural are incompatible (Gilroy 1987, 2004;[10] Anthias and Yuval-Davis 1992; Sayyid 2000, 2007; Joppke 2004;[11] Cannon 2006; O'Donnell 2007). Partly as a result, many Europeans think of multiculturalism as antithetical to rather than as a reformer of national identity. A dramatic illustration was the immediate public reception of the report of the Commission on Multi-Ethnic Britain (CMEB 2000). Despite its stated intention of placing issues of multiculturalism into the remaking of the national story, it was almost uniformly but mistakenly received by the press – broadsheet and tabloid alike – as being anti-patriotic (McLaughlin and Neal 2004), and sometimes welcomed for its alleged post-national vision (Robins 2001).

No one can deny that national identity, even where it has been connected to a national citizenship, has simultaneously or at other times been involved in ideological forms of nationalism which have led to exclusion, racism, military aggression, empires and much else. But looking at recent and contemporary history, especially in western Europe and countries like Canada, suggests that it is possible to disconnect national identities from strong forms of nationalism. Perhaps it is also possible to disconnect citizenship from national identities, and so from the national altogether, perhaps to invest our civic loyalties and sense of belonging into some principles of a human rights-based political order, what Habermas (1992) calls 'constitutional patriotism'. I would concede that recent trends in the countries mentioned above, where for many, especially younger people, citizenship can be prized but nationality is looked at with suspicion or indifference, are just as supportive of the idea of a fading of national identity as they are of a non-nationalism national identity.[12] Nevertheless, my judgement is that attitudes such as constitutional patriotism or cosmopolitanism are not affective enough for most people, especially the relatively non-political, and especially at times of crisis. They are unlikely to hold people together and to give them the confidence and optimism to see through the present crisis of multiculturalism as described in chapter 1. Indeed, what we see happening is that it is all too easy in these times of fear and panic for ordinary, decent people to be very anxious and – where multicultural national identities are weak or at least are not inclusive of Muslims – to wrap themselves in strong nationalisms, militarisms and other dichotomizing, confrontational ideologies.

Moreover, it does not make sense to encourage strong multicultural or minority identities and weak common or national identities; strong multicultural identities are a good thing – they are not intrinsically divisive, reactionary or fifth columns – but they need a framework of vibrant, dynamic, national narratives and the ceremonies and rituals which give expression to a national identity. It is clear that minority identities are capable of having an emotional pull for the individuals for whom they are important. Multicultural citizenship requires, therefore, if it is to be equally attractive to the same individuals, a comparable counterbalancing emotional pull. Many Britons say they are worried about disaffection amongst some Muslim young men and more generally a lack of identification with Britain amongst many Muslims in Britain. As a matter of fact, surveys over many years have shown Muslims have been reaching out for an identifica- tion with Britain. For example, in a Channel 4 NOP survey done in Spring 2006, 82 per cent of a well constructed national sample of Muslims said they very strongly (45 per cent) or fairly strongly (37 per cent) felt they belonged to Britain.[13] Yet the survey also found that many Muslims did not feel comfortable in Britain. For example, 58 per cent thought that extreme religious persecution of Muslims was very likely (23 per cent) or fairly likely (35 per cent); and 22 per cent strongly agreed (11 per cent) or fairly strongly agreed (11 per cent) that the 7/7 London bomb- ings were justified because of British support for the US war on terror – in each case the figures were higher amongst the young.[14] The last set of views are connected to foreign policy and so in some cases cannot be changed without a change in policy but nevertheless to not build on the clear support there is for a sense of national belonging is to fail to offer an obvious counterweight to the ideological calls for a jihad against fellow Britons.

A sense of belonging to one's country is necessary to make a success of a multicultural society. Not assimilation into an undifferentiated national identity; that is unrealistic and oppressive as a policy. An inclusive national identity is respectful of and builds upon the identities that people value and does not trample upon them. Simultaneously respecting difference and inculcating Britishness is not a naive hope but something that is happening, as pointed out in the previous chapter, and leads everyone to redefine themselves. Perhaps one of the lessons of the current crisis is that in some countries, certainly Britain, multiculturalists, and the left in general, have been too hesitant about embracing our national identity and allying it with progressive politics. The reaffirming of a plural, changing, inclusive British identity, which can be as emotionally and politically meaningful to British Muslims as the appeal of jihadi sentiments, is critical to isolating and defeating extremism. The lack of a sense of belonging to Britain that can stand up to the emotional appeal of transnational solidarities is due to several causes, including causes that belong to the majority society and not the minorities. One of these is exclusivist and racist notions of Britishness that hold that non-white people are not really British and that Muslims are an alien wedge. Another, and this time from the left, is the view that there is something deeply wrong about rallying round the idea of Britain, about defining ourselves in terms of a normative concept of Britishness – that it is too racist, imperialist, militaristic, elitist and so on – and that the goal of seeking to be British in the present and the future is silly and dangerous, and indeed, demeaning to the newly settled groups of population. But if the goal of wanting to become British, to be accepted as British and to belong to Britain is not a worthwhile goal for Commonwealth migrants and their progeny, what then are they supposed to integrate into? And if there is nothing strong, purposive and inspiring to integrate into, why bother with integration? And if inspiring and meaning-conferring identities can be found elsewhere – in some internationalist movement – that's just fine and if that's at the expense of your country and its citizens, well they don't really matter all that much in the ultimate scheme of significance. We cannot both ask new Britons to integrate and go around saying that being British (or English) is a hollowed-out, meaningless project whose time has come to an end. This will rightly produce confusion and will detract from the sociological and psychological processes of integration, and offer no defence against the calls of other loyalties and missions. Today's national identities certainly need to be re-imagined in a multicultural way but if this is thought impossible or unnecessary then multiculturalism is left not triumphant but with fewer emotive resources.

So integration – like multiculturalism as a whole – is not simply or even primarily a minority problem. If too many white people do not feel the power of Britishness, it will only be a legal concept and other identities will prevail, including ones that will be damaging to multicultural citizenship. Earlier in this chapter, I had to recognize that the development of a British Muslim identity was dependent on overseas events and international politics. I am now pointing out that whether and what kind of integrative citizenship takes place is inevitably dependent upon majority attitudes and interests. I believe that in many circumstances, as in Britain, the best support for multicultural citizenship is a national identity but I am unsure as to whether there is enough interest amongst white Britons in a British national identity. It is therefore to be welcomed when politicians of the left show an interest in British national identity. A leading example of this is Gordon Brown, the former Prime Minister. He has argued for the need to revive and revalue British national identity in a number of speeches, most notably at the Fabian 2006 Annual Conference, entitled 'Who do We Want to Be? The Future of Britishness' (Brown 2006). Brown wants to derive a set of core values (liberty, fairness, enterprise and so on) from a historical narrative yet such values, even if they could singly or in combination be given a distinctive British take, are too complex and their interpretation and priority too contested to be amenable to be set into a series of meaningful definitions. Every public culture must operate through shared values, which are both embodied in and used to criticize its institutions and practices, but they are not simple and uniform and their meaning is discursively grasped as old interpretations are dropped and new circumstances unsettle one consensus and another is built up. Simply saying that freedom or equality is a core British value is unlikely to settle any controversy or tell us, for example, what is hate speech and how it should be handled. Definitions of core values will either be too bland or too divisive and the idea that there has to be a schedule of value statements to which every citizen is expected to sign up is not in the spirit of a multilogical citizenship (Brown 2005). National identity should be woven in debate and discussion, not reduced to a list.

Let me return, in concluding, to one of my starting points, the CMEB report. It suggested that if people are to have a sense of belonging to society as a whole, to have a sense of sharing a common fate with fellow citizens and nationals they must be able to feel 'that their own flourishing as individuals and as communities is intimately linked with the flourishing of public institutions and public services' (CMEB 2000: 49). The report insisted that this sense of belonging required two important conditions: the idea that one's polity should be recognized as a community of communities as well as a community of individuals; and the challenging of all racisms and related structural inequalities (CMEB 2000: 56).[15] It is clear in the CMEB report, and I hope from this book, that the concepts of recognition and belonging are about much more than culture and cultural rights. They are interpretations of the idea of equality as applied to groups who are constituted by differentia that have identarian dimensions that elude socio-economic concepts. The realization of multicultural equality is not possible in a society in which the distribution of opportunities are restricted by 'difference' but it cannot be confined to socio-economic opportunities. For central to it is a citizenship and the right to make a claim on the national identity in which negative difference is challenged and supplanted by positive difference. We cannot afford to leave out these aspects of multicultural citizenship from an intellectual or political vision of social reform and justice in the twenty-first century. Rather, the turning of negative difference into positive difference should be one of the tests of social justice in this century.

This book is a response to the crisis of multiculturalism that has been brewing as a result of Muslim political assertiveness in the West, the support amongst some western Muslims for anti-imperialist Muslim causes in Muslim countries, and above all the terrorist activity by a few Muslims against fellow citizens. The book has taken the form of restating a conception of multicultural citizenship which makes a case for multiculturalism, arguing that the accommodation of Muslims is reasonable and just, should not be rejected as antithetical to progressive politics and can be achieved through dialogue and negotiation within a multicultural citizenship and an inclusive nationality. In most anglophone countries and in parts of western Europe we had begun moving in this direction. We need to reconnect with that movement. That is the best way to overcome the present state of fear, polarization and ultimately the suicide bombings in our cities. The 'best way', but I am conscious that multiculturalism offers only part of the answer, for it cannot itself flourish in a context of fear, terrorism and the neo-conservative US–UK international project of controlling Muslims. So, I cannot conclude on a clear note of optimism. But we do need some optimism and self-belief if we are even to limit the damage that is currently being done to our multicultural politics and prospects for the future. The twenty-first century is going to be one of unprecedented ethnic and religious mix in the West. In the past multicultural societies have tended to flourish only under imperial rule. If we are to keep alive the prospect of a dynamic, internally differentiated multiculturalism within the context of democratic citizenship, then we must at least see that multiculturalism is not the cause of the present crisis but part of the solution. Whether the sapling multiculturalism survives or not, we should at least know what it is we may be about to lose.

– 7 –

The Strange Non-Death
of Multiculturalism

That multiculturalism has failed, is in political retreat and even dead, especially in western Europe (Joppke 2004; Kundnani 2007; Bagguley and Hussain 2008; Abbas 2011; Husband and Alam 2011; and Lentin and Titley 2011)[1] is now so taken for granted that one can speak of 'The *ravages* of . . . the policy *disaster* of state multiculturalism' (Pathak 2008: 133; my italics) in leading academic journals without the support of a single reference. For these academics, assimilation and racism have replaced a movement towards multiculturalism.

There is of course considerable denunciation of multiculturalism. For example, seven European Premiers made high-profile attacks on multiculturalism in late 2010 and early 2011 (Fekete 2011). But with the notable exception of security responses to international terrorism and of the *niqab* bans of the new decade, which are proliferating, the policy changes that have accompanied the 'multiculturalism is dead' discourses have not been directed at ethnic-minority citizens but more or less confined to immigration and the acquisition of citizenship. A consequence is that the lesser or anti-multiculturalist countries, those who have fewer policies to undo according to the aggressive discourse, are having greater effects on ethnic minorities. Thus, those countries that have in the past not enabled or encouraged the taking up of (dual) citizenship are more able to directly change the position of settled ethnic-minority communities.[2] So, for example, the UK and Germany, beginning in very different places, have instituted similar changes in relation to nationality acquisition such that, by 2006, each country had very similar laws in place (Haverig 2011). But, as most non-European-origin people in Britain are British citizens, these changes have not affected them directly. In Germany, where even after a number of years of acceleration of naturalization it is estimated that 55 per cent of Muslims are not German citizens (Speigel Online 2009), the changes in law and policies in relation to immigration, right of residence and naturalization have a much greater effect on that population (mainly for the better by making citizenship acquisition a real option, a result that multiculturalists welcome, though it, especially dual citizenship, is still too difficult.). Indeed, in most countries, in relation to those who are already citizens multiculturalism is in most respects not retreating but growing, as measured by Keith Banting and Will Kymlicka's Multicultural Policy Index. While the popular belief is that multiculturalism died in the years following 9/11, analysis of policies in twenty-one countries shows that whilst there was substantial growth of post-immigration multicultural policies between 1980 and 2000, far from halting or retreating it progressed between 2000 and 2010, with only three countries having a lower score in 2010 than in 2000 (Kymlikca, 2012; MCP Index: http://www.queensu.ca/mcp/immigrant/table/Immigrant_Minorities_Table_2.pdf).[3]

While the discursive attack, then, is indeed substantial and significant, it cannot be accepted at face value. Rather than a wholesale retreat of multiculturalism, a more accurate analysis is that of a movement towards multiculturalism and towards a 'civic re-balancing' of multiculturalism of the kind argued for in this book.[4] It is true that the dominant discourse speaks of 'integration', but

throughout this book I have made clear that multiculturalism is not opposed to integration but is a mode of integration: 'multiculturalism assumes a two-way process of
integration but, additionally, it is taken to work differently
for different groups' (p. 44; see also p. 13). Multiculturalism, then, is a mode of integration that deals not just with
individuals but also groups.[5] Integration is the generic
over-arching term of which multiculturalism is a species
and so the two terms are on different levels rather than
being alternatives.

Integrating Difference

What do I mean by saying that integration is an over-
arching concept?[6] The need for integration arises when an
established society is faced with some people who are
perceived and treated unfavourably by standard members
of that society (and typically the former also perceive
themselves as 'different', though not necessarily in a negative way). This may relate to various areas or sectors of
society and policy, such as employment, education, housing
and so on. Someone is integrated into, for example, the
labour market when s/he is able to enjoy equality of opportunity in accessing jobs and careers, including accessing
the education and training necessary to compete for such
jobs, and where the labour market is not segmented into
different parts with radically different monetary rewards
and working conditions for those with broadly similar
qualifications and experience. It is particularly relevant to
ensure that the segmentation is not, formally or informally,
based on criteria such as race, ethnicity, religion and so
on, namely, the categories of 'difference' (as explained on
pp. 34–40). This does not just concern labour markets;
one can apply it more generally.

Core to the integration process is equality of opportunity in an unsegmented society, where no channelling into
or away from a particular sector of society takes place

based on criteria such as race and ethnicity. Inte₍
a number of components based on opportunit₍
ticipate that are context-specific but that need to b
by law and policy initiatives. It, however, also has ₍
tive and symbolic dimension, which again will ha₍
context-specific features, but which also has a more ₅₋₋₋eral
or macro character: how a minority is perceived by the
rest of the country and how members of a minority perceive their relationship to society as a whole. Sectoral
integration, even when achieved in a number of sectors, is
not full integration without some degree of subjective identification with the society or country as a whole – what
the Commission on Multi-Ethnic Britain called 'a sense of
belonging' (CMEB 2000: Introduction) – and with the
acceptance by the majority that you are a full member of
society with the right to feel that you belong.

Sectoral integration and the general sense of integration
can happen at an individual level. An individual may
choose to integrate or not; may be given opportunities to
participate or not. But what about such choices and opportunities when viewed at the level of groups or society
as a whole? A sense of belonging is dependent on how
others perceive and treat you, not just as an individual
but also as a member of a racial group or ethno-religious
community. Each policy area will have its own imperatives
and difficulties (e.g., whether concerning issues of qualification levels or residential segregation),[7] but there is also
a general understanding by members of society regarding
what their society is and what it is to be a member – a
macro-symbolic conception of society and of integration.
This informs popular understanding as well as political
ideas. Hence, it has been rightly said by a Commission
on these topics in Quebec, 'the symbolic framework of
integration (identity, religion, perception of the Other,
collective memory, and so on) is no less important than
its functional or material framework' (Bouchard and
Taylor 2008; see also Bouchard 2011). This is particularly
so because the sense of crisis about multiculturalism and

integration is operating at this macro-symbolic level. This is evident when one considers how few are the policies that could be said to be about integration, or how small the funds involved are compared to the headline importance that the issues regularly achieve. In thinking about a general ethos or policy orientation at a national level, it is therefore important to engage at this macro-symbolic level.[8]

I consider this larger, macro-symbolic sense of integration with its implied policy paradigms in terms of four modes of integration summarized in table 7.1, namely, assimilation, individualist-integration and two versions of multiculturalism, one of which I will call cosmopolitanism.[9] Each offers its own distinctive take on freedom, equality and civic unity (or 'fraternity'), the core values of democracy.[10] Different interpretations and prioritizations of these concepts suggest embryonic policy models. The issue or 'problem' addressed by these models is post-immigration 'difference' as defined in chapters 1 and 3 above. Those participating in large-scale immigration into the West from outside it have been people marked by 'difference'. The 'difference' is not confined to the fact of migration, or how long the migrants and their families have been in the West, or the fact that they come from less economically developed parts of the world – all aspects that can be stated structurally and quantitatively. 'Difference' here primarily refers to how people are identified and how they identify themselves (for example, as 'white', 'black', 'Chinese', 'Muslim', etc.), how they identify others (again, as 'white', 'black', 'Chinese', 'Muslim', etc.), and how they are identified by others ('white', etc.) (pp. 34–43).

These identities will no doubt be classed or gendered in specific or generalizable ways, but the important point from which everything else follows is that these identities are not reducible, or, stronger still, are not primarily socio-economic or 'objective' in classical sociological terms; the identities involve subjectivity and agency. The migrants

Table 7.1 Four modes of integration*

	Assimilation	Individualist-integration	Cosmopolitanism	Multiculturalism
Objects of policy	Individuals and groups marked by 'difference'.	Individuals marked by 'difference', especially their treatment by discriminatory practices of state and civil society.	Individuals marked by 'difference', especially their treatment by discriminatory practices of state and civil society, and societal ideas, especially of 'us' and 'them'.	Individuals and groups marked by 'difference', especially their treatment by discriminatory practices of state and civil society, and societal ideas, especially of 'us' and 'them'.
Liberty	Minorities must be encouraged to conform to the dominant cultural pattern.	Minorities are free to assimilate or cultivate their identities in private but are discouraged from thinking of themselves as minority, but rather as individuals.	Neither minority nor majority individuals should think of themselves as belonging to a single identity but be free to mix and match.	Members of minorities should be free to assimilate, to mix and match, or to cultivate group membership in proportions of their own choice.

(Continued)

Table 7.1 *Continued*

Equality	Presence of difference provokes discrimination and so is to be avoided.	Discriminatory treatment must be actively eliminated so everyone is treated as an individual and not on the basis of difference.	Anti-discrimination must be accompanied by the dethroning of the dominant culture.	In addition to anti-discrimination the public sphere must accommodate the presence of new group identities and norms.
Fraternity	A strong, homogeneous national identity.	Absence of discrimination and nurturing of individual autonomy within a national, liberal democratic citizenship.	People should be free to unite across communal and national boundaries and should think of themselves as global citizens.	Citizenship and national identity must be remade to include group identities that are important to minorities as well as majorities; the relationship between groups should be dialogical rather than one of domination or uniformity.

*In all cases it is assumed that a backdrop of liberal democratic rights and values are operative to a large degree, and what is highlighted here is in addition to or interaction with them.

and the 'hosts', or, more accurately, given that the migrations in question took place mainly in the third quarter of the twentieth century,[11] minority–majority relations, cannot be understood without the forms of difference. The relevant interactions cannot be explained, the position of different actors cannot be predicted (or even guessed at), and political preferences cannot be expressed without the explicit or implicit use of the forms of difference. It is commonly said that we must distinguish between multiculturalism as a social description and Multiculturalism as a political understanding of those social facts. Interestingly, the same could be but is rarely said about class/Class, nation/Nation or gender/Gender. In fact, social description and sociological concepts are not normally politically neutral. The concepts I analyse below are normative and policy-oriented but they presuppose a sociology, an understanding of what the social phenomenon is that needs a political response. The problem, then, is how to integrate difference or, to put it another way, the process whereby difference ceases to be problematic.

Four Modes of Integration

In the first edition I distinguished between three responses to 'difference':

(i)   Assimilation (pp. 47–8; p. 44 this volume)
(ii) Integration (p. 49; p. 44 this volume)
(iii) Multiculturalism (pp. 48–51; pp. 44–7 this volume).

I would now categorize them as four modes of integration:

(i)   Assimilation
(ii) Individualist-integration
(iii) Cosmopolitanism
(iv) Multiculturalism.

Assimilation remains as before; so does what was previously called 'integration' but its individualist character, as presented previously (p. 44) is highlighted by the term 'individualist-integration'. Cosmopolitanism is identified as a distinct mode of integration in an intermediate position between 'individualist-integration' and 'multiculturalism' because it is significant in its own right. I previously discussed it as a sociological critique of multiculturalism (pp. 95–101) but should have emphasized that it is a mode of integrating difference.

Cosmopolitanism emerges by accepting the concept of difference while critiquing or dissolving the concept of groups (Waldron 1991).[12] Disagreement about the extent to which post-immigration groups exist and/or ought to exist and be given political status means that there are two kinds of multiculturalism (Modood 1998; Meer and Modood 2009a). While in public discourse as well as in academia both are referred to as multiculturalism, and often without a full recognition that two different ideas are being expressed, I will reserve the term 'multiculturalism' for the sociological and political position in which groups are a critical feature.[13]

Cosmopolitanism goes beyond individualist-integration in two respects. Firstly, 'difference' is valued, especially novelty and the persons and lifestyles formed through free-mixing of peoples and cultures, with society taking the character of overlaps and fusions between different elements of society. Neither minority nor majority individuals should think of themselves as belonging to a single identity but be free to mix and match as suits each person because communal membership, including in relation to oppressed groups, can be oppressive of individuals and their life-chances (Appiah 1994). Inherited or ascribed identities which slot people into pigeonholes not of their choosing, giving them a script to live by, should be refused. They not only reduce the options of the kind of person one can be, but also divide society up into antagonistic groups.[14] Secondly, and consequently, it follows that groups, or indeed society or the country as a whole, cannot be characterized in terms of dominant or stable identities. Rather, people should be free to unite across communal and national boundaries and should think of themselves as planetary citizens. Cosmopolitianism, then, is a conception of multiculturalism as maximum freedom, for minority as well as majority individuals, to mix with, borrow and learn from all (whether they are of your group or not), so that individual identities are personal assemblages of bits from various groups and heritages and there is no one dominant social identity to which all must conform. The result will be a society composed of a blend of cultures, a 'multiculture'.

Multiculturalism proper, on the other hand, rather than individualist-integration or cosmopolitanism, stretches beyond individuals to accommodate groups. The groups in question, the post-immigration minorities, however, are not of one kind but are a 'multi' (pp. 40–3 above). For example, some people will identify with a colour identity like 'black' but there will be others for whom national-origin identities (like 'Algerian'), or a regional heritage (like 'Gujarati'), or a religious identity (like 'Sikh') may be much more meaningful, expressing forms of community and ethnic pride that are struggling for recognition and inclusion (pp. 40–1 above). And, of course, these minority identities will interact with wider, societal identities – 'woman', 'working class', 'Londoner', 'British' – in differing ways, expressing the varying experiences, locations and aspirations of different groups. So, both the alternative models of multiculturalism as cosmopolitanism, on the one hand, and, on the other hand, one which includes space for ethno-religious communities (for which I am reserving the term 'multiculturalism') have some grounding and meet the political aspirations of some minority groups. Neither works as a comprehensive sociological or political model and they should be viewed as complementary (Modood 1998; CMEB 2000; Modood and Dobbernack 2011). Moreover, while recognition of ethnic or religious groups may have a legal dimension, for the most part it will be at the level of civic consultations, political participation, institutional policies (for example, schools and hospitals) and discursive representations, especially in relation to the changing discourses of societal unity or national identity, and their remaking.

Regardless of the extent to which recognition of minority identities in this way is formal or informal, led by the state or the semi-autonomous institutions of civil society, it does not challenge, let alone displace, individual rights and the shared dimensions of citizenship. Indeed, for the most part, multiculturalist recognition is exercised through individual members' free choices rather than corporately. The legal recognition of the Sikh turban, for example, confers a right upon individual Sikh men, rather than upon a group entity, to exemption from wearing motorcycle helmets (Jones 1999). There may, however, be genuine concern that some groups at a particular time and in certain areas are becoming too inward-looking. Where the concern is primarily about a lack of positive mixing and interaction between groups at a local level, community cohesion measures – for example, a Christian school offering places to non-Christians or twinning with a non-Christian school – may be an appropriate response (Cantle 2001). Where the concern is about self-conceptions and discourses more generally, the issue will be about the national or societal identity. Whilst such inwardness has never been part of any theory or policy of multiculturalism, it is clear that it is a fundamental anxiety of the critics of multiculturalism, many of whom go as far as to define multiculturalism in terms of such separatism.[15] It is therefore important to emphasize both that accommodation of ethno-religious communities is a mode of integration, and that it, no less than hostility to minorities or other modes of integration, should be examined as a possible contributory cause of exclusion and segregation (Banting and Kymlicka 2008). However, while acknowledging that multiculturalism is 'a deeply (and intentionally) transformative project' (Kymlicka 2012: 9), we have to balance this with its 'conservative' aspect. A basic rationale for multiculturalism is that of protecting minority identities from misrecognition and external pressure to conform, allowing people to be themselves, to assert and live their 'mode of being', the identities that matter to them and that more powerful others should recognize. The sensibility that minority groups have a mode of being that is not wholly chosen, acknowledging the right of such groups to change in their own way and at their own pace, is one that conservatives should be able to appreciate (Oakeshott 1962). No group of citizens has a right to total exemption from the ethical duties of citizenship, but allowing people to be what they already are, showing respect for them as they are in themselves, rather than regarding them as objects of transformative criticism – or, worse still, as materials for a political project – is a requirement of egalitarian integration. Multiculturalism involves respect for historically prior and majoritarian attachments and identities, but seeks to extend the same respect to the new minorities whilst remaking the sense of commonalities and nationality.

Multiculturalism without Groups?

Multicultural citizenship is based on the idea that citizens have individual rights, while accepting that citizens do not consist of uniform types and acknowledging that their citizenship contours itself around the varied identities of citizens. Citizenship is not a monistic identity that is completely apart from or transcends other identities of importance to citizens. These group identities are ever present and each group has a right to be part of the civic whole, and to speak up for itself and for its vision of the whole.

Anne Phillips's *Multiculturalism Without Culture* (2007) was published at the same time as the first edition of this book, and I find myself in agreement with her on many points and broadly in sympathy, except for a core, theoretical difference. We both agree on a need to defend multiculturalism that is grounded in a concept of equal citizenship. This can mean, for example, the funding of ethno-religious community centres or increasing the number of persons from identifiable population groups in legislatures, governing bodies, consultative committees and so on. We both think that 'multiculture' and 'cosmopolitanism' are not enough, but we have an appreciation that 'culture' or groups are not holistic or closed, and that multiculturalism must be built upon anti-essentialism. Phillips combines her support for minority groups with a determination not to give power to groups (ibid.: 118) and, in opposing accommodation (ibid.: 163–4), she adopts an anti-group vocabulary and the term 'recognition' does not even feature in the index. She seems, therefore, to politically need, in however attenuated a form, a concept of 'group', but theoretically she makes no effort to provide one and simply notes the difficulties faced by conceptions of groups when they are connected to a reification of culture. I, on the other hand, maintain that accommodation and recognition are what multiculturalism is about. So, the very thing that Phillips wants to disallow is what I argue forms the core of multiculturalism. I appreciate that 'multi' in multiculturalism often refers to discrete groups, but work hard to put forward a distinctive view of 'multi' and 'groups' that overcomes that deficient reading by emphasizing that 'group' is not a univocal term, that there can be many different kinds of groups, more or less discrete, and that the theoretical conceptualization for this can be found in Wittgenstein's concept of 'family resemblance' (pp. 40–3, 40–112 above).[16]

Phillips wants to empower individual members of disadvantaged/minority groups, including the funding of ethnocultural associations and special measures to raise political representation. But she argues that this cannot be described as distributing power to cultural *groups*.

Moreover, she is opposed to enhancing the regulatory authority of a group, that is, of some of its members over others. Politically, the difference between Phillips's ideas and mine may be one of emphasis. For instance, she has a sensitive and sensible discussion of how some Muslim women in Europe appeal to *shariah* councils in order to obtain religiously validated divorces (Phillips 2007: 175–6). She rightly criticizes the position of the Norwegian Human Rights Service which encourages Muslim women to use a *shariah* council in London, but is opposed to the setting up of religious courts or councils in Norway. She concludes that:

> [f]aced with this problem, it seems disingenuous to rely on my distinction between recognising the rights and needs of individuals (good) and distributing powers and resources to groups (bad) as if that resolves all issues. We can aim at a multiculturalism without reified understandings of culture, but it would be unrealistic to think this will deliver us a multiculturalism without groups. And wherever there are groups, there is always the potential for coercion. (Ibid.)

I would endorse Phillips here: if a Muslim woman wants a *religious* divorce, then the state should empower her individual agency. Yet it is not possible for the state to allow her to have a religiously authoritative divorce without recognizing the authority of religious institutions and office-holders. If we have reasons to worry about the potential for coercion – again, which I share with Phillips – surely it is better to regulate and therefore make transparent such councils, to bring them within the law and so seek to safeguard the rights of the vulnerable, especially women and children, rather than let them flourish unregulated by law and unscrutinized by rights activists and public agencies.

Our difference is not in the pragmatics of such cases, but in Phillips not fully appreciating that the implications of her sensitivity to such dilemmas robs her of her theoretical distinction. As the above example shows, the distinction between the funding of ethnocultural associations and enhancing the regulatory authority of a group will often be a distinction without content. To take another simple case, suppose some funding is made available to a Muslim cultural centre: such measures enhance individual agency, for example, enable individuals to attend mosque classes or sessions in calligraphy, but at the same time they will clearly enhance the authority of the teachers and the religious organization that they are part of, and so on. The theoretical incoherence I am pointing to seems to be part of the larger problem of the absence of any theory of group or groupness, yet it should be obvious that these concepts are being asked to do critical political work.[17]

Ways in Which Multiculturalism is Not Dead

This unpacking of what I mean by 'multiculturalism' is also helpful in understanding those who say that multiculturalism has failed (Weldon 1989; see also Presseurop 2010 for Chancellor Angela Merkel's speech on the failure of *multikulti*) or that multiculturalism is dead (Cameron 2011). They may mean to endorse assimilation, individualistic integration or cosmopolitanism: there is not merely one alternative to multiculturalism.[18] But at the same time they are acknowledging and possibly reinforcing the sociological reality of group difference because their lament is that some groups (especially Muslims) are clearly visible as distinct groups when they should not be; they attribute this fact to a separatist tendency in the groups, allegedly encouraged by multiculturalist policies. Hence, paradoxical as it may sound, fierce critics of multiculturalism are usually deploying the sociology of group multiculturalism even while rejecting its political dimensions. If they thought these groups were merely the product of stereotypes and exclusion (in the sense that 'racial' groups are a product of racism), or were primarily socio-economic in character (perhaps a working-class 'fraction'), then that would be a sociological disagreement with the multiculturalists. The politicians I am referring to, however, are happy to engage in discourse about, for example, Muslim communities or to meet spokespersons for such communities, even while complaining about aspects of the behaviour of such communities. Moreover, the accusatory discourse that 'some groups are not integrating' may actually reinforce group identities, therefore contributing to the social conditions that give multiculturalism a sociological pertinence. On the other hand, a sociology that marginalized ethnicity in favour of, say, individuals, class and gender, would have a better fit with anti-multiculturalist politics but may be unable to explain or predict the relevant social reality, resulting in a weaker basis for politics. Our normative orientation – individualist or multiculturalist – suggests to us an ideal sociology (a place for non-pathological groups or not), but also recommends itself to us as feasible politics because we think *that* sociology is more accurate than not. We all aspire for our sociological analysis and politics to be mutually supportive, but anti-multiculturalists do not seem to be achieving this.

Moreover, it is not only at the level of sociology that anti-multiculturalists may use multiculturalist ideas; even while deploying an anti-multiculturalist discourse, they may enact multiculturalist policies. For example, they may continue with group consultations, representation and accommodation. The latter have actually increased. The British government has found it necessary to increase the scale and level of consultations with Muslims in Britain since 9/11, and, dissatisfied with existing organizations, has sought to increase the number of organized interlocutors and channels of communication. Avowedly anti-multiculturalist countries and governments have worked to increase corporatism in practice, for example, with the creation by Nicholas Sarkozy of the Conseil Français du Culte Musulman in 2003 to represent all Muslims to the French government in matters of worship and ritual (Akan 2009); and by the creation of the Islamkonferenz in

Germany in 2005, an exploratory body, yet with an extensive political agenda. These bodies are partly top-down efforts to control Muslims or to channel them into certain formations and away from others (Amir-Moazami 2011); nevertheless, such institutional processes cannot be understood within the conceptual framework of assimilation, individualist integration or cosmopolitanism. They are normatively less than the best of multiculturalism but they clearly are deploying a multiculturalist mode of integration (pp. 74–7, 134–5) and their presence offers the possibility of movement towards a more egalitarian, rather than a controlled top-down, multiculturalism (Meira 2012).

Hence, aspects of what is often understood as a backlash and denial of multiculturalism (Vertovec and Wessendorf 2010; Lentin and Titley 2011) are actually forms of multiculturalism, even if highly restrictive ones, which in countries such as France and Germany are illustrating a movement towards, not away from, multiculturalism. There is indeed a new intolerance regarding certain Muslim practices (for example, the *burqa*), which is leading to new laws or policies in many parts of Europe. I will discuss these in the next chapter, where I highlight the existence of a new radical secularism as a form of anti-multiculturalism, one that is being combined with crude forms of corporatist multiculturalism. The point is that we do not seem to be witnessing a clear paradigm shift, for example, from pluralistic integration to individualist integration. True, the anti-multiculturalist may not just be pointing to the visibility of groups like Muslims, but expressing the view that there is an insufficient participation of such groups in a common life or sharing of common values. My point is that some of the measures resorted to are not consistent with assimilation or individualism but acknowledge the social reality and political significance of groups.

Here, it may appear that I am obscuring the central difference between multiculturalism and its political critics, that is, that the latter but not the former emphasizes integration into a common life (discussed in Miller 2008

and Mason 2010). But this is mistaken. The multiculturalism in the writings of key theorists such as Charles Taylor,
Will Kymlicka, Bhikhu Parekh and Anne Phillips, and in
the relevant documents, laws and policies of Canada,
Australia and Britain are all aimed at integration (see
pp. 13–18 above for details). The difference between the
pro- and anti-multiculturalists lies not in the goal of
integration but, firstly, in the normative understanding
of integration. I have tried to bring this out by reference
to the alternative interpretations and prioritizing of the
normative concepts of liberty, equality and fraternity
(summarized in table 7.1). Secondly, there are different
judgements about contexts and about what will deliver
results and, more generally, how society works or what I
have been referring to as implicit sociologies.

The analytical framework offered helps us also to understand those who say they welcome diversity but seem to
be in agreement with the political critics of multiculturalism. Critics of multiculturalism are usually pointing to the
public assertion of strong group identities to mobilize a
group to achieve certain policies and/or to demand differential treatment. They are sometimes responded to by
those who point out how multiculturalism is working in
their neighbourhoods, which they say are multiethnic,
where people do not just live peaceably side by side but
mix freely, and where that mixing is valued above monoculturalism. This is, however, a weak response. For, such
views do not imply support for strong group identities and
related policies; on the contrary, their success may be seen
as dependent on the absence of the latter.[19] While this is a
reasonable response in its own terms, it does not counter
the above criticism of multiculturalism and in fact may
share it. It is the increasingly unpopular group-based multiculturalism that critics have in mind, and the weakness
of the rebuttal is obscured by the fact that advocates of
neighbourhood 'multiculturalism' are actually referring to
what I call 'cosmopolitanism'.

Similarly, it has been argued, for example, that the
majority of Australians welcome multiculturalism; indeed,

they see it as part of the country's identity, but they see it 'in terms of a mix of individuals rather than an ensemble of groups' (Brett and Moran 2011: 203; see also Fenton and Mann 2011 and Searchlight Educational Trust 2011 for a related discussion in relation to England). A group-based multiculturalism is much less popular than cosmopolitanism, but what we have to consider is: can integration of all post-immigration formations be achieved without the latter? Moreover, a group-based multiculturalism, membership of which is voluntary, may be part of the future in an unintended way. For instance, it is highly compatible with British Prime Minister Cameron's vision of a 'Big Society' in which civil society associations based on locality and faith take over some responsibilities currently undertaken by state agencies. A flagship policy of the Big Society agenda is the state funding to create new community-based non-state schools called 'free schools'. Over a quarter of these are led by religious groups; those that started in September 2011 included two Jewish, a Hindu and a Sikh school (Vasagar 2012). Of the 102 of the schools approved for funding in July 2012, three were Jewish, one was Hindu, four were Sikh and four were Muslim (BHA 2012). It is difficult to see how the new Big Society is a break with what is rejected as 'state multiculturalism' (Cameron 2011).[20] The same trend is found in France, where three Muslim schools have joined the many thousands (mainly Catholic) of state-supported religious schools (Akan 2009: 246–7), and in Germany, where there are no state-funded religious schools but where Islam is increasingly joining the religions for which the provincial government funds instruction within state schools (*The Local* 2011; see also DIK 2009).

Social Unity

The analysis offered here of related macro-symbolic ideas and policy orientations, each of which consists of a model of society and normative political ideas, includes also a sense of unity or fraternity. For modes of integration are not just about sociology (the first level) or politics (second level), but include ideas, however inchoate, of ourselves as a social unity (as displayed at the bottom of table 7.1). For assimilationists, this consists of a strong, homogeneous national identity. Individualist-integration emphasizes the liberal and democratic character of the national polity. Cosmopolitanism is uneasy with the national, an identity that craves some sort of allegiance from all citizens, whilst creating boundaries between ourselves and the rest of the world. With multiculturalism comes a positive vision of the whole remade so as to include the previously excluded or marginalized on the basis of equality and sense of belonging. It is at this level that we may fully speak of multicultural integration or multicultural citizenship (Taylor 1994; Parekh 2000; pp. 135–43 above). This third level of multiculturalism, incorporating the sociological fact of diversity, groupness and exclusion, but going beyond individual rights and political accommodation, is perhaps the level that has been least emphasized. At least, that is how it seems to many whose understanding of multiculturalism, sometimes polemical but sometimes sincere, is that multiculturalism is about encouraging minority difference without a counterbalancing emphasis on crosscutting commonalities and a vision of a greater good. This has led many commentators and politicians to talk of multiculturalism as divisive and productive of segregation.

Theorists of multiculturalism such as Taylor (1994) and Parekh (2000), related policy documents such as the report of the CMEB (2000), and enactments such as those in Canada and Australia, universally regarded as pioneers and exemplars of state multiculturalism, all appealed to and built on an idea of national citizenship.[21] Hence, from a multiculturalist point of view, though not from that of its critics, the recent emphasis on cohesion and citizenship – often called 'the civic turn' (Mouritsen 2008) or, better still, the civic-national turn[22] – is a necessary rebalancing of the political multiculturalism of the 1990s, which largely took the form of accommodation of groups while being ambivalent about national identity in some countries, notably Britain (Meer and Modood 2009a).[23] This does not invalidate the analysis offered here that integration without some degree of institutional accommodation is unlikely to be successful. Indeed, for multiculturalists a renewing of national identity has to be distinctly plural and hospitable to the minority identities. It involves 'rethinking the national story' with the minorities as important characters; not obscuring difference but weaving it into a common, multistranded identity that all can see themselves in and giving all a sense of belonging to each other (CMEB 2000: 54–6). Minority politics are common in the US but most groups, while honouring their origins, seek inclusion in the American dream. They seek to be and have come to be accepted as hyphenated Americans (Italian-Americans, Asian-Americans, etc.), a trend that is also present in parts of western Europe and, while not yet fully accepted, it may be that hyphenated nationalities will become the norm here too.

It is possible that all the attempted models of integration, especially national models, are in crisis. They are certainly perceived as such. Those who say 'multiculturalism has failed' do not have an alternative successful model to point to. Some, most notably the Council of Europe, believe that interculturalism is the successor policy concept but it is not clear that it has been given any content to distinguish it from multiculturalism, as a recent debate concluded in the *Journal of Intercultural Studies* (April 2012, kicked off by Meer and Modood 2012).[24] Some cited examples of failure in, say, multiculturalist Britain and the Netherlands may not be present in, say, antimulticulturalist France or Germany, but mostly they are. Indeed, the socio-economic marginalization of minorities, their over-representation in areas of deprivation and amongst those without jobs and higher qualifications, is worse in France and Germany than in Britain, not to mention levels of representation in higher-level occupations and public affairs. Yet, despite these exclusions and inequalities, and despite the large-scale religious intolerance and right-wing populism, France has been cited as a country achieving more successful integration of Muslims than the UK (Hansen 2011).[25] If multiculturalism is failing, it is still doing better than the alternatives.

Hence, the arguments about these different orientations are not only far from achieving a consensus, but suffer from numerous confusions, some of which I hope I have clarified. Whether there is a viable alternative to multiculturalism or not, we can at least have a better sense of what the issues are and how to address them, if we recognize that discourses of integration and multiculturalism are exercises in conceptualizing post-immigration difference, and, as such, operate at three distinct levels: as an (implicit) understanding of the relationship between individuals and groups in society; as a political response; and as a vision of the whole in which difference is to be integrated. Depending upon the understanding in question, certain political responses are more or less possible. The sociological and political assumptions are thus mutually dependent. If we could achieve at least this level of conceptual clarity we would make some progress, but I think we could go further.

Giving Each Mode of Integration Its Due

In reformulating and extending the idea of this book, namely, civic-national multiculturalism, I have offered a framework in which four distinct political responses (assimilation, individualist-integration, cosmopolitanism and multiculturalism) illuminate each other, and where each successive position attempts to include what is thought to be missing from its predecessor. Each position can in principle be attractive from different perspectives: some ethnic minorities may wish to assimilate, some to have the equal rights of integrated citizens, some to maintain the cultural differences of their group identities, and some to be free to choose cosmopolitan mixed identities suiting the roles they take on in a more diverse society. Moreover, a group may desire a particular combination (for example, individualist-integration in relation to law, but supplementary group representation in politics). Equally, the majority society may look on different minority groups in all these different ways. Each approach has a particular conception of equal citizenship, though the value of each can only be realized if it is not imposed but is the preferred choice of minority individuals and groups, who, of course, being 'multi', are bound to choose differently. Thus, no singular model is likely to be suitable for all groups – or perhaps even for any one group. To have a reasonable chance of integrating the maximum number of members of minorities, none of these political responses should be dismissed. Moreover, assimilation may be more appropriate in terms of national language acquisition before naturalization; individualist-integration may provide the model for non-discrimination in the labour market; yet multiculturalism may be the basis for supplementing electoral representation (where minorities are under-represented) and in creating new attitudes of inclusivity as well as rethinking national identities in a context of post-immigration 'difference'. Thus, perhaps the ultimate meaning of multiculturalism is not as one mode of integration but as the perspective which allows all four modes of integration their due, including, crucially, communitarian multiculturalism.

Communitarian multiculturalism may currently be viewed as undesirable by various publics and policymakers. Given how central Muslims have become to the prospects of integration on a number of fronts, it is unlikely that integration can be achieved without some element of this approach, which is practised even by those politicians who make anti-multiculturalist speeches. Perceptions of Muslims as groups, both by themselves and by non-Muslim majorities, are hardening. The key question is not how to

de-collectivize Muslims but whether they are to be stigmatized as outsiders or recognized as integral to the polity.
Most importantly, we must not overlook the third analytical level, which in many ways is not primarily about
minorities but about the majority. The enlargement,
hyphenation and internal pluralizing of national identities
is essential to an integration where all citizens have not
just rights but a sense of belonging to the whole, as well
as to their own 'little platoon' (Burke 1986: 135).[26] The
enlargement and remaking of national identities is more
easily seen in settler-societies such as the US, Canada and
Australia, which have a much greater sense of national
identity being always on the move, than in the settled-
societies of western Europe. Yet Britain, a relatively set-
tled-society, seems to be behaving more like one of the
settler-societies. I have mentioned (pp. 16–17) how the
report of the Commission on the Future of Multi-Ethnic
Britain (2000) made rethinking what it means to be British
central to its vision of Britain, for which it was widely
denounced as unpatriotic. A close study of the speeches of
Labour and Conservative senior politicians shows that
within a few years of making such denunciations they
moved from merely welcoming the multiculturalizing of
Britain to accepting the need for the state to actively engage
in the enlargement, hyphenation and pluralizing of Britishness (Uberoi and Modood forthcoming). While this multiculturalist advance is currently exceptional in Europe,
nevertheless the civic-national turn means that these states
can no longer pretend they are merely defined by liberal
principles, but are having to attend to their national identities – which, after all, is a necessary albeit not a sufficient
condition of recognizing and institutionalizing multicultural citizenship (Modood and Meer 2012; Modood 2012).
A national-identity dimension in which this challenge is
being actively felt is the civic place of religion and of religious groups, of church–state relations, and I turn to this
in the next chapter, updating and developing the argument
made in chapter 4 in favour of pluralizing moderate
secularism.

– 8 –
Multiculturalism and the 'Crisis of Secularism'

One of the distinctive features of this book is its placing questions about the nature and reform of political secularism as central to multiculturalism today, at least in western Europe. This is due to the triple contingency of the arrival and settlement of a significant number of Muslims; a multiculturalist sensibility which feels the need to respect 'difference'; and a moderate secularism, namely, that the historical compromises between the state and a church or churches in relation to public recognition and accommodation are still in place to some extent. In chapter 4, I argued that radical secularism or *laïcité* seems to be struggling to cope but the dominant version of secularism, far from being in crisis, offers a resource – suitably multiculturalized – for accommodating the new religious plurality of the region. An increasing number of academics think that we are experiencing a crisis of secularism.[1] Jürgen Habermas, who has western Europe very much at the forefront of his mind, has famously announced we are currently witnessing a transition from a secular to a 'post-secular society' in which 'secular citizens' have to express a previously denied respect for 'religious citizens', who should be allowed, even encouraged, to critique aspects of contemporary society and to find solutions to its problems from within their religious views (Habermas 2006). Instead of treating religion as sub-rational and a matter of private concern only, religion is once again to be recognized as a legitimate basis of public engagement and political action.[2] Some have gone further and speak of a global crisis. Even quite sober academics speak of 'a contemporary crisis of secularism' (Scherer 2010: 4), claiming that 'today, political secularisms are in crisis in almost every corner of the globe' (Jakelić 2010: 3). Olivier Roy, in an analysis focused on France, writes of 'the crisis of the secular state' (Roy 2007), and Rajeev Bhargava of the 'crisis of the secular state in Europe' (Bhargava 2010, 2011).[3] I think, however, that as far as western Europe is concerned, the 'crisis of secularism' is really the challenge of post-immigration multiculturalism.

There seems to be no endogenous slowing down in the decline of secularization in relation to organized religion, attendance at church services and traditional Christian belief and practice in western Europe. For example, to illustrate with the British case, church attendance of at least once a month has steadily declined from about 20 per cent in 1983 to about 15 per cent in 2008 amongst white people and with each younger age cohort (Voas and Crockett 2005; BRIN 2011; Kaufmann, Goujon and Skirbekk 2012).[4] This is not to say that religion has disappeared or is about to, but for many it has become more in the form of 'belief without belonging' (Davie 1994), or spirituality (Heelas and Woodhead 2005), or 'implicit religion' (Bailey 1997). For example, while belief in a personal God has gone down from over 40 per cent in the middle of the twentieth century to less than 30 per cent by its end, belief in a spirit or life source has remained steady at around 35–40 per cent, and belief in the soul has actually increased from less than 60 per cent in the early 1980s to an additional 5–10 per cent today (BRIN 2011). All these changes, however, are highly compatible with political secularism, if not with scientism or other rationalistic philosophies. Whether the decline of traditional religion is being replaced by no religion or new ways of being religious or spiritual, neither is creating a challenge for political secularism. Non-traditional forms of Christian or post-Christian religion in western Europe are in the main not attempting to connect with or reform political institutions and government policies; they are not seeking recognition or political accommodation or political power.[5]

The challenge to political secularism in western Europe lies not in any slowing down of secularization, but in the presence of Muslims.[6] With estimates of 12 to over 17 million Muslims in western Europe today, the Muslim population in the former EU 15 is only about 3–5 per cent and is relatively evenly distributed across the larger states (Peach 2007; Pew Forum 2010). In larger cities the proportion that is Muslim, however, is several times greater and, being young and fertile, is growing at a faster rate than most of the population (Lutz, Skirbekk and Testa 2007). In this context – with the riots in the *banlieues* of Paris and elsewhere, the Danish cartoon affair and other issues about offence and freedom of speech, and the proliferating bans on various forms of female Muslim dress just being a few in a series of conflicts focused on minority–majority relations – questions about integration, equality, racism and Islam, and their relation to terrorism, security and foreign policy, have become central to European politics.

The issue, then, driving the sense of a crisis of secularism in western Europe is the place of Muslim identities, or identities that are perceived to be ethno-religious (such as British Asian Muslim or Arab Muslim in France). This multicultural challenge to secularism is amongst the most profound political and long-term issues arising from the post-war western European hunger for labour migrants and the reversal of the population flows of European colonialism. The challenge is far from confined to secularism. It is a broad one: from socio-economic disadvantage and discrimination in the labour markets at one end, to a constitutional status or corporate relationship with the state at the other. Moreover, the awareness of this challenge began to manifest itself and was perceived before events such as 9/11; nor is it due to the fact that some Muslims, unlike other post-immigration groups, may have been involved in rowdy demonstrations and riots, because others (such as African Caribbeans in Britain) are associated with these without raising such profound normative questions.

Nor is it due to (Muslim) conservative values, especially in relation to gender and sexuality, though it is related to it. The core element of the challenge is the primacy given to religion as the basis of identity, organization, political representation, normative justification and so on. These matters were thought to be more or less settled (except in a few exceptional cases like Northern Ireland) until some Muslims began asserting themselves as Muslims in the public sphere of various west European countries. Some have thought that primacy could be given to, say, gender, ethnicity or class; others that primacy should not be given to any one or even a few of these social categories as identity self-concepts, but very few thought that religion should be in the select set (Modood 2005a; Modood, Triandafyllidou and Zapata-Barrero 2006).

The rising multicultural challenge and the gradual weakening of the political status of Christian churches, in particular, the national churches, has been taking place at the same time. The intersection of these two trajectories is nicely captured in two policy initiatives in the Netherlands in 1983. In that year, the national system of 'pillarization', which had made the country a bi-religious communal state, was formally wound up, with a new Minorities Policy (*Nota Minderhedenbeleid*) being announced (see Bader 2011; Lentin and Titley 2011: 107–8), which created post-immigration ethnic minorities (*allochtones*) as a mini-pillar, giving them state funding for faith schools, ethno-religious radio and TV broadcasting and other forms of cultural maintenance (Bader 2011). Some of that policy began to be reversed in the 1990s, but, looking beyond the Netherlands, the pivotal moment was 1988–9 and was, quite accidentally, marked by two events. These created national and international storms, setting in motion political developments that have not been reversed, and reveal contrasting responses by the two western European secularisms to the Muslim presence. The events were the protests in Britain against Sir Salman Rushdie's novel *The Satanic Verses*; and, in France, the decision by a school head teacher to prohibit entry to three girls unless they removed their headscarves in school premises.

Moderate and Radical Secularist Responses to Muslim Assertiveness

The Satanic Verses was not banned in the UK as the protestors demanded, and the conduct of some Muslims, especially those threatening the life of the author, certainly shocked and alienated many from the campaign. In that sense, the Muslim campaign clearly failed. In other respects, however, it galvanized many into seeking a democratic multiculturalism that was inclusive of Muslims. A national body was created to represent mainstream Muslim opinion, initially in relation to the novel (UK Action Committee on Islamic Action), but later, with some encouragement from both the main national political parties, especially New Labour, it led to the formation of a body to lobby on behalf of Muslims in the corridors of power. This new body, the Muslim Council of Britain (MCB), was accepted as a major consultee by the New Labour government of 1997, until about the middle of the next decade when it sought to diversify its Muslim interlocutors. The MCB was very successful in relation to its founding agenda (Modood 2010a). By 2001, it had achieved its aim of having Muslim issues and Muslims as a group recognized separately from issues of race and ethnicity; and of being itself accepted by government, media and civil society as the spokesperson

for Muslims. Another two achieved aims were the introduction of state funding of Muslim schools on the same
basis as Christian and Jewish schools; and in getting certain educational and employment policies targeted on the
severe disadvantage of the Pakistanis and Bangladeshis
(who are nearly all Muslims) as opposed to on minority
ethnicity generally. Additionally, it played a decisive role
in Tony Blair's inclusion of a religious question in the
2001 census despite ministerial and civil service advice
to the contrary (Sherif 2011). This laid the foundation
for a possible later introduction of policies targeting
Muslims to match those targeting groups defined by race
or ethnicity – or gender. The MCB had to wait a bit longer
for the legislative protection it sought. Laws against religious discrimination were introduced in 2003, strengthened in 2007 and again in 2010, making them much
stronger than anything available in the rest of the
European Union. Incitement to religious hatred, the legislation most closely connected to the protests over *The
Satanic Verses*, was introduced in 2006, though there is no
suggestion that it would have caught that novel. Indeed,
the protestors' original demand that the blasphemy law be
extended to cover Islam has been made inapplicable as
the blasphemy law was abolished in 2008 – with very
little protest from anybody. Moreover, even as the MCB,
because of its views on the government's foreign and security policies, fell out of favour, local and national consultations with Muslim groups has continued to grow and
probably now exceeds consultations with any Christian
body and certainly any minority group. Inevitably, this
has caused occasional friction between Christians and
Muslims. But on the whole these developments have taken
place not only with the support of the leadership of the
Church of England, but in a spirit of interfaith respect.[7]
(Given how adversarial English intellectual, journalistic,
legal and political culture is, religion in England is oddly
fraternal and little effort is expended in proving that the
other side is in a state of error and should convert.)

That, then, is one path of development from 1988 to 1989. It was a mobilization of a minority, with the extension of minority policies from race to religion in order to accommodate the religious minority. The other development, namely, the one arising from *l'affaire foulard* was one of top-down state action to prohibit certain minority practices. From the start, the majority of the country – whether it be the media, the public intellectuals, the politicians or public opinion – supported the head teacher who refused to have religious headscarves in school (Bowen 2007; Scott 2007).[8] Muslims either did not wish to or lacked the capacity to challenge this dominant view with anything like the publicity, organization, clamour or international assistance that Muslims in Britain brought to bear on Rushdie's novel.

The Conseil d'État, France's highest administrative court, emphasized freedom of religion as long as the religious symbols were not 'ostentatious', and so ruled that the issue should be treated on a case-by-case basis (Kastoryano 2006; see also Bowen 2007). This quietened things down till they blew up again in 1994 in relation to another state school. On that occasion, the Minister of Education forbade the wearing of any ostentatious symbols, which explicitly included the headscarf. The issue would not go away, however, and in 2003 President Chirac appointed a national Commission, chaired by Bernard Stasi, to consider the issue. The Stasi Commission recommended the banning of the wearing of conspicuous religious symbols in state schools, and a law to this effect was passed with an overwhelming majority by Parliament in February 2004. A few years later, the target of secularist and majoritarian disapproval was the full face-veil that revealed only the eyes (*niqab*; *burqa*), as favoured by a few hundred Muslim women. This was banned in public places in April 2011. Belgium followed suit in July 2011, and Italy is in the process of implementing a ban (*Guardian* 2011). Similar proposals are being discussed by governments and political parties across western Europe (e.g., the ruling Labour Party in Norway). Even in Britain there is popular support for a ban, though the major parties have no truck with it.

While the radical secularist (*laïcité*) trajectory of the banning of some headdress favoured by some Muslim women was taking place, another was simultaneously taking place in France and elsewhere, which is important to note as it does not so easily conform to the common understanding of French *laïcité*.[9] Since 1990 each French government, whether of the left or the right, has set about trying to create a national Muslim council that would be a corporate representative of Muslims in France and the official government consultee. It would be the state's recognition of Islam, comparable in some respects to its recognition of the Catholic Church, Protestant churches and the Jewish Consistory (p. 69 above). After at least three abortive attempts by previous Interior Ministers, Nicholas Sarkozy, when in that post, inaugurated the Conseil Français du Culte Musulman in 2003 (Modood and Kastoryano 2006: 174–5). Even now, this council is not yet accepted by the majority of Muslims in France and has little influence with the French media, civil society or government. Its importance for my argument does not depend on its effectiveness or on whether it has support amongst Muslims in France. Rather, it exhibits how even a laicist, anti-multiculturalist state, which is supported by most citizens in attacking fundamental religious freedom, is creating institutional linkages to govern Muslims in a way which is prima facie contrary to *laïcité*. It is not, however, contrary to the western European tradition of moderate secularism, and France is not alone in following a path of anti-multiculturalist rhetoric and refusal to offer accommodation on specifics[10] with a willingness to deal with Muslims not just as individual citizens, but also as a religious group. Chancellor Merkel's government in Germany assembled a group of Muslims in 2006 for an Islamkonfrenz at the highest level of government and this has been repeated every year. Interestingly, the secularist strand of opinion in Britain which looks to France as a model is opposed to special consultative status for Muslim organizations, and sees this as consistent with the older demand for the disestablishment of the Church of England, the removal of bishops from a democratized House of Lords and a reduction in the number of state-funded faith schools.[11] As explained on pp. 74–5 above, 'corporatist' accommodation is a form of multiculturalism, albeit less preferable than the bottom-up and civil-society-led approach that is more common in Britain, but clearly seems to be more in tune with certain European state models. British radical secularists fail to note, as discussed on pp. 74–5 and in the previous chapter, that such corporatist accommodation is part of the statist traditions of France and Germany and is an aspect of continental multiculturalism that is growing. It falls short of the ideal of multicultural citizenship sketched on pp. 115–18, which draws on a concept of citizenship which extends into voluntary associations and community activism – such that neighbourhood voluntary work can be said to exemplify 'active citizenship' or 'a good citizen'.

Additional Responses: Christian Values and Muscular Liberalism

Two responses, then, to Muslim action and claims-making have manifested themselves: the accommodationist, which through dialogue, negotiation and adaptation has tried to find a space for Muslims within an older, broad racial equality and multiculturalist orientation; and a radical secularist approach. Two other sentiments can also be identified, a Christianist and an intolerant or 'muscular' liberalism (which is not to say that Christians and liberals were not party to the first two approaches). The churches, especially the Church of England, have been actively involved in supporting British multiculturalism and developing interfaith dialogue, networks and policy coalitions with Muslims and other minorities. Similarly, what I refer to as liberal intolerance overlaps with the secularist intolerance that has already been discussed. What is distinctive about the two responses to Muslims is that one makes an explicit appeal to Christianity, and the other makes an explicit appeal to the limits of the prized value of toleration (Dobbernack and Modood forthcoming, 2013).

The reference to Christianity can be quite distant from policy. For example, it seems that the presence and salience of Muslims can be a factor in stimulating a Christian identity. An analysis of the voluntary question on religion in the 2001 UK census shows higher 'Christian' identification in areas near large Muslim populations (Voas and Bruce 2004). The emergence of a new, sometimes politically assertive, cultural identification with Christianity has been noted in Denmark (Mouritsen 2006), and, in Germany, Chancellor Merkel, in the speech already referred to, has asserted that '[t]hose who don't accept [Christian values] don't have a place here' (cited in Presseurop 2010, reported as 'Muslims in her country should adopt Christian values'). Since then, several senior Bavarian politicians have made the link between German nationalism and Christianity even more emphatically (Fekete 2011: 46).[12] Similar sentiments were voiced in the European Union Constitution debate and are apparent in the ongoing debate about Turkey as a future Union member (Casanova 2009). These assertions of public Christianity are not, as said earlier, accompanied by any increase in expressions of faith or church attendance, which continue to decline across Europe. What is at work is not the repudiation of a status-quo secularism in favour of Christianity, but a response to the challenge of multiculturalism (as Merkel made explicit by asserting that 'multi-kulti' had failed and was not wanted back). Giscard d'Estaing, the former President of France, who chaired the Convention on the Future of Europe, the body which drafted the (abortive) EU Constitution, expresses nicely the assertiveness I speak of: 'I never go to Church, but Europe is a Christian continent.'[13]

Such political views, however, are also being expressed by Christian organizations, especially by the Catholic Church. Early in his papacy, Pope Benedict XVI, in a speech at the Bavarian Catholic University at Regensberg, suggested that while reason was central to Christian divinity, this was not the case with the God of Islam, which licensed conversion by the sword and was deeply antithetical to the European tradition of rationality (November 2006, at <http://www.zenit.org/article-16955?l=english>). It has been argued that Pope John Paul II 'looked at the essential cleavage in the world as being between religion and unbelief. Devout Christians, Muslims, and Buddhists had more in common with each other than with atheists' (Caldwell 2009: 151). Pope Benedict, the same author contends, 'thinks that, within societies, believers and unbelievers exist in symbiosis. Secular Westerners, he implies, have a lot in common with their religious fellows' (ibid.). The suggestion is that secularists and Christians in Europe have more in common with each other than they do with Muslims, including European Muslims. That many secularists do not share Pope Benedict's view is evident from the fact that the proposed clause about Christianity was absent from the final draft of the abortive EU Constitution. Moreover, it is indicative of the place of Christianity in Europe relative to radical secularism, that it emerged as a third, not a first or second trend. That is to say, it joined a debate in which the running had been mainly made by an accommodationist multiculturalism and an exclusionist secularism allied with nationalism. Yet, while there is little sign of a Christian right in Europe of the kind that is strong in the USA, there is to some degree a reinforcing or renewing of a sense that Europe is 'secular Christian', analogous to the term 'secular Jew' to describe someone of Jewish descent who has a sense of Jewish identity but is not religiously practising and may even be an atheist.

A fourth trend focuses on Muslims' conservative or illiberal moral values and practices. These are likely to centre on issues of gender and sexuality and so this trend overlaps with that which has led to legal restrictions on the wearing of the headscarf and the face-veil, but goes much further and can be independent of questions of religion–state relations. It is alleged that the state needs to take special action against Muslims because their attitudes to, for example, gender equality and sexual orientation are threatening to reverse what has been achieved in western countries. This argument is found across the political and intellectual spectrum in the region, but is particularly strong in the Netherlands, where Pim Fortuyn's call for a halt to Muslim immigration because of their views on sex and personal freedom achieved considerable electoral success at the turn of the century (*The Economist* 2002). The Dutch government produced a video to be shown to prospective Muslim immigrants, which included a close-up of a topless woman on a beach and gay men kissing in a park, to assist in the process of assessing applicants for entry into the country (Monshipouri 2010: 51). In neighbouring Denmark, the newspaper *Jutlands Posten* famously published satirical and irreverent cartoons of the Prophet Muhammad, justified by its cultural editor as assisting Muslims in becoming acculturalized into Danish public culture (Levey and Modood 2009: 227).[14] Ayaan Hirsi Ali, a former Dutch MP of Somali Muslim origin, became an international figure through her argument that the subordination of women was a core feature of orthodox Islam. The position I am referring to could be called a form of liberal perfectionism – that is, the view, in contrast to a Rawlsian neutralism, that it is the business of a liberal state to produce liberal individuals and promote a liberal way of life (Mouritsen and Olsen forthcoming, 2013), perhaps what Charles Taylor once called, liberalism as 'a fighting creed' or what Prime Minister Cameron has called 'muscular liberalism'. Its actual political dynamic has been to create and lead popular anti-Muslim hostility as in the form of Geert Wilders's comparison of the Qur'an with *Mein Kampf* and campaign to ban the former as long as the latter is banned. His campaign against the 'Islamization of Europe' has many echoes across western Europe and is not limited to the Netherlands, where the party he founded in 2005, the Party for Freedom, became the third largest in the 2010 elections and a negotiating partner in the formation of a government (Wikipedia 2011).

This 'muscular liberalism' perhaps matches the radical secularism of the *hijab* and *burqa* bans – at least, that is how it has been interpreted by Joppke (2009a) and Hansen (2011), who argue that a ban on ostentatious religious dress is liberal if it does not name any particular religion but is equally restrictive of all of them! But I mention it separately as it is intellectually distinct,[15] and, more importantly, because it reveals how the dynamic that political secularism – and, indeed, liberalism – is being subjected to and is being tested on is that of the presence of Muslims combined with anti-Muslim hostility from various intellectual and political directions. Another example of this broad anti-Muslim coalition is the majority that voted in a referendum to ban the building of minarets in Switzerland in 2009. It has been analysed as including a wide range of motives – from those whose primary motivation is women's rights to those 'who simply feel that Islam is "foreign"', who may have no problems with Muslims per se but who are not ready to accept 'Islam's acquiring of visibility in public spaces' (Mayer 2009: 6) and who generally did not vote 'out of a desire to oppress anybody, but because they are themselves feeling threatened by what they see as an Islam invasion' (Mayer 2009: 8). So prejudiced or fearful perceptions of Islam are capable of uniting a wide range of opinion into a majority, including those who have no strong views about church–state arrangements, as indeed has been apparent from the beginning when Muslim claims became public controversies.

This means that the current challenge to secularism in western Europe is being debated not only in terms of the wider issues of integration and multiculturalism, but also in terms of a hostility to Muslims and Islam, based on stereotypes and scare stories in the media that are best understood as a specific form of cultural racism or 'Islamophobia' (Meer and Modood 2010; Sayyid and Vakil 2010; Morey and Yaqin 2011),[16] and as such is largely unrelated to questions of secularism. A meta-analysis of opinion polls between 1998 and 2006 in Britain concluded that 'between one in five and one in four Britons now exhibits a strong dislike of, and prejudice against, Islam and Muslims' (Field 2007: 465). A Pew survey in 2008 confirmed the higher figure and found its equivalent in France to be nearly double (38 per cent) and just over 50 per cent in Germany (Pew Research Center 2008). These views are growing, finding expression in the rise of extreme right-wing parties, and even in terrorism, as happened in Oslo and the island of Atoye in July, 2011 (Bangstad 2011). This, to put it mildly, is not a favourable context for accommodating Muslims and underscores the point that the so-called crisis of secularism is really about the presence and integration of Muslims, which of course partly depends on the behaviour of some Muslims, for example, those who commit acts of terrorism or make declarations of disloyalty to the country.

To Pluralize or Abandon Moderate Secularism?

So, looking at the four trends and the wider Islamophobic climate of opinion, it looks as if the radical secularist trend and the Christianist trend could unite through cultural nationalism or cultural Europeanism, animated by Islamophobia. I hope not. I would like to think that the spectre of a populist, right-wing nationalism – not to mention racism – would make enough people rally round a moderate secularism, which they would recognize has to be pluralized. But, either way, what this analysis suggests is that the real choice is between a pluralist, multifaith nationality or Europeanism and a monoculturalist nationalism or Europeanism. Or, put another way, the crisis of secularism is best understood within a framework of multiculturalism. Of course, multiculturalism currently has few advocates and the term is highly damaged.[17] Yet the argument of this book has been that the repeated declarations, such as from the senior politicians of the region, that 'multiculturalism is dead' (Fekete 2011) are a reaction to the continuing potency of multiculturalism which renders obsolete liberal takes on assimilation and integration in the face of new forms of public gender and public ethnicity, and now, public religion. Muslims are late joiners of this movement, but once they join, it slowly becomes apparent that the secularist status quo, with certain residual privileges for Christians, is untenable as it stands.

If multiculturalism were dead, we would not be having a debate about the role of public religion or proposals for dialogue with Muslims and the accommodation of Islam. The dynamic for change is not directly related to the historic religion or the historic secularism of western Europe; rather, the novelty – which then has implications for Christians and secularists and to which they are reacting – is the appearance of an assertive multiculturalism which cannot be contained within a matrix of individual rights, conscience, religious freedom and so on. If any of these were different the problems would be other than they are. For example, today we look at issues to do with, say, women or homosexuality not simply in terms of rights but in a political environment influenced by feminism and gay liberation, within a socio-political-intellectual culture in which the 'assertion of positive difference' or 'identity' is a shaping and powerful presence. It does not mean everybody is a feminist now, but the heightened consciousness of gender and gender equality creates a certain gender-equality sensibility. Similarly, my claim is that a multiculturalist sensibility is present in Europe and yet it is not comfortable with extending itself to accommodate Muslims, or able to find reasons for not extending to Muslims without self-contradiction.

The nature of the reform I proposed on pp. 72–8 is not one of abandoning or radically moving away from the status quo of the dominant moderate secularism of western Europe. A parallel approach has recently been proposed for Quebec (Bouchard and Taylor 2008: ch. 7; see also Taylor and Maclure 2011). Without endorsing the specifics of their understanding of a Quebecan 'open secularism', I recognize that their strategy is similar to mine. Moderate secularism can play a similar role in (much of) western Europe to the one that Bouchard and Taylor identify for open secularism in Quebec. Bhargava has mistakenly attributed to me the view that 'For [Modood], moderate secularism is a perfect ideal' (Bhargava 2011), but I do reject his analysis that leads him to conclude that moderate secularism is 'irretrievably flawed' and that, while it has accommodated Christians, it will not be able to accommodate Muslims.[18] Despite his suggestion that crisis can mean a turning point to 'recovery or mortality', the crisis that he believes exists for European moderate secularism is not of the kind that can be resolved through reform (Bhargava 2011). For me, it is the proverbial case of the bottle being half-full or half-empty: half-empty because it needs reforming to accommodate Muslims and religious diversity more generally; half-full because it acknowledges a place for religion within the state and/or supported by the state. The latter enable the possibility of the former, as argued in chapter 4. It also explains why talk of 'post-secular society' (like postmodern or post-national before it) has come to be seen as rather exaggerated. There now seems to be a consensus that the term 'post-secularism' means 'rethinking secularism' without any implication of anti-secularism or that it is time to move beyond secularism. While for some this is enough to make the case for using the term 'post-secular' (McLennan 2010), for me it makes evident that it is not an accurate term for what it is meant to capture, and if it is not to be abandoned it should at least be qualified as 'post-radical, post-uncritical secularism'. So a rethinking and opening up of political secularism in the light of contemporary multi-culturalism, especially the challenge of accommodating Muslims, is what I believe 'post-secularism' amounts to in western Europe.

Are the US and India Succeeding Where Europe is Failing?

While Bhargava's view of the 'irretrievably flawed' nature of European secularisms or church–state relations is based on a contrast with India, others take a similar view by comparing western Europe to the United States. Kymlicka, for example, has argued that 'American denominational-ism . . . has been successful precisely in relation to . . . reli-gious groups composed primarily of recent immigrants, and Muslims in particular', who are more likely than European Muslims 'to express the feeling that their reli-gion and religious freedoms are fully respected, and that they are accepted as citizens' (Kymlicka, 2009: 548). Simi-larly, it has been said of the US in explicit contrast to certain European countries such as Britain, that '[w]ithout the separation of church and state, we believe, the religions imported by past immigration streams could not have achieved parity with Protestant versions of Christianity' (Foner and Alba, 2008: 379). The claim that 'weak estab-lishment' or 'moderate secularism' of Britain alienates the majority of Muslims ignores the evidence about the strong sense of British identification and national pride amongst Muslims cited on p. 138 of this volume. Subsequent analy-ses of two Citizenship Surveys concluded: 'We find no evidence that Muslims or people of Pakistani heritage were in general less attached to Britain than were other religions or ethnic groups. Ethnic minorities show clear evidence of "dual" rather than "exclusive" identities' (Heath and Roberts 2008: 2). This has in fact been the finding of many surveys, including the most recent:

> Our polling shows that 88 per cent of Anglicans and Jews agreed that they were 'proud to be a British citizen' along-side 84 per cent of non-conformists and 83 per cent of Muslims – compared with 79 per cent for the population as a whole. (p. 39) [. . .] This optimism in British Muslims is significant as – combined with their high score for pride in being British – it runs counter to a prevailing narrative about Muslim dissatisfaction with and in the UK. While it is true that there are significant challenges to integration for some in the British Muslim community – and justified concern at the levels of radicalism and extremism in some British Muslim communities – overall British Muslims are more likely to be both patriotic and optimistic about Britain than are the white British community. (Wind-Cowie and Greogory 2011: 41)

Equally, we know that British Muslims include a large number of vociferous political groups, and between them they have mounted many arguments, not to mention campaigns, in relation to socio-economic deprivation, religious discrimination, incitement to religious hatred, various foreign policies, anti-terrorist policies and so on (Modood 2010b). Yet there is no record of any criticism by a Muslim group in relation to Establishment. On the other hand, many Muslims complain that Britain is too unreligious and anti-religious, too hedonistic, consumerist, materialist and so on. This suggests that the significant difficulty in Britain of integrating Muslims concerns more what Casanova himself identifies as the more important factor, namely, what he calls 'recent trends towards drastic secularization' (Casanova 2009: 141). Hence, if the US is better at integrating post-immigration religious minorities, this may not be due to its lack of an Establishment but to the greater presence of religion and in particular the greater social status of religion and its closeness to the mainstream of society (a point recognized by Casanova (2009) and offered as a factor by Foner and Alba (2008)). In this respect, it is important to note that while the US may be more of a secular state than Britain, the latter is more of a secular society and has an increasingly secularist political culture. It is as if two quite different social compacts were at work: in the British case, the deal is that the religious majority can have state recognition at the highest level but must exercise self-effacement in relation to the democratic process, if not public culture as well. The deal in the US, however, is that if all churches can agree to allow a certain limited area of public life as 'religiously neutral' and 'beyond religion', the rest of public life is an open field for religion. In the US, all religious groups are free to *lead the nation*, to seek to make the nation in their own image – as long as it is not through Establishment. It is not that politics is a no-go area, but Establishment is not considered an appropriate means to further religious ends (Modood 2009). While this may work well for the US, it is far from stress-free, as we have seen with the rise of an embittered Christian Right, alongside support for aggressive foreign policies with Islamophobic politics as extreme as those in Europe, but more conspicuously led by Christians.[19] Indeed, the US Tea Party has forged links with Islamophobic groups such as the English Defence League, and some of its luminaries are a source of nourishment for the mass murderer, Anders Breivik (Murray 2011). In this situation, where US state secularism sits alongside Christianist anti-Muslim political campaigns as aggressive as any found in Europe (except that, as we have seen, in Europe they are not primarily Christianist), and the Indian state secularism governs a society in which there can be a pogrom against Muslims, with perpetrators unpunished, it is disturbing that admirers of these state secularisms express pessimism regarding the capacity of moderate European secularism to reform and evolve. I hope I have offered some reasons for at least some Europeans to be more optimistic about their capacity to multiculturalize their own institutions in ways faithful to their own logic. This will certainly mean that there will be no singular European solution – the countries of Europe are too different for that. But one of the sources of hope is the moderate secularist legacy, with its varied forms in different states providing a plural set of resources, some of which may be more suitable for certain polities but from which there can be mutual learning and borrowing in the crafting of the multifaith and multicultural citizenships that are not so much dead as struggling to be born.

Notes

Chapter 1 *Is Multiculturalism Appropriate for the Twenty-first Century?*

1 In many ways the impetus for multiculturalism in each of these countries varied somewhat, not least because of the politics to do with long established populations like the Quebecois in Canada, African-Americans in the US and the aboriginal peoples in Australia, but my focus is on minorities formed through migration.

2 Which is not to say that one cannot learn from other histories and cultures. Muslim history is certainly relevant, though especially worth emphasizing is where different traditions have had to be synthesized, as in the case of India. Rajeev Bhargava has argued that multiculturalism 'has been an integral feature of public debate in India for more than a century' and the key lesson from it for the contemporary West is 'the need to rethink and reform another "ism" – secularism' (Bhargava 2004). I think Parekh 2000 is reflective of a sensibility informed by this Indian experience.

3 I use the term 'liberalism' as in contemporary anglophone political theory as the body of normative principles from which liberal politics receives its ultimate moral justification.

The work of John Stuart Mill and John Rawls are exemplars of liberalism and so the term is not identical to its uses in current political discourse, which of course varies even between anglophone countries and is only distantly related to 'neo-liberal', or any 'Liberal' political party.

4 For British right-wing criticism of multiculturalism-cum-anti-racism from this earlier period, see Palmer 1986 and Honeyford 1988.

5 For example, *Prospect*, *The Observer*, *The Guardian*, the Commission for Racial Equality, *openDemocracy*, Channel 4 and the British Council. In the light of this flood of open discussion and criticism it is extraordinary that comments by some academics were presented anonymously in the national professional paper, *The Higher*, 17 March 2006.

6 Not all of these commentators are of the centre-left and so highlight the new convergence against multiculturalism.

7 This is not surprising where the President describes his policy in Afghanistan and the Middle East as a 'crusade' and his religio-political allies describe Islam as 'wicked, violent and not of the same god' (Rev. Franklin Graham, *NBC, Nightly News*, 16 November 2001) and the Prophet Muhammad as 'a terrorist' (Rev. Jerry Falwell, CBS, *60 Minutes*, 6 October 2002).

8 The account of the Canadian legislation is based on the Department of Canadian Heritage website <http://www.pch.gc.ca/progs/multi/policy/act_e.cfm>.

9 I ought to declare an interest: I was the academic adviser to this Commission.

10 Not just in the media debates: see McLennan 2006: 101.

11 One of several difficulties that I have with the term 'multi-culturalism' is that it might be taken to be an '-ism' of the ideological kind that I discuss in chapter 6. I might have considered calling this book 'Multicultural Citizenship' had it not already been used by Will Kymlicka (1995) or 'Multicultural Politics', had I not already used it once (Modood 2005).

Chapter 2   A Liberal's Bias

1 We organized a very large international, interdisciplinary conference on Identity, Nationalism and Minority Rights at

the University of Bristol in 1999. Over two hundred papers were presented of which about thirty were in political theory; the overwhelming majority of the latter mentioned Kymlicka by name in the title or abstract. On 15 December 2012, he had a Google Scholar citation count of 25,601.

2 The Treaty of Westphalia (1648) is traditionally associated with the principle *cuius regio, eius religio*, in effect that the ruler decides the religion of his subjects, but it may be that this founding principle of the nation-state should be more identified with the Treaty of Augsburg (1555), for Westphalia included a clause in which a state's ruler had to accept that his subjects included persons of various denominations (Dreier 2006: 30). In any case, it is difficult to disagree that '[t]he era of religious wars was the era of nation-building in western Europe. Is not Sir Lewis Namier supposed to have said "religion is a sixteenth-century word for nationalism?"' (Wallerstein 2005: 125).

3 Kymlicka lists four types of minority rights claims, each differing from the other on the basis of the type of group involved: immigrant multiculturalism; multinational federalism; metic inclusion; religious exemptions (Kymlicka 2001b: 49, figure 1.1). Why religious groups are suited only for exemptions is not explained.

4 Interestingly, in a defence of Canadian multiculturalism, Kymlicka devotes a chapter to considering whether institutional multiculturalism should be extended to include some non-ethnic groups (primarily gays and lesbians and people with disabilities) but 'religion' is not even in the index (Kymlicka 1998).

5 For criticisms of 'societal culture' as suggesting an impossible discreteness of cultures, see Carens 1997, Young 1997 and Benhabib 1999. For a discussion of related criticisms of groups, see chapter 5 of this book.

6 Sometimes expressed in the slogan, 'We are over here because you were over there!' Kymlicka does recognize there are grey areas between incorporated peoples and voluntary migrants but wants to maintain distinctness.

7 In a later discussion he states that 'Canada's approach to the accommodation of groups formed by immigration is labelled "multiculturalism"' (Kymlicka 1998: 8) and is separate from Canada's treatment of 'national minorities'.

Chapter 3   Difference, Multi and Equality

1 One consequence of this is the iconic status enjoyed by Malcolm X (El-Hajj Malik El-Shabazz) amongst young, non-white, marginalized peoples in many cities, including for instance Bradford, Antwerp, Paris and Berlin. It is a status that has been boosted by the emergence of Muslim assertiveness in the West; certainly he is one of the two best known and most respected western Muslims, second only to Muhammad Ali.

2 It is interesting that while a black political identity is about half a century old in Britain, the first federation of 'Blacks of France' was created only in 2005, despite the French black population being twice that of the British (Lamont and Laurent 2006). This suggests that whatever might be said about multiculturalism, colour-blind republicanism may be losing some of its former hold in France.

3 This helps to explain the paradox that most continental European Muslims think that things are better for Muslims in Britain than most other parts of Europe but British Muslims are more critical of their political situation than any other Muslims in Europe (Klausen 2005). Reviewing the year 2004, a prominent international Muslim news website wrote: 'If a Muslim community in Europe was to be awarded first prize in integration and remarkable achievements, the British would be definitely singled out, and deservedly so' (Mohammad 2004).

4 An argument that is particularly well expressed by the late American feminist political theorist, Iris Young (e.g., Young 1990).

5 For the integration of the politics of redistribution and the politics of recognition, see Phillips 1999, Fraser and Honneth 2003 and Parekh 2004.

Chapter 4   Liberal Citizenship and Secularism

1 I am grateful to Joe Carens for this point.
2 One of the latest examples being the Euston Manifesto <http://eustonmanifesto.org/joomla/index.php?option=com_content&task=view&id=12&Itemid=41>.

3 It is clear that 'moderate' Muslim public figures in Britain are divided on homosexuality (Modood and Ahmad 2007) in just the way that all religions seem to be divided today.

4 The second half of this chapter builds on parts of Modood and Kastoryano 2006 and Modood 2009.

5 Not everybody thinks that terms such as 'secularist' and 'secularism' are helpful or should be reformed to give a positive meaning (e.g., Connolly 1999 and Bader 2007). Muslims in particular have an association of the term with European colonialism, atheism and anti-Islamic regimes. I think the term can and should be salvaged from such histories and associations.

6 This principle that recognized that Protestants and Catholics had a right to state resources and some publicly funded autonomous institutions officially ended in 1983. It is, however, still considered as a 'relevant framework for the development of a model that grants certain collective rights to religious groups' (Sunier and von Luijeren 2002) in such matters as state funding of Islamic schools. So, the accommodation of Muslims is, or at least was, being achieved through a combination of mild pillarization and Dutch minority policies.

7 While evocations of the Enlightenment and the need to (re)defend it is emerging as the dominant response amongst centre-left intellectuals in Europe, it is not (yet) necessarily so amongst policy-makers. Moreover, while there is little sign of a Christian right in Europe of the kind that is strong in the US, renewal of Christianity as a cultural marker is emerging as a response to the Muslim presence. It is visible in Denmark, in the UK 2001 Census and perhaps also in Germany, in the EU Constitution debate and debate about Turkey as a future EU member. These assertions of Christianity are not usually accompanied by any increase in expressions of faith or church attendance, which continue to decline across Europe.

Chapter 5   *Multiculturalism and Essentialism*

1 In parts of Europe a reason – sincere or tactical – given against ethnic monitoring is the uses of racial explicitness by

the Nazis (and sometimes also apartheid South Africa). This may be one reason why, even where Jews are officially acknowledged as a primary vulnerable group, they rarely feature on ethnic monitoring forms.

2 For example in relation to the Black Sections debate in the Labour Party and some of the large trades unions (e.g., NALGO (Unison) and NATFHE) the debate was a bit confused because they were organizations that stood for collective strength and for some version of corporate representation, and so the objection was ambiguous between a colour/difference-blind individualism, on the one hand and, on the other, the claim that any form of representation, other than an economic class representation, is divisive.

3 Actually, Brubaker's claim turns out to be even weaker than this for far from denying the reality of ethnicity, or even of ethnicity as a substantial entity or group, his ultimate claim is that it is sometimes possible to study ethnicity without necessarily positing groups, simply the process of group formation or 'groupness' (Brubaker 2005: 12). That Brubaker is not really intent on denying groups (as most people would understand them as social phenomena) becomes apparent in his exchange with Calhoun (2004a and 2004b; Brubaker 2004).

4 Parekh locates his multiculturalism within a discussion of human nature but it is clear that it is a humanity not conceived as a naturalistic object but one of enormous cultural variety within certain natural parameters (Parekh 2000).

5 On this and related issues, see the exchange between Bader (2001a and 2001b) and Baumann (2001).

6 For a good synopsis of how the handling of anti-essentialism and a number of other critical points can be used to offer a more sophisticated multiculturalism, sometimes called 'critical multiculturalism', see May 2002.

7 Most West Indians did not primarily think of themselves as 'black' prior to their arrival in Britain and the experience of a specific form of racial exclusion; and not all ever came to self-identify as black and this is true with subsequent generations too (Modood, Beishon and Virdee 1994: 81–4).

8 Where Muslims do not have to choose between identities, the identification with Britain is much higher: in an April 2006 survey of 1,000 Muslims in Britain, 82 percent

said they strongly or very strongly felt they belong to Britain, see <http://www.channel4.com/news/microsites/D/dispatches2006/muslim_survey/index.html>.

9 A related argument to that of 'new ethnicities' is the argument from 'superdiversity'. It is rightly argued that the new migrations to Britain (including refugees and asylum seekers) of the 1990s from a variety of new sources – Iran, Iraq, Somalia and various other parts of Africa, Turkish Kurdistan, Bosnia, Afghanistan, from Eastern Europe and South America – has meant that there is now such a diversity, so many micro-communities, that multiculturalism needs to be rethought (Vertovec 2006). This is a fair point but of course it does not mean that there are no larger, more settled ethno-religious groups; the latter still exist, and they too have a right to exist, and so must be included in a multiculturalism framework, sociologically and politically.

10 Cf. Morris 1968 and Handelman 1977.

Chapter 6 Multicultural Citizenship

1 The same point applies to my use of other singular terms, for example, in my use of the terms 'mode of being' and 'mode of oppression' in chapter 3. This is a general point about the use of words. R. G. Collingwood thought that variety in a genus was a characteristic of philosophical concepts (1933) whereas it seems to be a more general characteristic of concepts, or at least of concepts outside a scientific system.

2 The distinction between multicultural citizenship and ideology owes something I believe to Oakeshott's distinction between practical knowledge and ideology (Oakeshott 1962), and perhaps also to Ivan Hannaford's distinction between politics and race ideologies. I hope it is also apparent that my disagreement with each of these authors is also considerable. For example, Oakeshott offers a profound analysis displaying that reason and tradition are not an either/or but illegitimately concludes with traditionalism (Oakeshott 1962) or a very narrow conception of citizenship (1975). Hannaford wants to identify and protect an ideal of

citizenship from ideologies of race but assumes a purist conception of citizenship that I am opposing (Hannaford 1996).

3 Of course for some analysts working-class struggles too have always had cultural/recognition dimensions and class is ana-lysed in identarian as well as non-identarian terms (e.g., Fraser and Honneth 2003).

4 Perhaps to even talk about a 'religious' dimension is already to be thinking of Islam in terms of a western, Protestant originating category (Asad 2003), though it is a category that many Muslims, western and others, have by now made their own.

5 In fact, amongst Muslims, European French Muslims profess a very high degree of primary identity with nationality rather than religion (Pew Global Attitudes Project 2006).

6 Some leading examples of Islamic modernism in the West are Sardar 1987, Safi 2003, Ramadan 2004 and Aslan 2005; for a brief introduction, see Masood 2006b. Strictly speak-ing this modernist strand is just one of several opposed strands. For there is an alternative, radical Islamic modern-ism of figures such as the Ayatollah Khomeini (Sayyid 1997). While the former sees Islamic and western concepts and values in terms of overlap and the possibilities of co-devel-opment, the latter emphasizes alterity. Hence I would call the former 'moderate' Islamic modernism but for the fact that the term 'moderate Muslim' has been so sullied that it is refused by many Muslims I would use it of (Modood and Ahmad 2007); I have explained earlier in the chapter that I am defining 'moderate X' as compatibility of X with my conception of multicultural citizenship.

7 It has been argued that British Muslims can usefully learn from the appeal to the Prophetic Constitution of Madina by the Maulana Husain Ahmad Madani, a senior Muslim theologian who did not favour the religious parti-tion of India that took place in 1947 (Birt 2006; Madani 2005).

8 This is to correct an impression I may have given in Modood 2005a that Muslims were merely using without modifying western egalitarian discourses. I am grateful to Sean McLaughlin (2006) for pointing this out and also to a dis-cussion of this point with Bhikhu Parekh.

9 For a very helpful elaboration of nationality, though which in places takes too circumscribed a view of multiculturalism, see Miller 1995.

10 Gilroy 2004 presents most contemporary stirrings of English/British national identity as a form of melancholia, a depression introduced by a loss of empire.

11 I do not share the view that the 'national-identity dimension of multiculturalism has nothing in common with the minority-focused 'politics of recognition' (Joppke 2004: 244). Much of what Joppke describes as accommodation in fact is what I have argued is recognition and not, as Joppke thinks, toleration.

12 Of course for some, especially younger people, even citizenship is not prized and certainly not compared to entertainment and shopping. So, if all we wanted to do was to follow trends, even constitutional patriotism would look out of date.

13 Full survey at <http://www.channel4.com/news/microsites/D/dispatches2006/muslim_survey/index.html>.

14 'Justified' here does not necessarily mean approval of the bombings (for other questions about political violence elicited much less support) but more a sense that one thing causes another – the cause of the bombings lies in Anglo-American foreign policy. A Populous, *The Times* poll of British Muslims, 6 February 2006, found that 7 per cent agreed with 'There are circumstances in which I would condone suicide bombings on UK soil,' though in the same month the ICM/*Telegraph* survey found one per cent of Muslim respondents thought that those who bombed London were right to do so. That the latter may be closer to the true figure is indicated by a survey by the 1990 Trust. In answer to the question of whether it is justifiable to commit acts of terrorism against civilians in the UK, 96 per cent of respondents said it was unjustifiable, with two per cent saying it was justifiable. <www.blink.org.uk/docs/muslim_survey_report_screen.pdf>.

15 For an example of a discussion on how to challenge persistent employment inequalities, see the review of positive action in employment and concluding recommendations in Dhami, Squires and Modood 2007.

Chapter 7 The Strange Non-Death of Multiculturalism

1 Joppke has subsequently excluded Britain from this 'retreat' (Joppke 2008: 537, and 2009b: 462). For an alternative view of New Labour's national approach, see Meer and Modood (2009a) and Judith Squires's distinction between an acceptance of 'first level diversity' but not 'deep diversity', namely, not an erasure of 'difference' but its containment within a common citizenship (Squires 2007: 533); in the changes at the local level, as Paul Thomas shows in detail in relation to youth and community work, 'community cohesion' incorporated anti-racism and respect for minority identities (Thomas 2011). See also Rietveld (2012).

2 The opposite of the expectation of Soysal (1994), which argued that human rights were making the need for migrants to acquire citizenship passé. Her failure is due to her seeing 'the human rights revolution' of the twentieth century in highly individualistic ways (Soysal 2012); cf. Kymlicka (2007).

3 For a comparative framework for analysing multiculturalism across time and across countries, based on elements of the state rather than specific policies, see Modood and Meer (2012).

4 On the other hand, there is no evidence for the view that liberal multiculturalism is hegemonic and is a disguised form of racism (Zizek 2011); nor for the view that the monocultural hegemony involves the fantasy that multiculturalism is the hegemony and is a disguised form of racism (Ahmed 2008).

5 This is my central difference with the viewpoint of Phillips (2007), with which otherwise I have considerable sympathy; for discussion of similarity and differences between our conceptions of multiculturalism, see pp. 155–8 below and the symposium comprising of Squires (2008), Thompson (2008), Modood (2008), and Phillips (2008); see also Levey (2009). Other recent elaborations of related versions of multiculturalism built on the experience of Muslims in Britain include Meer (2010), Hellyer (2010), Malik (2010a), and Farrar (2012).

6 Most of the rest of the chapter is an adapted version of some parts of the booklet *Post-Immigration 'Difference' and Integration* (London: British Academy 2012).

7 Different groups may integrate to different degrees across sectors. For example, Jews in Britain are highly integrated in relation to employment, but are the most residentially segregated religious minority (Peach 2006). For an interesting moral argument questioning the assumption that segregation is bad, see Merry (2012).

8 For an alternative view that at a moment when general conceptions are confused, we can best grasp what the real issues are by focusing on 'the everyday', see Fox and Miller-Idris (2008). Concepts such as integration and national identity operate at different geographic scales and analytical levels, so that, for example, national identity is cashed out differently in different cities. I regret that some researchers are normatively driven to emphasize the local and the transnational not to complexify, and not to illuminate, but to dissolve the national. For a philosophical approach that seeks to allow all levels and aspects of identity their due rather than see them as either/or, see Parekh (2008).

9 The concern here is not primarily in relation to socio-economic integration, for which see Loury, Modood and Teles (2005), and Heath and Cheung (2007), but is a denial of the view that 'the problems addressed by difference theorists can all ultimately be reduced to problems of formal economic inequality' (Barry 2001: 319). The issues of 'difference', however, are as important as the socio-economic in relation to equal citizenship and have to be understood on their own terms. The bigger challenge, not attempted here, is to connect the socio-economic with the issues discussed here (Fraser and Honneth 2003; Parekh 2004).

10 In using this triad, I follow Charles Taylor's example in relation to the concept of secularism (Taylor 2009), though without claiming that he would wish to use it as I do in relation to integration. For recent discussions of how multiculturalism relates to some central democratic values, see Murphy (2012) and Sardoc (2011).

11 Migration to countries such as those of western Europe, and of North America, is a continuing phenomenon, and indeed saw new highs at the turn of the millennium but, as explained

on pp. 3–5, the area of multiculturalism focused on here emerges with settlement and citizenship, and I would add, the advent of an adult 'second generation'.

12 Here I do not mean the idea that there should be a world government; nor even the ethical view that one should be a citizen of the world. Rather, I am characterizing a mode of integration within a country that emphasizes a mixing of people from all over the world, as in the expression 'London is a cosmopolitan city'. British sociologists sometimes use the term 'multiculture', but this clearly has not carried over into public discourse. It has been suggested that the term 'interculturalism' best fits here, but this does not appear to include anything that is not or cannot be included in 'multiculturalism' (see Meer and Modood 2012). I also considered the term 'diversity', but that is too descriptive and generic, failing to pick out a mode of integration, or has been appropriated as 'diversity management' by human-resource professionals (cf. Faist 2009 and Kraus 2011).

13 This is how the term has been used by the leading political theorists such as Taylor (1994), Kymlicka (1995), and Parekh (2000), and by the Canadian government; it is also consistent with CMEB (2000) and other exponents of multiculturalism – see pp. 13–18 of this volume for details.

14 British exponents of this view tend, however, to put some collective identities in a normative, privileged position. This particularly applies to political blackness (Modood 1994b), and to some extent to non-cultural and non-religious political identities generally, especially those associated with class (Malik 2009; Lentin and Titley 2011) and gender (Patel 2008).

15 A review of the American social science literature found that '[t]he most common conception of multiculturalism in both scholarly circles and popular discourse is a negative one, having to do with what multiculturalism is not or what it stands in opposition to. Multiculturalism in this usage represents heterogeneity as opposed to homogeneity, diversity as a counterpoint to unity' (Hartmann and Gerteis 2005: 219). They found that if they looked at exponents, as opposed to critics, of multiculturalism, such simplistic dichotomies were unsustainable and they concluded:

'multiculturalism is best understood as a critical-theoretical project, an exercise in cultivating new conceptions of solidarity in the context of dealing with the realities of pervasive and increasing diversity in contemporary societies' (221–2). See also Kivisto (2012).

16 Despite explicit disavowals, some read me as working with essentialist, reificatory and primordial concepts of groups. For example, St Louis (2009) takes my 'mode of being' to be 'somehow pre- or extra-social'. But I mean pre-oppression, pre- a specific mode of oppression, not pre-social *as such*.

17 See the debate mentioned in note 5 of this chapter, above.

18 Some scholars prefer not to engage with rejections of multiculturalism, dismissing them as disguised racism, e.g., Lentin and Titley (2011), who simultaneously also reject multiculturalism without engaging with it as a normative political idea.

19 Hence the irony that anti-multiculturalists such as President Sarkozy have created corporate representations for Muslims in France, while pro-diversity authors have called for the cessation of government meetings with Muslim community leaders (Sen 2006; Malik 2011).

20 Another example of how state policies in this field can lead to unintended yet multiculturalist consequences is the British government's PREVENT programme, directed at preventing Muslim (violent) extremism, which has played an important part in increasing Muslim participation in local governance (O'Toole et al. 2012).

21 Uberoi (2009) offers detailed evidence that the framers of Canadian multiculturalism saw themselves as engaged in nation-building.

22 I emphasize the national to create a distance from the view that the real movement is a convergence towards liberal values and that the vocabulary of nationality is merely rhetorical and does not shape the nature of these values (Modood and Meer 2012: 37–9; Mouritsen 2012).

23 In the 1990s, cosmopolitanism and multiculturalism in Britain began to be linked to a national identity, and its modernization, to, for example, 'Cool Britannia' and 'rebranding Britain' (Leonard 1997), but others welcomed globalization as an era of the 'post-national' (Hall 1992b; Soysal 1994). The opening ceremony of the Olympic Games

in London in July 2012 was an excellent expression of a Britishness that New Labour tried to articulate without ever quite succeeding (Katwala 2012).

24 Interculturalism is actually nearly as old as multiculturalism, for the former was a Quebecan reaction to the latter, but what is understood by interculturalism in Europe is quite different, as explained in Meer and Modood (2012).

25 For evidence of the high levels that ethnic minorities, including Muslims, have of identification with Britain, see pp. 138 and 184–5.

26 'To be attached to the subdivision, to love the *little platoon* we belong to . . . we proceed towards a love of our country, and to mankind' (Burke 1986: 135).

Chapter 8 Multiculturalism and the 'Crisis of Secularism'

1 This chapter draws extensively on the Paul Hanly Furfey Lecture given at the Annual Conference of the Association of the Sociology of Religion, 19 August 2011, Las Vegas, and published as 'Is There A Crisis of Secularism?', *Sociology of Religion*, Summer 2012, 73(2): 130–49. This work was undertaken as part of an Arts and Humanities Research Council (AHRC) Fellowship award, for which I am grateful.

2 It is, though, doubtful whether Habermas has really abandoned his earlier reason–religion duality (Harrington 2007).

3 Bhargava has qualified what he means by crisis as 'only a critical turning point . . . to recovery or mortality', but continues to believe that secularism in some or all countries of western Europe is 'irretrievably flawed' (Bhargava 2011).

4 Immigration may, however, be masking some elements of decline in religious belief amongst 'natives' in western Europe, as well as in North America.

5 Some government policies may be seeking to delegate certain welfare responsibilities; that is not, however, based on rethinking secularism or Christianity, but on wishing to impose limitations for revenue or other reasons.

6 Roald (2012) offers a discussion of the effects of secularization on Muslims in Sweden; that most Muslims are 'privatizing' their beliefs while simultaneously projecting a public

ethno-religious Muslim group identity in the manner discussed in Modood (2010a: 11).

7 A study of aspects of Muslim participation in new forms of
governance in Britain is the subject of the project, Muslim
Participation in Contemporary Governance (http://www.
bristol.ac.uk/ethnicity/projects/muslimparticipation/index.
html).

8 The way that race, religion and ethnicity do not neatly
align today is illustrated by the fact that the head teacher
whose inflexibility created the national crisis was a black
African, while two of the three girls he excluded were supported by a Jewish father (thanks to David Lehmann for
sending me details of this, at: http://news.bbc.co.uk/1/hi/
world/europe/3149588.stm). It has in fact been argued with
some justification that the post-1989 *laïcité* is actually a
much stricter interpretation than what was initially in place
following the 1905 law that established *laïcité*; and that
those who reject the contemporary interpretation, which
includes some Muslim activists, are not anti-secularists but
true to the spirit of the 1905 law (Baubérot 2012).

9 Of course, neither does the idea that the French Republic
subsidizes religious schools, as mentioned in chapter 7
(p. 162). In fact, in both the *laïcité* Republic and 'Establishment' England about a quarter of all pupils attend state-
subsidized religious schools and the scale of subsidy is not
very different.

10 Sometimes refusal at a national level is accompanied by local
compromises (Bowen 2010).

11 See National Secular Society and the British Humanist
Association websites; for similar views amongst centre-left
Christians, see the website of the think tank, Ekklesia.

12 An interesting cross-national contrast is that, in Britain,
Muslims (79 per cent) and Hindus (74 per cent) are more
likely than Christians (70 per cent) to agree 'Our laws
should respect and be influenced by UK religious values'
(Nick Allen, *The Telegraph*, 24 February 2009; see also the
next note).

13 More recently, Prime Minister Cameron, who has confessed
to not being a steadfast believer, made a major speech
arguing that Britons should not be shy of asserting that
Britain is a Christian country (http://www.number10.gov.uk/

news/king-james-bible). While many secularists protested, the speech was welcomed by the chair of the Mosque and Community Affairs of the Muslim Council of Britain, Sheikh Ibrahim Mogra (http://www.bbc.co.uk/news/uk-16231223). See also the previous note.

14 Even though he, or at least his newspaper, took a different view of an anti-Christian cartoon earlier (Fouché 2006).

15 'Perfectionist liberalism is not intolerant *per se* . . . Intolerance (and conflict with traditional liberal pluralism) enters at the point where officially promoted ideals of good liberal citizenship come to be seen as so important, so threatened, and so much in conflict with specific *un-civic* (religious) practices and dispositions, concentrated in defined and targetable out-groups, that attempts to change, penalize or even outlaw them become legitimate' (Mouritsen and Olsen forthcoming, 2013). Levey (2012) offers a sophisticated and complex framework for evaluating whether putative non-liberal minority practices violate the ideal of liberal autonomy, warranting state intervention.

16 Interestingly, in Britain, the Christian media has been less hostile to Muslims than the mainstream media (Faimau 2010, 2011).

17 Which, as argued in chapter 7, does not mean subscription to the thesis that multiculturalism is in retreat.

18 For a fuller discussion of why I think Bhargava misunderstands western European secularisms, see Modood (2010b, 2011).

19 In relation to inflammatory politics around the 'Ground Zero Mosque', 'Shariah Law' and public burnings of the Qur'an, and how these controversies should be dealt with, see Nussbaum (2012).

References

Abbas, T. (2011) *Islamic Radicalism and Multicultural Politics: The British Experience*, London and New York: Routledge.

Ahmed, L. (1992) *Women and Gender in Islam: Historical Roots of a Modern Debate*, New Haven, CT: Yale University Press, p. 296.

Ahmed, S. (2008) '"Liberal Multiculturalism is the Hegemony – It's an Empirical Fact" – A response to Slavoj Žižek', *darkmatter Journal*, 19 February, <http://www.darkmatter101. org/site/2008/02/19//>. Last accessed 13 August 2011.

Akan, M. (2009) 'Laïcité and Multiculturalism: The Stasi Report in Context', *British Journal of Sociology*, 60(2): 237–56.

Al-Azmeh, A. (1993) *Islam and Modernities*, New York: Verso.

Alexander, C. (2004) 'Imagining the Asian Gang: Ethnicity, Masculinity and Youth after "The Riots"', *Critical Social Policy*, London: Sage Publications, 24(4): 526–49.

Alibhai-Brown, Y. (2000) *After Multiculturalism*, London: The Foreign Policy Centre.

Amin, A. (2002) 'Ethnicity and the Multicultural City: Living with Diversity', *Environment and Planning A*, 34: 959–80.

Amir-Moazami, S. (2011) 'Pitfalls of Consensus-Orientated Dialogue: The German Islam Conference (Duetsche Islam Konfrenz)', *Approaching Religion*, May, 1(2): 2–15.

Amos, V. and P. Parmar (1984) 'Challenging Imperial Feminism', *Feminist Review*, 17: 3–19.

Anderson, B. (1996) *Imagined Communities*, London and New York: Verso.

Anthias, F. and N. Yuval-Davis (1992) *Racialised Boundaries: Race, Gender, Colour and Class and the Anti-Racist Struggle*, London: Routledge.

Appiah, K. A. (1994) 'Identity, Authenticity, Survival: Multicultural Societies and Social Reproduction', in A. Gutmann (ed.), *Multiculturalism: Examining the Politics of Recognition*, Princeton, NJ: Princeton University Press.

Araujo, C. and A. I. Garcia (2006) 'Latin America: the Experience and Impact of Quotas' in D. Dahlerup (ed.), *Women, Quotas and Politics*, London: Routledge, pp. 83–111.

Asad, T. (2003) *Formations of the Secular*, Stanford, CA: Stanford University Press.

Asani, A. S. (2003) ' "So That You May Know One Another": A Muslim American Reflects on Pluralism and Islam', *The Annals of the American Academy of Political and Social Sciences*. Islam: Enduring Myths and Changing Realities, Special Editor: A. Syed, 588: 40–51.

Aslan, R. (2005) *No god but God*, London: William Heinemann.

Bader, V. (2011) 'Associational Governance of Ethno-Religious Diversity in Europe. The Dutch Case', in R. Smith (ed.), *Citizenship, Borders, and Human Needs*, Philadelphia, PA: Penn State University.

Back, L. (1993) 'Race, Identity and Nation within an Adolescent Community in South London', *New Community*, 19(2): 217–33.

Back, L. (1996) *New Ethnicities and Urban Culture: Racisms and Multiculture in Young Lives*, London: UCL Press.

Badawi, M. A. Z. (2003) 'Citizenship in Islam', *Association of Muslim Social Scientists (UK) Newsletter*, 6: 17–20.

Bader, V. (2001a) 'Culture and Identity', *Ethnicities*, 1(2): 251–73.

Bader, V. (2001b) 'Freedom-fighter Versus Stubborn Collectivist', *Ethnicities*, 1(2): 282–5.

Bader, V. (2005) (guest ed.) 'Multicultural Futures? International Approaches to Pluralism', *Canadian Diversity*, 4(1), Special Issue.

Bader, V. (2007) *Secularism or Democracy? Associational Governance of Religious Diversity*, Amsterdam: Amsterdam University Press.

Bagguley, P. and Y. Hussain (2008) *Riotous Citizens: Ethnic Conflict in Multicultural Britain*, Basingstoke: Ashgate.

Bailey, E. I. (1997) *Implicit Religion in Contemporary Society*, Kampen and Weinheim: Kok Pharos.

Baldwin, T. (2004) 'I Want an Integrated Society With a Difference (Trevor Phillips)', *The Times*, 3 April.

Bangstad, S. (2011) 'Norway: Terror and Islamophobia in the Mirror', *Open Democracy*, 22 August, <http://www.open democracy.net/sindre-bangstad/norway-terror-and-islamophobia-in-mirror>.

Banting, K. and W. Kymlicka (2008) *Multiculturalism and the Welfare State: Recognition and Redistribution in Contemporary Democracies*, Oxford: Oxford University Press.

Barry, B. (2001) *Culture Equality*, Cambridge: Polity.

Baubérot, J. (2012) *La Laïcité Falsifiée*. Paris: La Découverte.

Baubock, R. (2003) 'Public Culture in Societies of Immigration', in R. Sackmann, B. Peters and T. Faist (eds) (2003), *Identity and Integration, Migrants in Western Europe*, Aldershot: Ashgate.

Baumann, G. (1996) *Contesting Culture*, Cambridge: Cambridge University Press.

Baumann, G. (1999) *The Multicultural Riddle*, New York: Routledge.

Baumann, G. (2001) 'Culture and Collectivity', *Ethnicities*, 1(2): 274–82.

Benhabib, S. (1999) ' "Nous" et "les Autres": The Politics of Complex Cultural Dialogue in a Global Civilisation', in C. Joppke and S. Lukes (eds), *Multicultural Questions*, Oxford: Oxford University Press: 44–62.

Berger, P. L. and T. Luckmann (1967) *The Social Construction of Reality*, Harmondsworth: Penguin Books.

BHA (2012) 'BHA: Approved 2013 Free Schools include First "Faith" Special', *Alternative Provision Schools*, 16 July, <http://www.politics.co.uk/opinion-formers/bha-british-humanist-association/article/bha-approved-2013-free-schools-include-first-faith-special-a>.

Bhabba, H. (1994) *The Location of Culture*, London and New York: Routledge.

Bhargava, R. (2004) 'India's Model: Faith, Secularism and Democracy', *openDemocracy*, 3 November, <http://www.opendemocracy.net/arts-multiculturalism/article_2204.jsp>.

Bhargava, R. (2010) 'States, Religious Diversity, and the Crisis of Secularism', *Hedgehog Review*, <http://www.iasculture.org/publications_article_2010_Fall_Bhargava.php>.

Bhargava, R. (2011) 'States, Religious Diversity and the Crisis of Secularism', *Open Democracy*, 22 March, <http://www.opendemocracy.net/rajeev-bhargava/states-religious-diversity-and-crisis-of-secularism-0>.

Bi, F. (2006) '"Alienation": The London Bombs, one year on', *openDemocracy*, 3 July, <http://www.opendemocracy.net/articles/ViewPopUpArticle.jsp?id=3&articleId=3704>.

Birt, J. (2006) 'Between Nation and Umma: Muslim Loyalty in a Globalizing World', *Islam21*, 40, January: 6–11, <http://www.islam21.net/news%26pub/Quarterly%20Islam21/January2006.pdf>.

Bouchard, G. (2011) 'What is Interculturalism?', *McGill Law Journal*, 56: 435–68.

Bouchard, G. and C. Taylor (2008) *Building the Future: A Time for Reconciliation*, Quebec: Consultation Commission on Accommodation Practices Related to Cultural Differences.

Bowen, J. R. (2007) 'Why the French Don't Like Headscarves: Islam, the State, and Public Space', *European Review*, 15(3): 397–400.

Bowen, J. R. (2010) *Can Islam Be French?: Pluralism and Pragmatism in a Secularist State*, Princeton, NJ: Princeton University Press.

Bradley, H. (1996) *Fractured Identities: Changing Patterns of Inequality*, Polity.

Bradley, S. and J. Taylor (2004) 'Ethnicity, Educational Attainment and the Transition from School', *The Manchester School*, 72(3): 313–46.

Brett, J. and A. Moran (2011) 'Cosmopolitan Nationalism: Ordinary People Making Sense of Diversity', *Nations and Nationalism*, 17: 188–206.

BRIN (2011) 'Religious Affiliation and Church Attendance in Britain, 1983–2008', *British Religion in Numbers*, <http://www.brin.ac.uk/figures/#AffiliationAttendance>.

Brown, G. (2005) 'Roundtable: Britain Rediscovered', *Prospect*, 109, April: 20–5.

Brown, G. (2006) *Who do We Want to Be? The Future of Britishness*, Keynote Speech, Fabian Conference, on The

Future of Britishness, January, London, <http://www.fabian-society.org.uk/press_office/news_latest_all.asp?pressid=520>.

Brubaker, R. (1992) *Citizenship and Nationhood in France and Germany*, Cambridge, MA: Harvard University Press.

Brubaker, R. (2004) 'Neither Individalism nor "Groupism"', *Ethnicities*, 3(4): 553–7.

Brubaker, R. (2005) *Ethnicity Without Groups*, Cambridge, MA: Harvard University Press.

Bullock, K. (2002) *Rethinking Muslim Women and the Veil*, London: International Institute for Islamic Thought.

Burke, E. (1982) *Reflections on the Revolution in France*, Harmondsworth: Penguin.

Butler, J. (1990) *Gender Trouble: Feminism and the Subversion of Identity*, New York: Routledge.

Caglar, A. (1997) 'Hyphenated Identities and the Limits of "Culture"', in T. Modood and P. Werbner (eds), *The Politics of Multiculturalism in the New Europe: Racism, Identity and Community*, London: Zed Books.

Caldwell, C. (2009) *Reflections on the Revolution in Europe: Immigration, Islam and the West*, London: Allen Lane.

Calhoun, C. (2004a) '"Belonging" in the Cosmopolitan Imaginary', *Ethnicities*, 3(4): 531–53.

Calhoun, C. (2004b) 'The Variability of Belonging', *Ethnicities*, 3(4): 558–68.

Cameron, D. (2011) *PM's Speech at Munich Security Conference*, 5 February, <http://www.number10.gov.uk/news/speeches-and-transcripts/2011/02/pms-speech-at-munich-securityconference-60293>.

Cannon, B. (2006) 'Britishness, Multiculturalism and Globalisation', *Rising East Online*, 4 May, <http://www.uel.ac.uk/risingeast/currentissue/academic/cannon.htm>.

Cantle, T. (2001) *Community Cohesion: A Report of the Independent Review Team*, London: Home Office.

Carby, H. (1982) 'White Woman Listen! Black Feminism and the Boundaries of Sisterhood', in Centre for Contemporary Cultural Studies, *The Empire Strikes Back: Race and Racism in Seventies Britain*, London: Hutchinson: 212–35.

Carens, J. (1997) 'Liberalism and Culture' (Symposium on *Multicultural Citizenship*, Will Kymlicka), *Constellations*, 4(1): 35–47.

Casanova, J. (1994) *Public Religions in the Modern World*, Chicago: University of Chicago Press.

Casanova, J. (2007) 'Immigration and the New Religious Pluralism: A EU/US Comparison', in T. Banchoff (ed.), *The New Religious Pluralism and Democracy*, Oxford: Oxford University Press.

Casanova, J. (2009) 'Immigration and the New Religious Pluralism: A European Union – United States Comparison', in G. B. Levey and T. Modood (eds), *Secularism, Religion and Multicultural Citizenship*, Cambridge: Cambridge University Press.

Castles, S., B. Cope, M. Kalantzis and M. Morrisey (eds) (1992) *Mistaken Identity – Multiculturalism and the Demise of Nationalism in Australia*, Sydney: Pluto Press.

Cesari, J. (2004) *When Islam and Democracy Meet*, New York and Basingstoke: Palgrave.

Cohen, P. (ed.) (1999) *New Ethnicities, Old Racisms*, London: Zed Books.

Collingwood, R. G. (1933) *Essay on Philosophical Method*, Oxford: Oxford University Press.

Commission on British Muslims and Islamophobia (CMBI) (2002) *Response to the Commission on Racial Equality's Code of Practice*, London.

Commission on the Future of Multi-Ethnic Britain (CMEB) (2000) *The Future of Multi-Ethnic Britain*, London: Profile Books.

Connolly, C. (1990) 'Washing our Linen: One Year of Women Against Fundamentalism', *Women Against Fundamentalism*, 1.

Connolly, W. (1999) *Why I Am Not a Secularist*, Minneapolis: University of Minnesota Press.

Connor, H., C. Tyers, T. Modood and J. Hilage (2004) *Why the Difference? A Closer Look at Minority Ethnic Students and Graduates*, Research Report 552, Department for Education and Skills, July.

Davie, G. (1994) *Religion in Britain since 1945: Believing without Belonging*, Oxford: Blackwell.

Dhami, R., J. Squires and T. Modood (2007) *Developing Positive Action Policies: Learning from the Experiences of Europe and North America*, London: Department of Works and Pensions.

DIK (2009) 'Islamic Religious Education Trials in Schools', 16 February, <http://www.deutsche-islam-Konferenz.de/nn_1875202/SubSites/DIK/EN/ReligionsunterrichtImame/ReligionBildung/Schulversuche/schulversuche-node.html?__nnn=true>.

Dirlik, A. (1990) 'Culturalism as Hegemonic Ideology and Liberating Practice', in J. Mohamed and D. Lloyd (eds), *The Nature and Context of Minority Discourse*, New York: Oxford University Press.

Dobbernack, J. and T. Modood (eds) (forthcoming, 2013) *Hard to Accept: New Perspectives on Tolerance, Intolerance and Respect*, Basingstoke: Palgrave.

Donald, J. and A. Rattansi (eds) (1992) *'Race', Culture and Difference*, London: Sage.

Doomernik, J. (2005) 'The State of Multiculturalism in the Netherlands', *Canadian Diversity*, Multicultural Futures? International Approaches to Pluralism, 4(1): 32–5. Guest editor V. Bader.

Dreier, H. (2006) 'Stages of the Secularization of the State', *Workshop on The Secular, Secularizations and Secularism*, Wissenschaftskolleg zu Berlin, June 7.

Du Bois, W. E. B. (1999 [1903]) *The Souls of Black Folk: Centenary Edition*. H. L. Gates Jr and H. Oliver (eds), London: Norton Critical Edition.

Durkheim, E. (1964) *The Division of Labour in Society*, trans. G. Simpson, New York: The Free Press.

Economist, The (2002) 'A Wind of Change in the Netherlands – and across Europe', 16 May, <http://www.economist.com/node/1136775>.

Emmerson, M. (2011) *Interculturalism: Europe and its Muslims, in Search of Sound Societal Models*, Brussels: Centre for European Policy Studies.

Faimau, G. (2010) 'The Discursive Representation of Islam and Muslims in the British Christian Media: Socio-Cultural Construction of Recognition', PhD thesis, University of Bristol, UK.

Faimau, G. (2011) 'Naming Muslims as Partners: The Discursive Representation of Islam and Muslims in a British Catholic Newspaper', *Journalism Studies*, August, 12(4): 474–89.

Faist, T. (2009) 'Diversity – a New Mode of Incorporation?', *Ethnic and Racial Studies*, 32(1): 171–90.

Farrar, M. (2012) 'Multiculturalism in the UK – A Contested Discourse', in M. Farrar, S. Robinson, Y. Valli and P. Wetherly (eds), *Islam in the West – Key Issues in Multiculturalism*, Basingstoke: Palgrave.

Favell, A. and T. Modood (2003) 'Multiculturalism and the Theory and Practice of Normative Political Theory', in A. Finlayson (ed.), *Contemporary Political Thought*, Edinburgh: Edinburgh University Press: 484–95.

Fekete, L. (2008) *Integration, Islamophobia and Civil Rights in Europe*, London: Institute of Race Relations.

Fekete, L. (2011) 'Understanding the European-wide Assault on Multiculturalism', in H. Mahamdallie (ed.), *Defending Multiculturalism: A Guide for the Movement*, London: Bookmarks.

Fenton, S. (2003) *Ethnicity*, Cambridge: Polity.

Fenton, S. and R. Mann (2011) ' "Our Own People": Ethnic Majority Orientations to Nation and Country', in T. Modood, and J. Salt (eds), *Global Migration, Ethnicity and Britishness*, Basingstoke: Palgrave.

Feuchtwang, S. (1990) 'Racism: Territoriality and Ethnocentricity', in A. Cambridge and S. Feuchtwang (eds), *Antiracist Strategies*, Aldershot: Avebury.

Field, C. D. (2007) 'Islamophobia in Contemporary Britain: The Evidence of the Opinion Polls, 1988–2006', *Islam and Christian–Muslim Relations*, 18: 447–77.

Foner, N. and R. Alba (2008) 'Immigrant Religion in the US and Western Europe: Bridge or Barrier to Inclusion?', *International Migration Review*, 42: 360–92.

Forum Against Islamophobia and Racism (FAIR) (2002) *A Response to the Government Consultation Paper, 'Towards Equality and Diversity: Implementing the Employment and Race Directives'*, London.

Fouché, G. (2006) 'Danish Paper Rejected Jesus Cartoons', *Guardian*, 6 February, <http://www.guardian.co.uk/media/2006/feb/06/pressandpublishing.politics>.

Fox, G. (1996) *The Hispanic Nation: Culture, Politics and the Constructing of Identity*, New Jersey: Secacusus.

Fox, J. and C. Miller-Idriss (2008) 'Everyday Nationhood', *Ethnicities*, 8(4): 536–63.

Fraser, N. and A. Honneth (2003) *Redistribution or Recognition*, London: Verso.

Fukuyama, F. (2005) 'A Year of Living Dangerously', *The Wall Street Journal*, November.

Fuss, D. (1989) *Essentially Speaking*, New York: Routledge.

Galeotti, A. (2002) *Toleration as Recognition*, Cambridge: Cambridge University Press.

Gans, H. (1979) 'Symbolic Ethnicity: the Future of Ethnic Groups and Cultures in America', *Ethnic and Racial Studies*, 2(1): 1–20.

Gates, H. J., Jr (1986a) *'Race', Writing and Difference*, Chicago: University of Chicago Press.

Gayle, V., D. Berridge and R. Davies (2002) 'Young People's Entry into Higher Education: Quantifying Influential Factors', *Oxford Review of Education*, vol. 28, no.1, pp. 1–20.

Gillborn, D. (1995) *Racism and Antiracism in Real Schools*, Bristol, TN: Open University Press.

Gilroy, P. (1987) *There Ain't No Black in the Union Jack: The Cultural Politics of Race and Nation*, London: Heinemann.

Gilroy, P. (1990) 'The End of Anti-Racism', *New Community*, (17): 71–83.

Gilroy, P. (1993) *The Black Atlantic: Modernity and Double Consciousness*, London: Verso.

Gilroy, P. (2000) *Between Camps: Nations, Cultures and the Allure of Race*, Harmondsworth: Allen Lane.

Gilroy, P. (2004) *After Empire: Melancholia or Convivial Culture?* Abingdon: Routledge.

Gilroy, P. (2005) 'Melancholia or Conviviality: The Politics of Belonging in Britain', *Soundings*, 29 (Spring): 35–46.

Glazer, N. (1998) *We Are All Multiculturalists Now*, Cambridge, MA: Harvard University Press.

Glazer, N. (2006) 'The Reality of Multiculturalism in America', in B. Chandra and S. Mahajah (eds), *Composite Culture in a Multicultural Society*, New Delhi: Longman.

Goldthorpe, J. H. (2000) *On Sociology: Numbers, Narratives, and the Integration of Research and Theory*, Oxford: Oxford University Press.

Greely, A. (1995) 'The Persistence of Religion', *Cross Currents*, 45 (Spring): 24–41.

Guardian (2011) 'Italy Approves Draft Law To Ban Burqa', 3 August, <http://www.guardian.co.uk/world/2011/aug/03/italy-draft-law-burqa>.

Habermas, J. (1992) 'Citizenship and National Identity: Some Reflections on the Future of Europe', *Praxis International*, vol. 12, no. 1, pp. 1–19.

Habermas, J. (2006) 'Religion in the Public Sphere', *European Journal of Philosophy*, 14(1): 1–25.

Hall, S. (1992a) 'The Question of Cultural Identity', in S. Hall and T. McGrew (eds), *Modernity and its Futures*, Cambridge: Polity.

Hall, S. (1992b) 'New Ethnicities', in J. Donald and A. Rattansi (eds), *'Race', Culture and Difference*, London: Sage.

Hall, S. (2000) 'Conclusion: Multi-cultural Questions', in B. Hesse (ed.), *Un/settled Multiculturalisms: Diasporas, Entanglements, Transruptions*, London: Zed Books.

Hamburger, P. (2002) *Separation of Church and State*, Cambridge, MA, and London: Harvard University Press.

Handelman, D. (1977) 'The Organisation of Ethnicity', *Ethnic Groups*, 1: 187–200.

Hannaford, I. (1996) *Race: The History of an Idea in the West*, London: The Johns Hopkins University Press.

Hansen, R. (2011) 'The Two Faces of Liberalism: Islam in Contemporary Europe', *Journal of Ethnic and Migration Studies*, July, 37(6): 881–97.

Harrington, A. (2007) 'Habermas and "the Post-Secular Society"', *European Journal of Social Theory*, 10(4): 543–60.

Hartman, D. and J. Gerteis (2005) 'Dealing with Diversity: Mapping Multiculturalism in Sociological Terms', *Sociological Theory*, 23(2): 218–40.

Haverig, A. (2011) Managing the 'Enemy Within' – The Re-evaluation of Citizenship in Germany and the United Kingdom post-2001, PhD thesis, University of Kent.

Heath, A. and S. Y. Cheung (2007) *Unequal Chances: Ethnic Minorities in Western Labour Markets*, Oxford: published for the British Academy by Oxford University Press.

Heath, A. F. and J. Roberts (2008) *British Identity: Its Sources and Possible Implications for Civic Attitudes and Behaviour.* Research Report for Lord Goldsmith's Citizenship Review. <http://webarchive.nationalarchives.gov.uk/+/http:/www.justice.gov.uk/docs/british-identity.pdf> last accessed 6 August 2012.

Heelas, P. and L. Woodhead (2005) *The Spiritual Revolution: Why Religion is Giving Way to Spirituality*, Malden, MA: Wiley-Blackwell.

Hellyer, H. A. (2010) *Muslims of Europe: The 'Other' Europeans*. Edinburgh: Edinburgh University Press.

Hollinger, D. A. (1995) *Postethnic America: Beyond Multiculturalism*, New York: Basic Books.

Honeyford, R. (1988) *Integration or Disintegration?* London: The Claridge Press.

Husband, C. and Y. Alam (2011) *Social Cohesion and Counter-Terrorism: A Policy Contradiction?* Bristol: Policy Press.

Jacobson, J. (1997) 'Religion and Ethnicity: Dual and Alternative Sources of Identity among Young British Pakistanis', *Ethnic and Racial Studies*, 20(2).

Jakelić, S. (2010) 'Secularism: A Bibliographic Essay', *The Hedgehog Review*, <http://www.iasc-culture.org/publications_article_2010_Fall_Jakelic.php>.

Jakubowicz, A. (2005) 'Pluralism in Crisis – Challenges to Multicultural Agendas in the UK, the USA, Canada, and Australia', *Ideas in Action: Social Inquiry Seminar Series*, September, Sydney: University of Technology Sydney.

Jedwab, J. (2005) 'Muslims and Multicultural Futures in Western Democracies: Is Kymlicka's Pessimism Warranted?', *Canadian Diversity*, 4(3): 92–6.

Jones, P. (1999) 'Group Rights and Group Oppression', *Journal of Political Philosophy*, 7(4): 533–7.

Jones, P. (2006) 'Equality, Recognition and Difference', *Critical Review of International Social and Political Philosophy*, 9(1): 23–36.

Jones, T. (2006) 'Candidate Finds Past Ties a Real Bind', *Chicago Tribune*, 30 June, <http://www.chicagotribune.com/news/nationworld/chi-0606300131jun30,1,5656742.story>.

Joppke, C. (2004) 'The Retreat of Multiculturalism in the Liberal State: Theory and Policy', *The British Journal of Sociology*, 55(2): 237–57.

Joppke, C. (2008) 'Immigration and the Identity of Citizenship: The Paradox of Universalism', *Citizenship Studies*, 12(6): 533–46.

Joppke, C. (2009a) *Veil: The Mirror of Identity*, Cambridge: Polity.

Joppke, C. (2009b) 'Limits of Integration Policy: Britain and Her Muslims', *Journal of Ethnic and Migration Studies*, 35(3): 453–72.

Kabbani, R. (1989) *Letter to Christendom*, London: Virago Press.

Kastoryano, R. (2006) 'French Secularism and Islam: France's Headscarf Affair', in T. Modood, A. Triandafyllidou and R. Zapata-Barrero (eds), *Multiculturalism, Muslims and Citizenship*, London and New York: Routledge: 57–69.

Katwala, S. (2012) 'An Island Story: Boyle's Olympic Opening was Irresistibly British', *Open Democracy*, 31 July, <http://www.opendemocracy.net/ourkingdom/sunder-katwala/island-story-boyles-olympic-opening-was-irresistibly-british>.

Kaufmann, E., A. Goujon, and V. Skirbekk (2011) 'The End of Secularization in Europe? A Socio-demographic Perspective', *Sociology of Religion*, 73(1): 69–91.

Keith, M. (2005) *After the Cosmopolitan: Multicultural Cities and the Future of Racism*, London and New York: Routledge.

Kepel, G. (2005) 'Europe's Answer to Londonistan', *openDemocracy*, 24 August, <http://www.opendemocracy.net/ conflict-terrorism/londonistan_2775.jsp#]>.

Khan, M. A. M. (2002) *American Muslims: Bridging Faith and Freedom*, Beltsville, MD: Amana Publications.

Kivisto, P. (2005) *Incorporating Diversity: Rethinking Assimilation in a Multicultural Age*, Boulder, CO: Paradigm Publishers.

Kivisto, P. (2012) 'We Really Are All Multiculturalists Now', *The Sociological Quarterly*, 53(1): 1–24.

Klausen, J. (2005) *The Islamic Challenge: Politics and Religion in Western Europe*, Oxford: Oxford University Press.

Kraus, P. A. (2012) 'The Politics of Complex Diversity: A European Perspective', *Ethnicities*, 12(1): 3–25.

Krook, M., J. Lovenduski and J. Squires (2006) 'Western Europe, North America, Australia and New Zealand: Gender Quotas in the Context of Citizenship Models', in D. Dahlerup (ed.), *Women, Quotas and Politics*, London: Routledge: 194–221.

Kundnani, A. (2007) *The End of Tolerance: Racism in 21st Century Britain*, London: Pluto Press.

Kymlicka, W. (1989) *Liberalism, Community and Culture*, Oxford: Oxford University Press.

Kymlicka, W. (1995) *Multicultural Citizenship*, Oxford: Oxford University Press.

Kymlicka, W. (1998) *Finding Our Way*, Ontario: Oxford University Press.

Kymlicka, W. (1999) 'Comments on Shachar and Spinner-Halev: An Update from the Multiculturalism Wars', in C. Joppke and S. Lukes (eds), *Multicultural Questions*, New York: Oxford University Press.

Kymlicka, W. (2001a) *Politics in the Vernacular*, New York: Oxford University Press.

Kymlicka, W. (2001b) 'Western Political Theory and Ethnic Relations in Eastern Europe', in W. Kymlicka and M. Opalski (eds), *Can Liberal Pluralism be Exported?* New York: Oxford University Press: 13–105.

Kymlicka, W. (2005) 'The Uncertain Futures of Multiculturalism', *Canadian Diversity*, Multicultural Futures? International Approaches to Pluralism, 4(1): 82–5, Guest editor V. Bader.

Kymlicka, W. (2007) *Oxford: Multicultural Odysseys: Navigating the New International Politics of Diversity*, Oxford: Oxford University Press.

Kymlicka, W. (2009) 'Review Symposium: Historic Settlements and New Challenges' (Veit Bader, Secularism or Democracy? Associational Governance of Religious Diversity, Amsterdam: Amsterdam University Press, 2008), *Ethnicities*, December, 9(4): 546–52.

Kymlicka, W. (2012) *Multiculturalism: Success, Failure, and the Future*, Washington, DC: Migration Policy Institute.

Laclau, E. (ed.) (1994) *The Making of Political Identities*, London: Verso.

Laclau, E. (ed.) (1996) *Emancipations*, London: Verso.

Laclau, E. and C. Mouffe (1985) *Hegemony and Socialist Strategy*, London: Verso.

Lamont, M. and E. Laurent (2006) 'France Shows Its True Colours', *The Boston Globe*, 3 June, <http://www.boston.com/news/globe/editorial_opinion/oped/articles/2006/06/03/france_shows_its_true_colors/>.

Lentin, A. and G. Titley (2011) *The Crises of Multiculturalism: Racism in a Neoliberal Age*, London: Zed Books.

Leonard, K. I. (2003) *Muslims in the United States: The State of Research*, New York: Russell Sage Foundation.

Leonard, M. (1997) *Britain TM: Renewing our Identity*, London: Demos.

Levey, G. B. (2009) 'What is Living and What is Dead in Multiculturalism', *Ethnicities*, 9(1): 75–93.

Levey, G. B. (2012) 'Liberal Autonomy as a Pluralistic Value', *The Monist*, 95(1): 103–26.

Levey, G. B. and T. Modood (2009) 'Liberal Democracy, Multicultural Citizenship, and the Danish Cartoon Affair', in G. B. Levey and T. Modood (eds), *Secularism, Religion and Multicultural Citizenship*, Cambridge: Cambridge University Press.

Lister, R. (2003) *Citizenship: Feminist Perspectives*, consultant ed. J. Campling, Basingstoke: Palgrave Macmillan, 2nd edn, xi: p. 323.

Local, The (2011) 'Islamic Studies Gain Foothold in State Schools', 22 December <http://www.thelocal.de/education/20111222-39667.html>.

Loury, G., T. Modood and S. Teles (eds) (2005) *Ethnicity, Social Mobility and Public Policy in the US and UK*, Cambridge: Cambridge University Press.

Lutz, W., V. Skirbekk and M. Testa (2007) 'The Low-fertility Trap Hypothesis: Forces That May Lead to Further Postponement and Fewer Births in Europe', *Vienna Yearbook of Population Research 2006*, Vienna: Vienna Institute of Demography: 167–92.

Mac an Ghaill, M. (1999) *Contemporary Racisms and Ethnicities*, Buckingham: Open University Press.

McGhee, D. (2008) *The End of Multiculturalism? Terrorism, Integration and Human Rights*, Milton Keynes: Open University Press.

McLaren, P. (2001) 'Wayward Multiculturalists', *Ethnicities*, 1(3): 408–19.

McLaughlin, E. and S. Neal (2004) 'Misrepresenting the Multicultural Nation', *Policy Studies*, 25(3): 155–74.

McLennan, G. (2006) *Sociological Cultural Studies: Reflexivity and Positivity in the Human Sciences*, Houndmills: Palgrave Macmillan.

McLennan, G. (2010) 'The Postsecular Turn', *Theory Culture Society*, July, 27(4): 27: 3.

Madani, H. A. (2005) *Composite Nationalism and Islam*, trans. A. H. Hussain and H. Iman, Delhi: Manohar.

Malik, K. (2009) *From Fatwa to Jihad*, London: Allen and Unwin.

Malik, K. (2011) 'I Am Still a Critic of Multiculturalism, Honest', 10 February, *Pandemonium*, <http://kenanmalik.wordpress.com/2011/02/10/still-a-critic-of-multiculturalism/>.

Malik, M. (2010a) 'Progressive Multiculturalism: The British Experience', in A. Slij (ed.), *European Multiculturalism Revisited*, London: Zed Books.

Malik, M. (ed.) (2010b) *Anti-Muslim Prejudice: Past and Present*, London: Routledge.

Marshall, T. H. (1973) 'Citizenship and Social Class', in T. H. Marshall (ed.), *Class, Citizenship, and Social Development*, Westport, CT: Greenwood Press.

Marx, K. (1955) *The Poverty of Philosophy*, Moscow: Progress Publishers.

Mason, A. (2010) 'Integration, Cohesion and National Identity: Theoretical Reflections on Recent British Policy', *British Journal of Political Science*, 40: 857–74.

Masood, E. (2006a) 'Muslim Britain: the End of Identity Politics?', *openDemocracy*, 3 July, <http://www.opendemocracy.net/globalization/muslim_britain_3700.jsp>.

Masood, E. (2006b) 'Islam's Reformers', *Prospect*, 124, July.

May, S. (ed.) (1999) *Critical Multiculturalism*, London: Falmer Press.

May, S. (2002) 'Multiculturalism', in D. T. Goldberg and J. Solomos (eds), *A Companion to Racial and Ethnic Studies*, Oxford: Blackwell Publishers.

May, S., T. Modood and J. Squires (2004) 'Ethnicity, Nationalism and Minority Rights: Charting the Disciplinary Debates', in S. May, T. Modood and J. Squires (eds), *Ethnicity, Nationalism and Minority Rights*, Cambridge: Cambridge University Press: 1–23.

Mayer, J.-F. (2009) 'Analysis: A Majority of Swiss Voters Decide to Ban the Building of New Minarets', Religioscope Institute, <http://religion.info/english/articles/article_455.shtml>.

Meer, N. (2006) ' "Get off your knees" ', *Journalism Studies*, 7(1): 35–9.

Meer, N. (2010) *Citizenship, Identity & the Politics of Multiculturalism*. Basingstoke: Palgrave.

Meer, N. and T. Modood (2009a) 'The Multicultural State We're In: Muslims, Multiculture and the "Civic Re-balancing" of British Multiculturalism', *Political Studies*, 57: 473–97.

Meer, N. and T. Modood (2009b) 'Refutations of Racism in the "Muslim Question"', *Patterns of Prejudice*, 43: 335–54.

Meer, N. and T. Modood (2010) 'The Racialization of Muslims', in S. Sayyid and A. Vakil (eds), *Thinking Through Islamophobia: Global Perspectives*, London and New York: Hurst and Columbia University Press.

Meer, N. and T. Modood (2012) 'How Does Interculturalism Contrast with Multiculturalism?', *Journal of Intercultural Studies*, 33(2): 175–96.

Meira, F. (2012) 'Not a One-Way Road? Integration as a Concept and as a Policy', in A. Triandafyllidou, T. Modood and N. Meer (eds), *European Multiculturalisms: Cultural, Religious and Ethnic Challenges*, Edinburgh: Edinburgh University Press.

Mendus, S. (1989) *Toleration and the Limits of Liberalism*, London: Macmillan.

Mernissi, F. (1991) *Women and Islam: an Historical and Theological Enquiry*, trans. M. J. Lakeland, Oxford: Blackwell Publishing: xi, 228.

Merry, M. S. (2012) 'Segregation and Civic Virtue', *Educational Theory*, 62(4): 465–86.

Metcalf, H., T. Modood and S. Virdee (1996) *Asian Self-Employment*, Poole: Policy Studies Institute.

Miller, D. (1995) *On Nationality*, Oxford: Oxford University Press.

Miller, D. (2008) 'Immigrants, Nations and Citizenship', *The Journal of Political Philosophy*, 16(4): 371–90.

Modood, T. (1988) '"Black", Racial Equality and Asian Identity', in *New Community*, 14(3): 397–404.

Modood, T. (1990) 'British Asian Muslims and the Rushdie Affair', *The Poltical Quarterly*, 61: 143–60.

Modood, T. (1992) *Not Easy Being British: Colour, Culture and Citizenship*, London: Runnymede Trust/Trentham Books.

Modood, T. (1994a) 'Establishment, Multiculturalism and British Citizenship', *Political Quarterly*, 65(1): 53–73.

Modood, T. (1994b) 'Political Blackness and British Asians', *Sociology*, 28(4): 859–76.

Modood, T. (ed.) (1997) *Church, State and Religious Minorities*, London: Policy Studies Institute.

Modood, T. (1998) 'Anti-essentialism, Multiculturalism and the "Recognition" of Religious Minorities', *Journal of Political Philosophy*, 6: 378–99.

Modood, T. (2001) 'Multiculturalism', in J. Krieger (ed.), *The Oxford Companion to Politics of the World*, Oxford: Oxford University Press: 562–4.

Modood, T. (2004) 'Capitals, Ethnic Identity and Educational Qualifications', *Cultural Trends*, Special Issue on Cultural Capital and Social Exclusion, guest editors T. Bennett and M. Savage, June, 13(2): 50.

Modood, T. (2005a) *Multicultural Politics: Racism, Ethnicity and Muslims in Britain*, University of Minnesota Press and University of Edinburgh Press.

Modood, T. (2005b) 'Ethnicity and Political Mobilisation in Britain', in G. Loury, T. Modood and S. Teles (eds), *Ethnicity, Social Mobility and Public Policy in the US and UK*, Cambridge: Cambridge University Press: 457–74.

Modood, T. (2005c) 'A Defence of Multiculturalism', in *Soundings*, 29: 62–71.

Modood, T. (2006) 'The Liberal Dilemma: Integration or Vilification?' *openDemocracy* website, 8 February, <http://www.opendemocracy.net/conflict-terrorism/liberal_dilemma_3249.jsp>.

Modood, T. (2008) 'Multiculturalism and Groups', *Social & Legal Studies*, December, 17(4): 549–53.

Modood, T. (2009a) 'Muslims, Religious Equality and Secularism', in G. B. Levey and T. Modood (eds), *Secularism, Religion and Multicultural Citizenship*, Cambridge: Cambridge University Press.

Modood, T. (2009b) 'Introduction: Odd Ways of Being Secular', *Social Research: An International Quarterly*, 76(4): 1169–72.

Modood, T. (2010a) *Still Not Easy Being British: Struggles for a Multicultural Citizenship*, Stoke-on-Trent: Trentham.

Modood, T. (2010b) 'Moderate Secularism, Religion as Identity and Respect for Religion', *The Political Quarterly*, 81: 4–14.

Modood, T. (2011) 'Moderate Secularism: A European Conception', *openDemocracy*, 8 April <http://www.opendemocracy.net/tariq-modood/moderate-secularism-european-conception> last accessed 5 August.

Modood, T. (2012) 'Multiculturalism and the Nation', Network Global Governance Programme website, November', available at: <http://network.globalgovernanceprogramme.eu/multiculturalism-and-the-nation/>.

Modood, T. and F. Ahmad (2007) 'British Muslim Perspectives on Multiculturalism', *Theory, Culture and Society*, Special Issue on Global Islam, guest editors B. Turner and F. Volpi: 24(2): 187–212.

Modood, T. and J. Dobbernack (2011) 'A Left Communitarianism? What about Multiculturalism?', *Soundings*, 48: 55–64.

Modood, T. and R. Kastoryano (2006) 'Secularism and the Accommodation of Muslims in Europe', in T. Modood, A. Triandafyllidou and R. Zapata-Barrero (eds), *Multiculturalism, Muslims and Citizenship: A European Approach*, London and New York: Routledge.

Modood, T. and N. Meer (2012) 'Framing Contemporary Citizenship and Diversity in Europe', in A. Triandafyllidou, T. Modood and N. Meer (eds), *European Multiculturalisms: Cultural, Religious and Ethnic Challenges*, Edinburgh: Edinburgh University Press, 33–60.

Modood, T., S. Beishon and S. Virdee (1994) *Changing Ethnic Identities*, London: Policy Studies Institute.

Modood, T., R. Berthoud, J. Lakey, J. Nazroo, P. Smith, S. Virdee and S. Beishon (1997) *Ethnic Minorities in Britain: Diversity and Disadvantage*, London: Policy Studies Institute.

Modood, T., R. Hansen, E. Bleich, B. O'Leary and J. Carens (2006) 'The Danish Cartoon Affair: Free Speech, Racism, Islamism and Integration', *International Migration*, 44(5): 3–57.

Modood, T., H. Metcalf and S. Virdee (1998) 'British Asian Entrepreneurs: Culture and Opportunity Structures', in P. Taylor-Gooby (ed.), *Choice and Public Policy*, Basingstoke: Macmillan.

Modood, T., A. Triandafyllidou and R. Zapata-Barrero (eds) (2006b) *Multiculturalism, Muslims and Citizenship: A European Approach*, London and New York: Routledge.

Mohammad, H. (2004) 'British Muslims a Success Story in 2004', IslamOnline.net, 28 December <http://www.islamonline.net/English/News/2004-12/28article06.shtml>.

Monshipouri, M. (2010) 'The War on Terror and Muslims in the West', in J. Cesari (ed.), *Muslims in the West after 9/11: Religion, Politics and Law*, London: Routledge.

Morris, H. S. (1968) 'Ethnic Groups', in D. L. Sills (ed.), *International Encyclopaedia of the Social Sciences*, New York: Macmillan/Free Press.

Mouritsen, P. (2006) 'The Particular Universalism of a Nordic Civic Nation: Common Values, State Religion and Islam in Danish Political Culture', in T. Modood, A. Triandafyllidou and R. Zapata-Barrero (eds), *Multiculturalism, Muslims and Citizenship: A European Approach*, London: Routledge.

Mouritsen, P. (2008) 'Political Responses to Cultural Conflict: Reflections on the Ambiguities of the Civic Turn', in P. Mouritsen and K. E. Jørgensen (eds), *Constituting Communities: Political Solutions to Cultural Conflict*, London: Palgrave.

Mouritsen, P. and T. V. Olsen (forthcoming, 2013) 'Liberalism and the Diminishing Space of Tolerance', in J. Dobbernack and T. Modood (eds), *Hard to Accept. Perspectives on Intolerance, Toleration and Respect*, Basingstoke: Palgrave.

Mullard, C. (1985) *Race, Power and Resistance*, London: Routledge and Kegan Paul.

Murphy, M. (2012) *Multiculturalism: A Critical Analysis*, London and New York: Routledge.

Murray, C. (2011) 'Norwegian Killer Linked to Tea Party and EDL', July 23, <http://www.craigmurray.org.uk/archives/2011/07/norwegian-killer-linked-to-tea-party-and-edl/> last accessed on 13 August 2012.

Ngata, J. A. (1981) 'In Defence of Ethnic Boundaries: the Changing Myths and Charters of Malay Identity', in C. Keyes (ed.), *Ethnic Change*, Seattle: University of Washington Press: 87–116.

Nussbaum, N. (2012) *The New Religious Intolerance: Overcoming the Politics of Fear in an Anxious Age*, Cambridge, MA: Harvard University Press.

Oakeshott, M. (1962) *Rationalism in Politics*, London: Methuen.

Oakeshott, M. (1975) *On Human Conduct*, London: Oxford University Press.

O'Donnell, M. (2007) ' "We" Need Human Rights Not Nationalism "Lite": Globalisation and British Solidarity', *Ethnicities*, June, 7(2): 248–69.

Omi, M. and H. Winant (1986) *Racial Formation in the United States from the 1960s to the 1980s*, London: Routledge.

O'Toole, T., D. N. DeHanas and T. Modood (2012) 'Balancing Tolerance, Security and Muslim Engagement in the UK: The

Impact of the "Prevent" Agenda', *Critical Terrorism Studies*, 5(3): 373–89.

Palmer, F. (ed.) (1986) *Anti-Racism – An Assault on Education and Value*, London: Sherwood Press.

Parekh, B. (1991) 'British Citizenship and Cultural Difference', in G. Andrews (ed.), *Citizenship*, London: Lawrence and Wishart.

Parekh, B. (2000) *Rethinking Multiculturalism: Cultural Diversity and Political Theory*, Basingstoke: Macmillan.

Parekh, B. (2004) 'Redistribution or Recognition: a Misguided Debate', in S. May, T. Modood and J. Squires (eds), *Ethnicity, Nationalism and Minority Rights*, Cambridge: Cambridge University Press, pp. 199–213.

Parekh, B. (2005) 'British Commitments', *Prospect*, September, <http://prospectmagazine.co.uk/article_details.php?search_term=parekh&id=7003&issue=509&AuthKey=51e3e0b168fd1b98c34d1cb9f08e4fe9>.

Parekh, B. (2008) *A New Politics of Identity: Political Principles for an Interdependent World*, Basingstoke and New York: Palgrave Macmillan.

Park, A., J. Curtice, K. Thomson, M. M. Phillips, E. Clery and S. Butt (eds) (2010) *British Social Attitudes: The 26th Report*, London: Sage.

Patel, P. (2008) 'Defending Secular Spaces', *New Statesman*, 4 August, <http://www.guardian.co.uk/education/2012/jul/13/third-new-free-schools-religious>.

Pathak, P. (2008) 'Making a Case for Multiculture: From the "Politics of Piety" to the Politics of the Secular?', *Theory, Culture & Society*, 25(5): 123–41.

Peach, C. (2006) 'Islam, Ethnicity and South Asian Religions in the London 2001 Census', *Transactions of the Institute of British Geographers*, 31: 353–70.

Peach, C. (ed.) (2007) 'Muslim Population of Europe: A Brief Overview of Demographic Trends and Socioeconomic Integration, with Particular Reference to Britain', in *Muslim Integration: Challenging Conventional Wisdom in Europe and the United States*, Washington, DC: Center for Strategic and International Studies.

Pew Global Attitudes Project (2006) 'Muslims in Europe: Economic Worries Top Concerns about Religious and

Cultural Identity', <http://pewglobal.org/reports/display.php? ReportID=254>.

Pew Forum (2010) 'Muslim Networks and Movements in Western Europe', 16 September, <http://pewresearch.org/pubs/ 1731/muslim-networksmovements-western-europe>.

Pew Research Center (2008) 'Unfavorable Views of Jews and Muslims on the Increase in Europe', Pew Research Center, <http://pewglobal.org/2008/09/17/unfavorable-views-of-jews-and-muslims-on-the-increase-in-europe/>.

Pfaff, W. (2005) 'A Monster of Our Own Making', *Observer*, 21 August, <http://www.guardian.co.uk/alqaida/story/0,124 69, 1553504,00.html>.

Phillips, A. (1999) *Which Equalities Matter?* Cambridge: Polity.

Phillips, A. (2007) *Multiculturalism Without Culture*, Princeton, NJ: Princeton University Press.

Phillips, A. (2008) 'More on Culture and Representation', *Social & Legal Studies*, 17(4): 555–8.

Platt, L. (2005) 'New Destinations? Assessing the Post-migration Social Mobility of Minority Ethnic Groups in England and Wales', *Social Policy and Administration*, 39(6): 697–721.

Platt, L. (2006) 'Understanding Ethnic Group Differences in Britain: the Role of Family Background and Education in Shaping Social Class Outcomes', in S. Delorenzi (ed.), *Going Places*, London: Institute for Public Policy Research: 72–89.

Portes, A. and M. Zhou (1993) 'The New Second Generation: Segmented Assimilation and Its Variants among Post-1965 Immigrant Youth', *Annals of the American Academy of Political and Social Science*, 530: 74–98.

Presseurop (2010) 'Mutti Merkel handbags Multikulti', 18 October, <http://www.presseurop.eu/en/content/article/3640 91-mutti-merkelhandbags-multikulti>.

Ramadan, T. (2004) *Western Muslims and the Future of Islam*, Oxford: Oxford University Press.

Rawls, J. (1971) *A Theory of Justice*, Oxford: Oxford University Press.

Rawls, J. (1993) *Political Liberalism*, New York: Columbia University Press.

Richardson, R. (2000) 'Children Will Be Told Lies', *Runnymede's Quarterly Bulletin*, 324, December: 12–17.

Rietveld, E. (2012) 'Beyond the "Crisis of Multiculturalism":
     Moves in Theory and Practice', *Unedited Workshop Proceed-
     ings: Debating Multiculturalism 1*, London: Dialogue Society.
Robins, K. (2001) 'Endnote: To London: The City beyond the
     Nation', in D. Morley and K. Robins (eds), *British Cultural
     Studies*, New York: Oxford University Press: 473–93.
Roche, M. (1992) *Rethinking Citizenship: Ideology, Welfare and
     Change in Modern Society*, Cambridge: Polity.
Roy, O. (2004) *Globalised Islam*, London: C. Hurst.
Roy, O. (2005) 'A Clash of Cultures or a Debate on Europe's
     Values?', in ISIM (International Institute for the Study of Islam
     in the Modern World) Review, Spring 2005: 6–7.
Roy, O. (2007) *Secularism Confronts Islam*, New York: Colum-
     bia University Press.
The Royal Commission on Reform of the House of Lords (2000)
     A House for the Future, London: Cm 4534.
Rumbaut, R. G. (2005) 'Assimilation, Dissimilation, and Ethnic
     Identities: The Experience of Children of Immigrants in the
     United States', in M. Rutter and M. Tienda (eds), *Ethnicity
     and Causal Mechanisms*, New York: Cambridge University
     Press: 301–34.
Sacranie, I. (2006) 'Secretary General's Speech, Muslim Council
     of Britain Annual General Meeting', 4 June, <http://www.mcb.
     org.uk/uploads/SECGEN.pdf>.
Saeed, A., N. Blain and D. Forbes (1999) 'New Ethnic and
     National Questions in Scotland: Post-British Identities Among
     Glasgow Pakistani Teenagers', *Ethnic and Racial Studies*,
     22(5): 821–44.
Safi, O. (ed.) (2003) *Progressive Muslims*, Oxford: One World.
Said, E. W. (1985) *Orientalism*, Harmondsworth: Penguin.
St Louis, B. (2009) 'On the Necessity and Impossibility of Identi-
     ties: The Politics and Ethics of "New Ethnicities"', *Cultural
     Studies*, 23(4): 559–82.
Sandel, M. (1994) 'Review of Rawls' Political Liberalism',
     Harvard Law Review, 107: 1765–94.
Sardar, Z. (1987) *The Future of Muslim Civilisation*, 2nd edn,
     London: Mansell.
Sardar, Z. (2004) *Beyond Difference: Cultural Relations in the
     New Century*, London: British Council.
Sardoc, M. (2011) 'Citizenship and Civic Equality: Tensions,
     Problems and Challenges', *Annales*, 21(2): 225–36.

Savage, T. (2004) 'Europe and Islam: Crescent Waxing, Cultures Clashing', *The Washington Quarterly*, 27(3): 25–50.

Sayyid, B. (1997) *A Fundamental Fear: Eurocentricism and the Emergence of Islamism*, London and New York: Zed Books.

Sayyid, S. (2000) 'Beyond Westphalia: Nations and Diasporas – the Case of the Muslim *Umma* and Diasporic Logics', in B. Hesse (ed.), *Un/settled Multiculturalisms*, New York: Zed Books, pp. 33–50.

Sayyid, S. (2007) 'Contemporary Politics of Secularism', in G. B. Levey and T. Modood (eds), *Secularism, Religion and Multicultural Citizenship*, Cambridge: Cambridge University Press.

Sayyid, S. and A. Vakil (eds) (2010) *Thinking through Islamophobia*, London: C. Hurst & Co.

Scherer, M. (2010) 'Landmarks in the Critical Study of Secularism', *The Immanent Frame*, <http://blogs.ssrc.org/tif/2010/11/12/landmarks-secularism/>.

Schierup, C.-U. and A. Alund (1991) *Paradoxes of Multiculturalism: Essays on Swedish Society*, Aldershot: Ashgate.

Schiffauer, W. (2006) 'Enemies within the Gates: the Debate about the Citizenship of Muslims in Germany', in T. Modood, A. Triandafyllidou and R. Zapata-Barrero (eds), *Multiculturalism, Muslims and Citizenship*, Abingdon: Routledge: 94–116.

Scott, J. W. (2007) *The Politics of the Veil*, Princeton, NJ: Princeton University Press.

Searchlight Educational Trust (2011) *Fear and Hope Project Report*, February, <http://www.fearandhope.org.uk/project-report/>.

Seglow, J. (2003) 'Theorising "Recognition"', in B. Haddock and B. Sutch (eds), *Multiculturalism, Identity and Rights*, London: Routledge.

Sen, A. (2006) *Identity and Violence*, London: Allen Lane.

Sherif, J. (2011) 'A Census Chronicle – Reflections on the Campaign for a Religion Question in the 2001 Census for England and Wales', *Journal of Beliefs & Values*, 32(1): 1–18.

Sivanandan, A. (1982) *A Different Hunger*, London: Pluto Press.

Sivanandan, A. (1985) 'RAT and the Degradation of the Black Struggle', *Race and Class*, XXVI, 4.

Song, M. (2001) 'Comparing Minorities' Ethnic Options', *Ethnicities*: 57–82.

Soysal, Y. (1994) *Limits of Citizenship: Migrants and Post National Membership in Europe*, Chicago, IL: Chicago University Press.

Soysal, Y. N. (2012) 'Citizenship, Immigration, and the European Social Project: Rights and Obligations of Individuality', *The British Journal of Sociology*, 63(1): 1–21.

Spiegel Online (2009) 'Germany Has 1 Million More Muslims than Previously Thought', 24 June, <http://www.spiegel.de/international/germany/challenging-stereotypes-germany-has-1-million-more-muslims-than-previously-thought-a-632290.html>.

Squires, J. (2007) 'Negotiating Equality and Diversity in Britain: Towards a Differentiated Citizenship?', *Critical Review of International Social and Political Philosophy*, 10(4): 531–59.

Squires, J. (2008) 'Multiculturalism, Multiple Groups and Inequalities', *Social & Legal Studies,* 17(4): 535–42.

Sunier, T. and M. von Luijeren (2002) 'Islam in the Netherlands', in Y. Haddad (ed.), *Muslims in the West: From Sojourners to Citizens*, New York: Oxford University Press: 144–58.

Swann, Lord (1985) *Education for All: Final Report of the Committee of Inquiry into the Education of Children from Ethnic Minority Groups*, Cmnd 9453, London: HMSO.

Taylor, C. (1992) 'Multiculturalism and "The Politics of Recognition"', in A. Gutmann (ed.), *Multiculturalism and 'The Politics of Recognition'*, Princeton: Princeton University Press.

Taylor, C. (2009) 'Foreword: What is Secularism?', in G. B. Levey and T. Modood (eds), *Secularism, Religion and Multicultural Citizenship*, Cambridge: Cambridge University Press.

Taylor, C. and J. Maclure (2011) *Secularism and Freedom of Conscience*, trans. J. T. Todd, Cambridge, MA: Harvard University Press.

Thomas, P. (2011) *Youth, Multiculturalism and Community Cohesion*, Palgrave Politics of Identity and Citizenship. Basingstoke: Palgrave Macmillan.

Thompson, S. (2008) 'Multiculturalism without Multiple Cultures?', *Social & Legal Studies*, 17(4): 543–7.

Travis, A. (2002) 'The Need to Belong – But with a Strong Faith', *The Guardian*, 17 June: 4.

Tribalat, M. (1995) *Faire France: une enquête sur les immigrés et leurs enfants*, Paris: La Découverte.

Tribalat, M. (ed.) (1996) *De l'immigration à l'assimilation: une enquête sur la population étrangère en France*, Paris: INED.

Tripp, A., D. Konate and C. Lowe-Morna (2006) 'Sub-Saharan Africa: On the Fast Track to Women's Political Representation', in D. Dahlerup (ed.), *Women, Quotas and Politics*, London: Routledge: 112–37.

Troyna, B. (1993) *Racism and Education*, Buckingham: Open University Press.

Turner, B. S. (1993) 'Contemporary Problems in the Theory of Citizenship', in B. S. Turner (ed.), *Citizenship and Social Theory*, London: Sage.

Uberoi, V. (2009) 'Multiculturalism and the Canadian Charter of Rights and Freedoms', *Political Studies*, 57(4): 805–27, December.

Uberoi, V. and T. Modood (forthcoming) 'Inclusive Britishness: A Multiculturalist Advance,' *Political Studies*. Early view online available from 30 October 2012, at: <http://onlinelibrary. wiley.com/doi/10.1111/j.1467-9248.2012.00979.x/pdf>.

Vasagar, J. (2012) 'Third of New Free Schools Are Religious', *Guardian*, 13 July, <http://www.newstatesman.com/uk-politics/ 2008/08/religious-state-secular>.

Vertovec, S. (1996) 'Multiculturalism, Culturalism and Public Incorporation', *Ethnic and Racial Studies*, 19: 49–69.

Vertovec, S. (2006) 'The Emergence of Super-Diversity in Britain', Working Paper no. 5, University of Oxford: Centre on Migration, Policy and Society (COMPAS).

Vertovec, S. and S. Wessendorf (eds) (2010) *The Multiculturalism Backlash: European Discourses, Policies and Practices*, Abingdon and New York: Routledge.

Voas, D. and S. Bruce (2004) 'Research Note: The 2001 Census and Christian Identification in Britain', *Journal of Contemporary Religion*, 19(1): 23–8.

Voas, D. and A. Crockett (2005) 'Religion in Britain: Neither Believing nor Belonging', *Sociology*, 39(1): 11–28.

Wadud, A. (1999) *Qur'an and Woman: Rereading the Sacred Text from a Woman's Perspective*, New York: Oxford University Press.

Waldron, J. (1991) 'Minority Cultures and the Cosmopolitan Alternative', *University of Michigan Journal of Law Reform*, 25: 751.

Wallerstein, I. (2005) 'Render Unto Caesar? The Dilemmas of a Multicultural World', *Sociology of Religion*, 66(2): 121–34.

Waters, M. (1990) *Ethnic Options*, Berkeley: University of California Press.

Weber, M. (1949) *The Methodology of the Social Sciences*, translated and edited by E. A. Shils and H. L. Finch, Basingstoke: Macmillan.

Weldon, F. (1989) *Sacred Cows*, London: Chatto & Windus.

Werbner, P. (2004) 'The Predicament of Diaspora and Millennial Islam: Reflections on September 11, 2001', *Ethnicities*, 4(4): 451–76.

Wikipedia (2011) 'Dutch General Election, 2010', <http://en.wikipedia.org/wiki/Dutch_general_election,_2010>.

Wittgenstein, L. (1922) *Tractatus Logico-Philosophicus*, London: Routledge and Kegan Paul.

Wittgenstein, L. (1968) *Philosophical Investigations*, trans. G. E. M. Anscombe, Oxford: Blackwell.

Wolf, M. (2005) 'When Multiculturalism is a Nonsense', *Financial Times*, 31 August 2005, <http://news.ft.com/cms/s/4c751acc-19bc-11da-804e-00000e2511c8.html>.

Women Against Fundamentalism (1990) 'Founding Statement', *Women Against Fundamentalism Journal*, 1(1).

Wyn Davies, M. (1988) *Knowing One Another: Shaping an Islamic Anthropology*, London: Mansell.

Young, I. M. (1990) *Justice and the Politics of Difference*, Princeton: Princeton University Press.

Young, I. M. (1997) 'A Multicultural Continuum: A Critique of Will Kymlicka's Ethnic-Nation Dichotomy', Symposium on *Multicultural Citizenship* by Will Kymlicka, in *Constellations*, 4(1): 48–53.

Yuval-Davis, N. (1992) 'Fundamentalism, Multiculturalism and Women in Britain', in J. Donald and A. Rattansi (eds), *Race, Culture and Difference*, Sage: London.

Žižek, S. (1997) 'Multiculturalism or the Cultural Logic of Multinational Capitalism', *New Left Review*, I/225, September–October.

Žižek, S. (2011) *Living in the End Times*, London: Verso.

Zolberg, A. and L. Woon (1999) 'Why Islam is like Spanish', *Politics and Society* (Spring).

Index